Accession no.
36133424

WITHDRAWN

D0548030

SOCIAL ISSUES, JUSTICE AND STATUS SERIES

DOCTORING MEDICAL GOVERNANCE: MEDICAL SELF-REGULATION IN TRANSITION

SOCIAL ISSUES, JUSTICE AND STATUS SERIES

SOCIAL ISSUES, JUSTICE AND STATUS SERIES

DOCTORING MEDICAL GOVERNANCE: MEDICAL SELF-REGULATION IN TRANSITION

JOHN M. CHAMBERLAIN

LIS - LIBRARY

Date	Fund
13|09|12	h-che

Order No.

234662x

University of Chester

Nova Science Publishers, Inc.

New York

Copyright © 2009 by Nova Science Publishers, Inc.

All rights reserved. No part of this book may be reproduced, stored in a retrieval system or transmitted in any form or by any means: electronic, electrostatic, magnetic, tape, mechanical photocopying, recording or otherwise without the written permission of the Publisher.

For permission to use material from this book please contact us:
Telephone 631-231-7269; Fax 631-231-8175
Web Site: http://www.novapublishers.com

NOTICE TO THE READER

The Publisher has taken reasonable care in the preparation of this book, but makes no expressed or implied warranty of any kind and assumes no responsibility for any errors or omissions. No liability is assumed for incidental or consequential damages in connection with or arising out of information contained in this book. The Publisher shall not be liable for any special, consequential, or exemplary damages resulting, in whole or in part, from the readers' use of, or reliance upon, this material. Any parts of this book based on government reports are so indicated and copyright is claimed for those parts to the extent applicable to compilations of such works.

Independent verification should be sought for any data, advice or recommendations contained in this book. In addition, no responsibility is assumed by the publisher for any injury and/or damage to persons or property arising from any methods, products, instructions, ideas or otherwise contained in this publication.

This publication is designed to provide accurate and authoritative information with regard to the subject matter covered herein. It is sold with the clear understanding that the Publisher is not engaged in rendering legal or any other professional services. If legal or any other expert assistance is required, the services of a competent person should be sought. FROM A DECLARATION OF PARTICIPANTS JOINTLY ADOPTED BY A COMMITTEE OF THE AMERICAN BAR ASSOCIATION AND A COMMITTEE OF PUBLISHERS.

LIBRARY OF CONGRESS CATALOGING-IN-PUBLICATION DATA

Chamberlain, John M.
 Doctoring medical governance : medical self-regulation in transition / John M. Chamberlain.
   p. ; cm.
 Includes bibliographical references and index.
 ISBN 978-1-60876-119-7 (hardcover : alk. paper)
 1. Medicine--Great Britain. 2. Physicians--Great Britain. 3. Professional socialization. I. Title.
 [DNLM: 1. Education, Professional--standards--Great Britain. 2. Professional Autonomy--Great Britain. 3. Professional Competence--Great Britain. 4. Education, Professional--history--Great Britain. 5. Sociology, Medical--standards--Great Britain. W 21 C443d 2009]
 R690.C4145 2009
 610--dc22
                2009028869

Published by Nova Science Publishers, Inc. ✛ New York

CONTENTS

PREFACE

This book is concerned with the sociological analysis of the professions and professional self-regulation. This is the view that professionals such as doctors should be left alone to manage their own affairs in regards to members training, practice and discipline. Over the last two decades social scientists from the United States, Europe, Canada, Australia and New Zealand have discussed how governments are increasingly acting to open up the previously 'closed shop' field of professional regulation. Indeed, many have been vocal advocates of the need to promote greater inter-professional cooperation and managerial and public involvement in the regulation of professional forms of expertise. The United Kingdom is no exception. A series of high profile medical malpractice cases have caused sociologists to join patient rights advocates, lawyers, politicians and the media in calling for reforms in the regulation of doctors. Grounded in contemporary health and social policy developments in the United Kingdom, including the 2008 Health and Social Care Act, this book undertakes an in-depth analysis of the development of the principle of professional self-regulation in relation to the evolution of the modern medical profession and contemporary calls for reform in the governance of doctors. In doing so it highlights how medical elites are advocating a new medical professionalism, sometimes called professionally-led medical regulation, as they seek to maintain the principle of medical self-regulation, albeit in a new more publicly accountable form. Against this background the results of original empirical research undertaken with doctors to identify their experiences and perceptions of these reforms is presented and analyzed in light of current policy developments as well as relevant theoretical sociological frameworks.

Chapter 2 - This chapter and the next provide an historical overview of the development of the principle of medical self-regulation, as institutionalised in the United Kingdom in the form of the General Medical Council. They give a necessary background to subsequent discussion in chapters four and five of sociological perspectives pertaining to the study of professional regulation. For many sociologists, medical power ultimately rests on the professions ability to exclude third parties – be they patients, other professional groups or the state - from the technical evaluation of group members' activities. This may well be true and the 1858 Medical Act certainly established professional control over entry onto and exit from a legally underwritten register of state approved medical practitioners. However, before the 1858 Act is discussed it is necessary to tell the story of the development of modern scientific medicine to draw out a key theme for subsequent exploration in relation to the theoretical frameworks sociologists have utilised when analysing the professions. Namely, that the state may well have acted in recent times to limit the amount of occupational control the medical profession collectively possesses over the regulation of medical training and practice, but nevertheless medical and state forms of governance are interdependent, as well as to no small degree, mutually sustaining. Indeed, as will become clear as the next five chapters unfold, perhaps *the* key challenge facing current sociological theorising of contemporary reforms in medical regulation is how best to understand the nature of contemporary changes in the governance of the professions in relation to broader social-political changes in the nature and goal of legitimate governing regimes (Rose 2000). Consequently, it is necessary to tell the story of the development of modern medicine and its governance from its early beginnings. This requires going back in time well over two thousand years.

Chapter 3 - Chapter three discusses the historical development of medical regulation after the 1858 Medical Act up until the 2008 Health and Social Care Act. In doing do it sets the scene for the subsequent discussion of relevant sociological literature in chapter four. As chapter two discussed, under the guise of improving standards to ensure public safety, the 1858 Act did achieve its key goal of introducing a register of approved practitioners who have completed a quality assured training programme. But one thing it could not do was completely resolve existing tensions within the profession between general practitioners and physicians and surgeons. General practitioners resented the increasing importance of hospitals, particularly the teaching hospital, but they also felt that some of their colleagues were engaged in *'competitive undercutting, fee-splitting, canvassing for patients and other unethical practices'* (Titmus 1958: 172). The Act had led to the public being less clear about the various roles and relationships between the different elements of the profession. A doctor was a doctor and all that mattered was that there name was on the medical register. By the 1890s the problem of competition amongst doctors for patients had become so intense that it took the collective power of the British Medical Association – the professions trade union - the Royal Colleges and the GMC to advert a potentially *'really ugly internecine feud'* (Gould 1985: 73). It was agreed that hospital specialists would only see patients referred to them by a general practitioner for a second opinion. This created a division of labour between general practitioner – the generalist - and hospital consultant – the specialist – which remains in place today. However, this was a small (but still important) victory for the general practitioners as they were still seen to at the bottom of the medical hierarchy. Despite being the equal of their physician and surgeon peers in the eyes of the law. The Royal College of Physicians and Surgeons were the most important examining bodies. Their members' occupied key places within the teaching hospitals, universities and the GMC. It would not be until the middle of the twentieth century before general practitioners were granted their own Royal charter to create a college.

Chapter 4 – Chapter four provides an account of the development of the sociological analysis of professional regulation with a particular emphasis on the medical profession. As such it provides a bridge between the empirical research discussed in chapter six and the empirical and policy analysis literature relating to contemporary challenges to the principle of medical self-regulation explored in chapter five. It does this against the background of the historical narrative provided in chapters two and three. These chapters traced the unfolding trajectory of medical autonomy in the United Kingdom through detailing the changing social-political and health policy context surrounding the regulatory body which since 1858 has embodied the principle of professional self-regulation in medicine – the GMC. Here the entwined nature of medical governance with the development of the modern state was first noted. As was that a key paradox surrounding recent challenges to the principle of medical self-regulation is that they have occurred at a time when the success of medical knowledge and technology to promote public health is greater than it has been previously. These two themes are explored in this chapter and the next. But to do this the chapter must start with discussing the perspective which has dominated sociological analysis of professional regulation for the last four decades: the neo-Weberian viewpoint. This in turn requires the chapter initially focus upon delineating the development of the sociological study of the professions.

Chapter 5 - Chapter five discusses the development of the restratification thesis to illustrate the value of recognising points of agreement between the neo-Weberian and Governmentality perspectives. It achieves this through exploring how sociologists conceptualised social changes that were held to be challenging medical autonomy, in the form of clinical freedom 'at the bedside' and the principle of self-regulation, from the 1980s onwards. As will become clear, this opens up an important line for empirical inquiry that is examined further in chapter six.

Chapter 6 - The previous chapter concluded by arguing for the need to investigate the implementation of portfolio based performance appraisal within the medical profession. Chapter six outlines the findings of research conducted to fill this gap within the academic literature. The process of data collection and analysis occurred between 2007 and 2008. Revalidation was an unknown quantity when the research started, so the decision was made to focus upon exploring the introduction of appraisal within medicine through discussing with doctors their experience of annual appraisal as well as conducting trainee appraisal during clinical training placements.

Chapter 7 - The research detailed in chapter six was undertaken after a review of the sociological literature revealed that, first, little research had been undertaken by social scientists on recent challenges to medical autonomy from the perspective of doctors themselves, and second, what had been undertaken had been concerned with analysing doctors perceptions of challenges to their clinical freedom 'at the bedside', rather than with what is happening within the training and regulatory sphere. It therefore represents the first attempt to analyse doctors educational autonomy in the context of contemporary sociological debate concerning 'the decline and fall' of medical autonomy and the future of the principle of professional self-regulation.

DEDICATION

For my daughter Freyja …
Having your hand to hold makes the hard times easier
and the good times even better.

And for Nemira…
Because she loves sunflowers and 'nana plants' just as much as I do.

Chapter 1

INTRODUCTION

'[Medicine]...must be enthused with a spirit of openness, driven by the conviction that...decisions must be routinely open to inspection and evaluation, like the openness that pervades science and scholarship'.
Freidson (1994: 196)

This book is concerned with the sociological study of the medical profession and the principle of medical self-regulation. This is the view that medical professionals should be left alone to manage their own affairs in regards to members training, practice and discipline. Like in many other Western nation-states, in the United Kingdom (UK) professions such as medicine, dentistry and law have traditionally possessed monopolistic control over entry onto and exit from a legally underwritten state approved register of qualified practitioners. Furthermore in the UK the principle of professional self-regulation has been embodied by the public institution which for the last one hundred and fifty years has symbolized the principle of professional self-regulation within medicine: the General Medical Council (GMC). However there have been substantial changes in the governance of professional expertise in recent times. Growing concern over the effectiveness of existing self-regulatory arrangements has caused the state to act to 'open up' the previously 'close shop' field of professional regulation, and in doing so it called for greater inter-professional cooperation and managerial and lay involvement in the regulation of professional expertise. This has directly challenged the traditional viewpoint held by professional elites that they should be left alone to manage their own affairs. A similar trend has been recognised internationally by sociologists in Europe (Kuhlmann and Allsop 2008), Canada (Coburn et al 1997), Australia (Coburn and Willis 2000), New Zealand (Doolin 2002) and USA (Freidson 2001). Consequently, although its empirical case study is grounded in the UK, this book is of international relevance to social scientists concerned with how medical practitioners are reacting to contemporary shifts in the regulation of expert services (Kuhlmann and Saks 2008).

It may have long been recognised internationally by sociologists that doctors are becoming increasing subject to formal calculative regimes, such as audit and appraisal, which seek to contractualize and formalize their working arrangements and professional judgements to economise health service provision. However two important points need to be recognised here. First, little sociological research has been undertaken on recent challenges to medical autonomy from the perspective of doctors themselves, and furthermore, what has been published is primarily concerned with doctor's perceptions of a possible decline in their clinical freedom 'at the bedside'. Second, no published research has focused on exploring the relationship between contemporary challenges to the principle of medical self-regulation and medical practitioners' educational activities. This is not too much of a surprise given that the sociological study of professional regulation in general was seen to be a 'backwater topic' until the late 1990s (Davies 2004). This book seeks to fill a recognised gap in the current 'sociological corpus' that has been recognised as needing to be filled for quite some time (i.e. Elston, 1991). It achieves this by, firstly, reviewing the current 'state of the art' of the sociological literature concerned with professional regulation in light of contemporary shifts in the practice of state governance, and secondly, by documenting the findings of empirical work undertaken with doctors in the UK examining the impact of portfolio-based performance appraisal on how they supervise medical trainees and keep themselves up to date and fit to practice in their chosen speciality.

The system of medical training and regulation in the UK has undergone substantial reform in recent times. As they have responded to external pressure for reform, medical elites such as the GMC, medical schools and the Royal Colleges have enforced a move towards a structured competence-focused outcome-based approach to training and career progression by means of formal appraisal. They advocate a 'new medical professionalism', sometimes called 'professionally-led' medical regulation, as they seek to maintain the principle of self-regulation, albeit in a new more publicly accountable form. For the contemporary political climate requires medical elites themselves adopt a more open, transparent and inclusive governing regime which relies upon a 'best evidenced' approach to medical governance (see Irvine 1997 2001 2003, Catto 2006 2007). So it should come as no surprise to learn that this 'new professionalism' has also signalled the beginning of a proactive surveillance, inspection and control programme by the GMC and the Royal Colleges of the delivery of medical training at undergraduate, postgraduate and continuing levels. Clear quality assurance standards are used to govern their content and outcomes (Bateman 2000, Searle 2000). As the ex-chairman of the GMC, Donald Irvine, (2001: 1808) notes *the essence of the new professionalism is clear professional standards'*.

A key tool that medicines elites have used to support their new open and accountable governing regime is the 'learning portfolio' or 'portfolio of achievement' (Challis 1999, Southgate 2001). Portfolios support the implementation of a 'best evidenced' outcome based performance appraisal within the medical club (Snadden 1998, Wilkinson 2002). Indeed, today's medical students will encounter portfolio based professional development planning and performance appraisal throughout their professional careers (Davis 2001). For paper-based and electronic portfolios are being used throughout medical school and junior doctor training, in later specialist training, as well as to support the implementation of Annual Appraisal of doctors as part of their National Health Service (NHS) contract (BMA 2005). Many things are called 'portfolios', including logbooks of activity, observational 'check lists', records of critical incidents and collections of personal reflective narratives (Redman 1995, Morrison 1996). Yet the political utility of portfolio learning as a governing strategy that supports the renewal of principle of professional self-regulation lies in the fact that a completed portfolio acts as a personalised bureaucratic surveillance record of key events and turning points in the career biography of individual workers (Gilbert 2001). Their increased use within medicine is due to their ability to act as a concrete record of an individual doctor's competence and career development. Furthermore, they are completed in an apparently inclusive manner under the banner of promoting individual and institutional transparency and accountability, as required by medicines 'new professionalism'. In short, portfolios act as one of medicines new *'visible markers of trust [which as]...tools of bureaucratic regulation fulfil [a] function as signifiers of quality'* (Kuhlmann 2006b: 617). The purpose of the research detailed in chapter seven of this book was to explore the application of appraisal to ascertain the reliability of this new trust marker.

The book consists of seven interlocking chapters. After the introduction provided in this chapter, chapter two outlines the ancient origins of the modern medical profession, tracing its unfolding development up until the 1858 Medical Act, which is held to be a landmark in the history of the organisation of medical governance within the UK. Chapter three continues this narrative. By tracking the development of the principle of professional self-regulation it details contemporary challenges to medical autonomy from both within and outside of the NHS. In doing so it highlights how elites within the medical profession have been criticised for possessing a 'closed shop' club mentality towards the issue of who should regulate doctors' activities, as well as for consistently placing their own professional interests above those of the general public. It concludes by discussing the 2008 Medical Act, which has instigated a series of fundamental reforms to medical governance, including the implementation of revalidation nationally in 2010. Against the background of the historical policy analysis in chapter three, chapter four provides an account of the development of sociological analysis of medical self-regulation against the broader context of the sociological study of the professions. In doing so, it covers neo-Weberian, neo-Marxist, Feminist and Governmentality perspectives as it seeks to analyse the entwined nature of the development of the modern state and professions. Chapter five leads on from this discussion, noting how there is a lack of empirical literature relating to the sociological study of medical training and regulation. This is particularly true from the perspective of doctors themselves and concerning the affect on their actions, if any, of recent reforms within medical education. Based on this gap in the literature, the chapter concludes by proposing an investigation into the introduction of portfolio based performance appraisal within medicine. Chapter six presents the findings of research conducted in light of this proposal. Embedding its discussion within the context of the historically situated policy analysis provided in chapters two and three, as well as the theoretical perspectives and empirical literature discussed in chapters four and five, it details how the doctors interviewed adopted a stance of 'paperwork compliance' toward portfolio based performance appraisal. Chapter seven discusses this findings contribution to the sociological literature concerned with the study of professional regulation in general, and the medical profession and the principle of medical self-regulation in particular.

Chapter 2

FROM ANCIENT BEGINNINGS TO THE 1858 MEDICAL ACT

'The primitive does not distinguish between medicine, magic and religion. To him they are one, a set of practices intended to protect him from evil forces.'
Sigerist (1951: 127)

This chapter and the next provide an historical overview of the development of the principle of medical self-regulation, as institutionalised in the United Kingdom in the form of the General Medical Council. They give a necessary background to subsequent discussion in chapters four and five of sociological perspectives pertaining to the study of professional regulation. For many sociologists, medical power ultimately rests on the professions ability to exclude third parties – be they patients, other professional groups or the state - from the technical evaluation of group members' activities. This may well be true and the 1858 Medical Act certainly established professional control over entry onto and exit from a legally underwritten register of state approved medical practitioners. However, before the 1858 Act is discussed it is necessary to tell the story of the development of modern scientific medicine to draw out a key theme for subsequent exploration in relation to the theoretical frameworks sociologists have utilised when analysing the professions. Namely, that the state may well have acted in recent times to limit the amount of occupational control the medical profession collectively possesses over the regulation of medical training and practice, but nevertheless medical and state forms of governance are interdependent, as well as to no small degree, mutually sustaining. Indeed, as will become clear as the next five chapters unfold, perhaps *the* key challenge facing current sociological theorising of contemporary reforms in medical regulation is how best to understand the nature of contemporary changes in the governance of the professions in relation to broader social-political changes in the nature and goal of legitimate governing regimes (Rose 2000). Consequently, it is necessary to tell the story of the development of modern medicine and its governance from its early beginnings. This requires going back in time well over two thousand years.

Ancient Beginnings

Western philosophy typically views ancient Greek civilization as the cradle of rational enquiry and modern science. According to canonical tradition, modern science in the form of natural philosophy is said to have begun when Thales of Miletus predicted an eclipse of the sun in 585 BC. Thales was the first in a succession of thinkers known as the Pre-Socratic philosophers who lived before or during the lifetime of Socrates (470-399 BC). These individuals did not belong to any unified school of thought, but shared a commitment to rational empirical inquiry and the belief that the natural world could be explained in terms that did not refer to anything beyond nature itself. This viewpoint influenced the early teachers of Greek society – the Sophists - and Socrates whose pupil Plato established his Academy as a learning institution built upon dialectical argument and the cultivation of the mind. It is also what separates early Greek from Egyptian and Babylonian thought. True, the Babylonians and Egyptians made advances in mathematics, astronomy and medicine that informed the development of early Greek philosophy and science, but unlike the Greeks they did not possess a thorough going commitment to observation, reason and experiment. For example, the famous Edwin Smith papyrus, which dates from at least 1600 BC, contains an account of forty eight surgical cases divided into sections pertaining to title, examination, diagnosis and treatment. Illustrating that the Egyptians were committed to recording empirical data in much the same way as later Hippocratic doctors did (Allen et al 2005). Yet even this text, which is generally free of superstition, turns in case nine to supernatural aids when it details a charm that is to be recited to ensure a recommended remedy is effective. Conversely, early Greek medical texts in the Hippocratic tradition, for instance the treatise *On the Sacred Disease* (400 BC), illustrate a growing refutation of superstitious beliefs. In this case in regards to epilepsy:

'I do not believe that the "Sacred Disease" is any more divine or sacred than any other disease but, on the contrary, has specific characteristics and a definite cause. Nevertheless, because it is completely different from other diseases, it has been regarded as a divine visitation by those who, being only human, view it with ignorance and astonishment.'
Chadwick and Mann (1950: 1)

Hippocrates (450 BC to 370 BC) is best known for his oath, which combined the practice of medicine with moral values which are still highly relevant today. Including a duty to help the sick, to reframe from doing harm as well as maintain patient confidentiality. The oath also includes a call for an apprenticeship model of medical learning with masters passing on 'trade secrets' to selected apprentices. This being an early sign of medicines exclusive attitude towards outsiders – Hippocrates believed that medicine should be practiced by a special elite group of people (i.e natural philosophers) who share knowledge and insights freely with each other but not patients (King 2001). Additionally, the oath precluded practitioners from carrying out surgery, it being deemed not suitable for early Greek gentlemen of learning to perform surgical procedures as these were deemed to be manual work. So creating early on the distinction which is still with us today between physician and surgeon. While the all male make up of the ancient Greek medical club somewhat supports the view of authors operating from a Feminist perspective that far from being a 'gender neutral' enterprise medicine in fact has historically reflected, and indeed in many ways reinforced, the patriarchal nature of society through endorsing social practices which seek to place women firmly within the private sphere of home and family (Riska 2001). A point discussed in more detail in chapter four.

The Hippocratic Oath of the early Greek medical club can be said to have began the long public relations exercise still present today of viewing doctors as an elite group of individuals providing a disinterested service to the needy with absolute integrity and honesty. Hippocrates successor and the father of western learned medicine, Galen (129 to 200 AD), similarly stressed that a good physician should possess a detailed knowledge of the body, a love of philosophy and respect for human life. Given that it is Galen's theoretical framework that medieval medicine in Europe drew upon until the rise of modern scientific biomedical model in the eighteenth and nineteenth centuries, it is necessary to outline its main features and historical trajectory.

Galen's Humors

'Certain basic physiological concepts and associated therapeutic methods – notably humoral theory and the practice of bloodletting to get rid of bad humors – had a continuous life extending from Greek antiquity into the nineteenth century.'
Siraisis (1990: 70 - 71)

Though it was first challenged as early as the sixteenth century by the Swedish physician Paracelsus (1493 to 1541) it is generally accepted by medical historians (i.e. Siraisis 1990 and Porter 1995) that the Galenic humoral tradition dominated western medicine throughout the middle ages and was influential until the beginning of the nineteenth century. As Turner (1995: 29) notes, *'Galen's work 'On the Conduct of Anatomies' became the definitive source for medical understanding of the structure and function of the human body until it was successfully challenged in the late sixteenth century'*. The chapter will discuss the challenges to the Galenic tradition in a moment but first it will briefly outline the main features of the Galenic worldview.

The ancient Greek Hippocratic-Galenic medical tradition, along with much of early Greek science and philosophy, was transmitted from Arabic and Latin texts to the West in the twelve and thirteen centuries as the first modern centres of academic learning – the University - were established in Italy, France, Germany and England (O'Malley 1970). As would be expected the Galenic tradition believed in natural causes for disease. Indeed it perceived disease to be an environmental but ultimately an individual humoral phenomena. The world was conceived in terms of consisting of four elements – fire, earth, air and water - and individuals as having four humors – black bile, yellow or red bile, blood and phlegm – as well as four personality types – sanguine, phlegmatic, choleric and melancholic (Lindeman 1999). Those individuals with a preponderance for phlegm tended to be heavy and slow, those with to much blood sanguine, those with too much yellow or red bile quarrelsome and, finally, those with to much black bile melancholic (Temkin 1973). Good health rested on the proper balance of a person's four humors in line with their personality type. Illness and disease came about due to their imbalance. A state of affairs that could be influenced by the environment, for instance, having hot summers when ones personality type and humors required a mild one could cause illness. Particularly as disease was specific to individuals and any alteration in their humors due to changing environmental conditions could place them in mortal danger. Standard therapies to readjust imbalances included inducing vomiting and, of course, bleeding (a tradition which went back to ancient Greece). Yet humoral medicine was also heavily focused on prevention.

> *'In humoral medicine, prevention...was as important as treatment. The best means of maintaining health was to practice moderation in all things, especially in the use of...(1) air, (2) sleep and waking, (3) food and drink, (4) rest and exercise, (5) excretion and retention and (6) the passions or emotions. A healthy regimen was predicted on observing these rules of nature and avoiding exhaustion, overheating, overeating, excessive consumption of spirits, and immoderate desires. Such ideas were prevalent, and informed not only medical theories but more popular versions of health and illness as well.'*
> Lindeman (1999: 10)

Galenic Medicine and the Christian Worldview

This focus on prevention as much as cure reflects humoral medicines origin in ancient Greece and its affiliation with natural philosophy and concern with the good life. To be sure, as Turner (1995: 20) notes, *'there was considerable conflict between the secular assumptions of Greek Medicine and the spiritual aims of Christian religious practice'*. But it equally can be argued that there was considerable congruence between the two, particularly given humoral medicines' focus on moderation and the need for the individual to take responsibility for their humor to ensure healthy living. In short, both operate within a moral discourse which promotes a set of practices for the regulation of the body and the mind (and the Christian concept of the soul) at the level of the individual and the population. Indeed, at this point in time the church had powers to license practitioners due to its control of the early universities. With Henry VIII for example making it offence in 1511 to practice 'physic' without a university degree or license directly obtained from a bishop (Copeman 1960).

The decline of the Galenic worldview and the ecclesiastic stranglehold over medical practice started with the Renaissance and ended with the Enlightenment and the rise of hospital medicine (Tenkin 1973). Renaissance artists such as Michelangelo (1475-1564) and da Vinci (1452 – 1519) familiarised themselves with human anatomy, producing detailed drawings of the body as perhaps only an artist can, and in doing so highlighted that Galen had actually dissected animals, not humans, when constructing his anatomical principles. This viewpoint was supported by the Flemish physician Vesalius (1514 – 1564) in his anatomical text *On the fabric of the human body* (1543) (Siraisis 1990). For instance, Vesalius showed that the human breastbone actually has seven segments not three as Galen held. Meanwhile, William Harvey (1578 – 1657) established the circulatory system demonstrating the attachment of veins and arteries and the movement of blood in a circular motion around the body. A point of view which was at odds with the essentially static conception of blood that existed in the humoral system (Tenkin 1973). While Paracelsus (1493 to 1541) broke completely with the Galenic tradition of seeing disease as the result of humoral imbalance and laid the foundations for modern medical practice by conceiving it as an entity – an *archeus* - which entered the human body (Siraisis 1990).

The Enlightenment and the Clinical Gaze of the Biomedical Model

'At the end of the eighteenth century a new type of medicine swept away the old humoral theories of illness that had dominated clinical practice for hundreds of years. The distinctive feature of the new medicine was its claim that illness existed in the form of localized pathological lesions inside the body....The new model of disease – often called biomedicine because it reduced illness to a biological abnormality inside the body – led to enormous resources being invested in the examination of anatomical and physiological processes, both normal and abnormal, to identify the underlying basis of pathology.'
Armstrong (1995: 1)

Though he had what can be said to be a modern view of disease Paracelsus relied on mystical and magical explanations in some of his teachings. For instance he held that the stars influenced a person's health. Yet his obsession with dissection promoted a scientific basis for medical practice by refocusing it away from the rote learning of ancient texts and towards the gaining of direct experience through conducting anatomical experiments (Siraisis 1990). Inspired by Paracelsus and Harvey, Bichat (1772 to 1802) examined the tissues of organs and searched for disease in decidedly natural origins (Carter 1991). Similarly Morgagni (1682-1771) used an early microscope to identify, amongst other things, the clinical features of pneumonia, while Baillie (1761 – 1823) accurately described cirrhosis of the liver. Morgagni, Baillie and Bichat signify the beginning of medicines focus on abnormality as much as normality and its use of morbid anatomy as a methodology to further medical knowledge and practice. Indeed, Bichat is quoted by Carter (1991: 543) as saying *'open up a few corpses (and) you will dissipate at once the darkness that observation alone could not dissipate'*. For though corpses had been dissected since the thirteenth century at least humoral medicines' dominance had meant that symptoms expressed in life were until now not directly related to findings made during a dissection.

Medicine in the Eighteenth Century

The decline of humoral medicine was not however a straight forward affair divorced from broader socio-economic changes and the power dynamics at play between the different social groups essential to the organisation of medical training and practice. Medical historians typically hold that at the beginning of the eighteenth century they were three categories of medical practitioner in England. Each reflected an elemental aspect of medicine: as learned profession (the Physician), as craft (the Surgeon) and as trade (the Apothecaries) (Parry and Parry 1976). Although they were provincial affiliated societies based in major towns and cities, each aspect had its headquarters in London – The Royal College of Physicians, The Royal College of Surgeons and the Worshipful Company of Apothecaries. The Royal College of Physicians of London was established in 1518. Surgeons joined the Barbers in 1540 to form the Barber-Surgeons Company, but they broke this association in 1745 and subsequently the Royal College of Surgeons of London was established in 1800. Apothecaries were at first medicinal shopkeepers, but they were granted a Royal Charter as the society of Apothecaries of London in 1617. This was primarily because though Physicians may prescribe medicinal remedies, as gentlemen they certainly were not going to engage in trade and actually sell such items. As Carr-Saunders and Wilson (1933: 421) note: *'A gentleman might be rich and might even seek riches. But certain roads to the acquisition of riches were closed to him; in particular he must not seek riches through the avenue of 'trade'.*

Entry to each of these three occupational corporations (which were all male) was different with each possessing their own tests of competence. Entry into the Royal College of Physicians was available only to men of good social reputation who held a degree from Oxford or Cambridge, though those with Scottish medical degrees could become affiliated members. Surgeons and apothecaries, unlike physicians, learnt their trade by apprenticeship. When a surgeon or apothecary took on an apprentice, they signed a legally binding contractual agreement with them. More than often, given the apprentice was a child, this agreement was made with their parents. The apprenticeship process was designed to teach the trade, the mystery and the business of surgery or apothecary. For instance, the physician prescribed drugs and the apothecary sold them. Therefore, as Latin was the preferred language of the learned physician, the apothecaries' apprenticeship typically also included some Latin. The apprenticeship system by and large did produce competent practitioners but there was concern that *'at its worst, if the master neglected his duties, or the pupil was idle and cared little to learn, the period of apprenticeship too often represented so much precious time wasted'* (Muirhead-Little 1932: 6).

Two factors are immediately apparent about these early arrangements for the organisation of medical practice and training. First, as will be discussed in more detail later in relation to the 1858 Act, although women administered medical care in the domestic and local community, they were excluded from these early formalised arrangements for ensuring the quality of 'state licensed' medical training and practice (Porter 1997). Second, the system was centralised in London and largely concerned on a day-to-day basis with a geographical area of roughly seven miles outside of the city. At the time, the three medical corporations possessing little control over countryside areas. The only real control the corporations exercised outside of London was in the main cities through various provincial societies (Porter 1995). In short the medical marketplace in the countryside was unorganised, largely unregulated and dominated by women and 'quacks' (defined by the colleges as individuals who has not passed their exams) who operated in direct competition with a few officially licensed practitioners (typically apothecaries). It can be said that nationally at this time it was still a buyer's market with the sick actively involved in choosing their treatment. The state of affairs outside of London was about to become even more fluid, as the beginning of the industrial revolution and ascent of enlightenment ideals led to a huge increase in urban populations, the development of new industrial cities and the application of *laissez faire* philosophies to marketplace economics. As Holloway (1966: 114) notes: *'Administrative difficulties, partly the result of the sudden growth of the new industrial towns, and a doctrinaire belief in the efficacy of free competition to ensure the interests of the consumer, led to the decay of...the mediaeval system of local regulation'.*

The Industrial Revolution, the Growth of Modern Medicine and the Birth of the Clinic

The stable system of separate medical streams, centralised in London with associated provincial societies in the countryside, had its origins in the early commercial guilds and was well suited to the essentially static social order of the medieval era. However, the industrial revolution brought with it liberal ideals and marketplace economics which engendered an upward mobility for medical practitioners that gradually broke down the old compartmentalised view of medical practice. This breakdown happened first between the 'trade' and 'craft' elements of medicine - the apothecary and the surgeon - creating the surgeon-apothecary. Indeed, by 1783 they were some 2,067 registered surgeon-apothecaries, compared to 89 surgeons and 105 apothecaries (Lane 1985). At the same time, physicians educated in Scotland were clashing with those educated in London. This was mainly over their lack of voting rights in regards to College decision-making machinery, which was monopolised by the medical men of Oxford and Cambridge. In addition, Scottish medical training was heavily influenced by 'the birth of the clinic' in Europe, so it therefore rejected the Galenic tradition that had long lain at the heart of the traditional Oxbridge approach to medical training and practice.

It is often asserted that the pre-eminence of the modern medical profession lies in its scientific knowledge base and, in turn, this is linked to the historical development of pathological anatomy and the establishment of the hospital clinic as a site for the application of the biomedical model. Certainly many medical sociologists would hold that modern medicine's technological and diagnostic advancements and successes throughout the last hundred and fifty years, have led to a biomedical discourse dominating contemporary debate surrounding public health as well as the organisation and delivery of health care (Lupton 1995). Here it is argued that biomedicine is a *cultural system comprised of numerous variations, the many medicines...[it is]..a more or less coherent and self-consistent set of values and premises, including an ontology, an epistemology and rules of proper action/interaction, embodied and mediated through significant symbols'* (Gaines and Hahn 1985: 4). Although it is a somewhat diverse entity, biomedicine at heart is reductionist and materialistic: it largely seeks to explain the phenomena of health and ill health in terms of cellular and molecular processes and events. This approach has generally proven to be diagnostically successful throughout the last hundred years or more. Here it must be remembered that the work of Foucault (1989) highlights that the new mode of medical perception and understanding bound up with the birth of the clinic, and which gradually replaced Galenic humoral medicine, was founded upon the discipline of pathological anatomy. This enabled the doctor to treat disease in the form of lesions and processes located within the organs and systems of the body. Observable signs and symptoms were increasingly matched to the findings of pathological science. With emerging techniques such as palpation, auscultation and percussion reinforcing the legitimacy of this new approach to medical practice. Consequently, the individual body was firmly established as a site for social surveillance and inspection as well as the advancement of rational, scientific, medical knowledge (Turner, 1995). The hospital increasingly became a location for medical research and training as the body was sampled, measured and generally coerced into revealing its secrets by a growing number of specialist medical disciplines, departments and laboratories. As Armstrong (1983: 2) notes: *'[the] medical gaze, in which is encompassed all the techniques, languages and assumptions of modern medicine...[established]...by its authority and penetration an observable and analysable space in which...[was]...crystallised that apparently solid figure – which has now become familiar – the discrete human body'*.

Foucault (1989) notes that in addition to laying the foundation stones of modern medicines formal scientific knowledge base, the birth of the clinic also placed the emphasis of medical training and practice on gaining direct personal experience of a phenomenon. This laid the foundation stones for the development of modern medicine's 'craft expertise', as a direct result of a doctor's own direct scrutiny of a patient becoming paramount. Indeed, Foucault (1989: xvii) says that: *"clinical experience ...was soon taken as a simple, unconceptualised confrontation of a gaze and a face, or a glance and a silent body, a sort of contact prior to all discourse, free of the burdens of language, by which two living individuals are trapped in a common, but non-reciprocal situation."*

Although not necessarily influenced by the work of Foucault, this emphasis on the primacy of tacit clinical knowledge and expertise gained through obtaining direct clinical experience under apprenticeship, has been a regular feature of sociological accounts of medical training. Becker (1961: 225) comments on how personal expertise gained from actual clinical experience is often contrasted by clinical teachers to available scientific knowledge, '*[so even] though it substitutes for scientifically verified knowledge, it can be used to legitimate a choice of procedures for a patients treatment and can even be used to rule out the use of some procedures that have been scientifically established".* Similarly, Atkinson (1981: 19) in his ethnographic study of bedside teaching and learning in Edinburgh, comments that students experience a '*recurrent reinforcement of the primacy of clinical knowledge over 'theory'.* Sinclair (1997), in his more recent study of medical training in London, highlights that during clinical training students encounter an occupational culture that reinforces the primacy of personal knowledge gained through experience. Students are told *"quite explicitly...that they must learn how to think in a medical way, that preclinical teaching has stopped them being able to think and so on"* Sinclair (1997: 223).

The Clinical Gaze and the Doctor-Patient Relationship

Foucault (1989) recognised that 'hands on' clinical training existed in *protoclinics* before the establishment of the clinic in 1790's France. For example, Rutherford (1695 to 1779) was giving bedside clinical teaching to medical students in Edinburgh in 1748. What was different for Foucault was not that clinical teaching at Paris was no longer undertaken on an ad hoc basis. Nor was it because there was potentially a vast number of patients involved – 20,000 or so – when compared with *the protoclinic* numbers of roughly less than 100 patients per annum. This in itself obviously did signify a significant break with the past. What separated *the protoclinic* from *the clinic* proper was its application of the medical gaze as a diagnostic and teaching tool. This not only led to new ways of defining, understanding and classifying disease, but also engendered a change in the doctor-patient relationship. In the clinic, the disease not the patient mattered. This was reinforced, as Foucault notes, by the lowly social status and poverty-stricken nature of those treated. Here we see how the clinic contributed to the formation of the modern medical profession through the separation of medical and lay worlds and the reversal of the doctor-patient power relationship. As both Johnson (1972) and Jewson (1974 and 1976) note, whereas traditionally the patient acted as a patron and largely determined the dynamics of the medical encounter as well as the course of treatment, the shift to hospital medicine across Europe in the nineteenth century gradually led to the subordination of the patient to medical authority. In other words, the patients' narrative of their personal experience of illness and disease became secondary to the doctor's esoteric clinical-anatomical experimental expertise. As Jewson (1976: 235) states: *'Henceforth the medical investigator was accorded respect on the basis of the authority inherent in his occupational role rather than on the basis of his individually proven worth. The public guarantee of the safety and efficacy of theories and therapies no longer rested upon the patients' approval of their contents.'*

In summary, by the middle of the eighteenth century the continental 'medical gaze' of modern medicine was entering England via Scottish medicine and beginning its rise to prominence. It was creating a new type of medical practitioner, the early forerunner of the modern general practitioner, who had been trained in medicine, surgery, midwifery, chemistry and pharmacy. These well trained doctors needed to generate an income and began to enter general practice (mainly but not solely in the Middle and North of England treating the middle class) and brought with them the idea of the differential fee: the wealthy paying more than the poor. This practice upset their London based counterparts, just as much as Scottish medicines rejection of the Galenic medical tradition did. It was this mixture of economic and epistemological difference between the various elements of the medical profession that ultimately led to the 1815 Apothecaries Act, and so laid the foundations for the 1858 Medical Act.

The 1815 Apothecaries Act

The Royal College of Physicians may have accepted the licensing privileges of the surgeons and apothecaries but it had rejected the idea that these tradesmen possessed the same social status of the physician *as gentleman*. Certainly, the College claimed their profession was different to the apothecaries' trade, as no gentleman would allow himself to be seen to be a tradesman. Indeed, while the surgeons and apothecaries could conduct examinations and issue licenses, Physicians were the regulatory elite. For instance, Physicians claimed the right to supervise the preparations of the apothecaries. The surgeons and apothecaries resented the elevated position of the physician and saw the upward social mobility inherent in the changing world around them as an opportunity to reap social and economic rewards. However, by the middle of the 18th century the apothecaries in particular had their own problems. The potential for upwards social mobility brought about by the industrial revolution was a two way street. The apothecaries increasingly found themselves coming under pressure from shopkeepers trading in drugs. These individuals - the early forerunner of the modern chemist - were marketplace entrepreneurs who retailed and dispensed medicines. The latter part of the eighteenth century as well as the early part nineteenth century was seen by many individuals to be the golden age of charlatans and quacks. However, the rise of the druggist meant the *'apothecaries, the largest order of medical practitioners, began to feel themselves encroached on from below. The result was that when unqualified practice grew to sufficient proportions the apothecaries felt that something should be done'* (Newman 1957: 58).

The apothecaries wanted a review of the regulation of the medical marketplace and had the support of the Royal College of Physicians - only because the College elite were worried about the rise of the general medical practitioners. Who were increasingly registering as surgeon-apothecaries and calling for reform of the existing training and practice arrangements. As Louden (1995: 238) notes *'the surgeon-apothecaries/general practitioners wanted to run their own show by being in charge of the selection, examination and certification of those who chose their branch of the profession. They had no intention of being subservient to any superior body'.* The College of Physicians saw an opportunity to stamp their authority on medical practice and training. They sponsored the 1815 Apothecaries Act, which endorsed apothecary control over medical dispensation. More importantly, the Act made it a legal requirement for general practitioners to take Apothecaries examinations. It also reinforced the subservience of the apothecary to the physician. In one stroke, the Physicians reminded the apothecary and the general practitioner of their place in the medical hierarchy. Holloway (1966: 128) notes that *'the general practitioners demand for an Act of Parliament to further their advancement was so skilfully manipulated by the College of Physicians that the Act passed tended to degrade rather than to elevate the rank and file of the profession. The general practitioner was subjected to the direct control of a London mercantile company, still largely engaged in the wholesale drug trade, and to the indirect supervision of the College of Physicians, whose policy was to make permanent the subordinate and inferior status of the apothecary.'*

An Upwardly Mobile Profession

The College of Physicians seemed to have put the general practitioner in their place. However, the 1815 Act took place against a background of increasing discontent amongst provincial physicians, surgeons and surgeon-apothecaries regarding the standard of medical education in some universities and teaching hospitals. That is in addition to the continued activities of unlicensed medical practitioners, including cooks, blacksmiths, druggists and grocers, amongst others. It soon became apparent that the Society of Apothecaries did not possess the work force to prosecute quackery. The grocer and the blacksmith who also treated the sick did so without fear of prosecution. Indeed, the 1841 census revealed that of the 30,000 individuals who declared themselves 'doctors' only 11,000 appeared on approved registers (Moran and Wood 1993). Additionally, incensed by the fact that they were viewed as tradesmen instead of members of a learned profession, general practitioners fanned the flames for reform by lobbying parliament for the establishment of a Royal College of General Practitioners. This was unsuccessful because the Royal College of Surgeons would not agree to general practitioners conducting surgical examinations. In turn, the general practitioners could not conceive of a college that did not conduct surgical examinations. However, a National Association of General Practitioners in Medicine, Surgery and Midwifery was formed in 1842. This contributed to the growing realisation by Royal College's of Physicians and Surgeons that the organisation of the regulatory and training arrangements had to be re-evaluated.

A key factor that heavily influenced the College of Physician's eventual support for reform was that by the mid-Nineteenth century a generation of London Physicians had been directly influenced by Scottish and French medicine. A large number spent a 'gap year' in France as part of their initial clinical education. Consequently, *'experience, from the dissection table and the hospital wards, flowed through the careers of multitudinous young Englishmen as they made the journey out and back....The year in France was, far from a passive period of observation, a veritable tour de main'* (Maulitz 1987: 136). Additionally, the recent introduction of the stethoscope was beginning to secure modern medicine's future in English medicine. Physicians were as conscious of the possibility of upward social mobility as their fellow surgeons, apothecaries and general practitioners. They saw that the growing association of medicine with science was changing the nature of the doctor-patient relationship to their advantage and they realised the political utility in establishing a united medical profession whose practitioners were self-governing and equal in the eyes of the law. As an editorial in the medical periodical *Lancet* reported after the enactment of the 1858 Medical Act: *'Medicine in this country has, both in regards to Science and Polity entered into a new era...with our free institution there is scarcely a limit to the influence which the profession may come to exert in the state now that it acquired a collective and political existence'* (Lancet editorial 1858: 148*)*.

The 1858 Medical Act

The 1858 Medical Act established the General Council of Medical Education and Registration (subsequently shortened to the General Medical Council). This body would be responsible to Parliament through the Privy Council, but in practice it was autonomous. Its responsibilities were essentially twofold – to maintain a register of qualified medical practitioners and to define the nature of the qualifications necessary to obtain registration. The 1858 Act is often held to be a landmark in the modernisation of medical training and regulation in the United Kingdom. Even today, it is held by many to be a measure that ensures patient safety. For through its enactment the profession entered into a regulatory bargain with the state: it gained the privilege of professional self-regulation in return for promising the public that they could trust the competence of registered medical practitioners. Yet the Act also ensured the continuation of the status quo as the existing medical elites made sure their qualifications alone were accepted by the GMC for the purpose of registration (Gladstone 2000). In addition, their members controlled the GMC's board. Indeed, of the initial twenty four board members board, nine represented directly the Royal Colleges, twelve the universities whose representatives were naturally senior members of the Colleges, and the remaining three were nominated on the advice of the Privy Council (these were usually medical men). There was no space for general practitioners. This did change until an amendment to the Act in 1886, which allowed the profession to elect by postal vote five doctors from the profession as a whole. It was not until the 1926 that the Privy Council chose to include one layperson on the GMC board. This will be discussed in detail in the next chapter.

Victorian Club Government and Medicine's 'Club Mentality'

'In 1858 the GMC was effectively a gentlemen's club. Its promise that the public could trust those it registered amounted to ensuring that there were no 'bounders' in the medical fraternity [sic] who would do dastardly things such as no gentleman would do...'.
Stacey (1992: 204)

It is commonly asserted that medicine's altruistic principles and close association with science naturally led to its being granted the privilege of professional self-regulation. In contrast, this chapter has argued that the organisation of medical regulation occurred in particular social and political circumstances that shaped the nature of the institutional arrangements surrounding the establishment of the GMC. These, it has been argued, favoured the institutionalisation of medical privilege and autonomy. The 1858 Medical Act was designed to regulate the burgeoning health care marketplace and to generate public trust in the competence of medical practitioners. However, it also established a medical hierarchy (with the Royal Colleges at the top) which was in a good position to take full advantage of subsequent developments in the public health sphere, such as the introduction of the National Health Service (NHS). The 1858 Act and the GMC were reflections of the essentially pre-democratic, oligarchic, political structure in which they were founded. As Moran (2004: 28) notes *'because government was the product of an era of oligarchy, deference and social elitism it was the government of clubs…[and] the government of doctors was patterned on the club system'*. He cites Marquand (1988: 178) who says of the ideology of the broader Victorian governing style that *'[the] atmosphere of British government was that of a club, whose members trusted each other to observe the spirit of the club rules, the notion that the principles underlying the rules should be clearly defined and publicly proclaimed was profoundly alien'*. Indeed, medicine's lack of transparency and accountability continued for the next hundred years. Stacey (1992: 204-5) noted when she joined the GMC as a lay member in the 1970s that it still retrained the air of being an exclusive 'gentlemen's club': *'One felt that change was accepted reluctantly and that tradition dominated. It was really a place for white men…The few women were tolerated and treated very civilly (albeit their toilets were in basement or attic) but the ethos was male…Life on the Council was not entirely nineteenth century of course; the founding fathers would have felt out of place in a number of ways. But given their pervasive legacy, they would have felt happier there than in many parts of the outside world'*.

Sorry Mrs, These are 'Men Only' Clubs

An interrelated feature of medicine's 'club mentality' and the wider club government system of the time was their gender bias. Women had been involved in the practice of healing and childbirth for many centuries. However, it was not until the rise of the biomedical model that the medical fraternity deliberately excluded women as they collectively pursued their project to obtain occupational control of the medical register. Ehrenrich and English (1973) trace historical portrayals of women as physically and mentally weak. In doing so they illustrate how these served the interests of male doctors by disqualifying women as healers and qualifying them as patients. The rise of scientific interest in reproductive biology in the eighteenth and nineteenth centuries transformed the female body into an object for detailed examination, with evolutionary theory being used to justify patriarchal social roles. The overwhelming consensus of the male dominated sciences of the time was that *'women were inherently different from men in their anatomy, physiology, temperament and intellect. In the evolutionary development of the race women had lagged behind men, much as 'primitive people' lagged behind Europeans. Even as adults, they remained childlike in body and mind. The reasons for women's arrested development were the need to preserve her energies for reproduction'* (Russett 1989: 11). The corollary of such ideas was that women were perceived as mentally and morally weak and fragile. These assumptions were used to justify the allocation of an inferior social status of women. The division of labour between men and women was seen as being pre-determined by nature: men produced and women reproduced.

Interestingly, though women were actively excluded from medical practice, the wording of the 1858 Medical Act did not specifically exclude women from becoming a registered medical practitioner. Indeed, the Act stipulated that a person could practice medicine if they possessed a British University degree or a licentiate membership or fellowship in one of the medical corporations. It should be no surprise to learn then that women managed to break into the profession, though not without some difficulty. The first, Elizabeth Blackwell, gained a medical qualification in the USA in 1849. On returning to England, she subsequently obtained a diploma from the Irish College of Physicians. This enabled her to gain admittance onto the medical register in 1858. In typical gentleman club style the GMC at once changed their rules so that in future women with a foreign degree could not be included on the medical register. Despite experiencing considerable social hostility, Blackwell gave lectures and encouraged other women to become doctors. She inspired Elizabeth Garrett, who in 1865 became the first women to qualify in Britain after studying at the Society of Apothecaries, which was the only medical corporation that did not specifically exclude women. She subsequently helped other women lobby for equality and eventually in 1899 an Act of Parliament removed all remaining legal barriers to women training as doctors. However, social and cultural barriers would persist for several generations. For instance in the 1890s William Osler jokingly told his students that humankind could be divided into three categories – men, women and women physicians (Moldow 1987).

Women and the Modern Medical Profession

Women who wished to practice medicine during the first part of the twentieth century faced were actively encouraged by family and friends to be nurses. Nursing was seen to be a more suitable occupation for a woman (Riska and Wegar 1993). The fact of the matter was that female medical students were actively kept in the minority through an informal quota system (roughly 10% of medical school places). It was not until after the 1968 Todd report on medical education that women would enter medical school in greater numbers. In contemporary times, women are now in the majority as the proportion of women entering medical school has risen to almost 55% (McManus 1997). Indeed, in 2001 3,355 women from the UK were given places at UK medical schools compared to 2,320 men (Carvel 2002). This trend is expected to continue and seems to reflect broader social changes in regards to traditional perceptions surrounding the appropriate position of women in the public sphere in general, and health care and medicine in particular. Recent figures show that the percentage of female hospital consultants has grown from 16% to 22% (Department of Health 2001). This trend indicates that medicine's traditional male bias has been slowly disappearing over the last several decades. Inequalities between the sexes remain. Not only are they less women consultants than men, but women are also unevenly distributed across the medical specialists. With the majority being in paediatrics (38%) and the minority surgery (6%) (Department of Health 2001). Providing a full historical exploration of the topic of modern medicine's gender imbalance is not the purpose of this book. However, it is important to note that there has been a change in the general social perception of which individuals are appropriate to practice medicine. For this highlights, first, the culturally and historically embedded nature of the organisation of medical practice and regulation, and second, that it is possible for social inequalities to be successfully challenged. Even those that at a particular point in time are perceived by society as 'natural'. Indeed, the central argument of this chapter has been that the particular form of medical regulation in the UK with the establishment of the 1858 Medical Act – i.e. medical self-regulation – was not a natural consequence of the nature of medical expertise, but rather was very much a product of its time.

Medical Science, the Principle of Self-Regulation and the Doctrine of Clinical Autonomy

At first sight there does seem to be a logical consistency between the scientific foundations of modern medical expertise, the principle of medical self-regulation and the doctrine of clinical autonomy. Patients want doctors to possess the freedom to decide the best course of treatment for them (i.e. clinical freedom). While it can be argued that the esoteric nature of medical knowledge means only a doctor's peers can be said to be sufficiently qualified to judge the quality of her work (i.e. medical self-regulation). Yet the rational scientific basis of modern medical knowledge means it is open to codification, routinization and cross-site comparison and evaluation by outsiders. A point that will be discussed in more detail in subsequent chapters. Additionally, even if one admits that there is an inherent indeterminacy present when clinical decisions are made in complex practice situations, it does not necessarily follow that a particular course of action lies beyond the moral evaluation of an outsider, or even the patient themselves for that matter. Regardless of the persuasiveness of arguments in support of medical self-regulation in particular and clinical autonomy in general, the possession of an esoteric knowledge base alone does not necessarily lead to a 'closed shop' approach to medical regulation, as was established by the 1858 Medical Act. Indeed, this chapter has focused upon how the process by which the principle of medical autonomy became institutionalised in the form of the GMC took place within a broader social and political context. This supported the development of an occupational culture within medicine built upon paternalistic practices during doctor-patient encounters and occupational elitism in the professional-public relationship. In short, the particular form medical regulation took with the introduction of the 1858 Medical Act (i.e. self-regulation) reflected an elitist model of 'club government' characteristic of the organisation of the state in the Nineteenth century (Moran 2004). The patterning of medical regulation on the Victorian gentleman's club reflected doctor's individualistic image of themselves *as autonomous, self sufficient practitioners with personal responsibility for their patients'* (Davies, 2004: 59). An emphasis on voluntary compliance and self-regulation has historically been a common feature of the government of social elites in the United Kingdom. The informal 'old boy network' of the gentleman's club stressed informal and unwritten gentleman's agreements and emphasised self-discipline (Baggott 2004). The direct control of fellow members was seen to be distasteful and ungentlemanly, as well as largely unnecessary. Relatively few 'bad apples' were expected to exist. How could such people get into the club in the first place? No matter how attractive to the medical profession this method of governance was, it could only last as long as the general public accepted its legitimacy. Indeed, it is medical regulations historical journey away from being an exclusive Victorian member's only club that the next chapter is concerned with.

Chapter 3

FROM CLUB GOVERNANCE TO STAKEHOLDER REGULATION

'Until the General Medical Council is composed of hard-working representatives of the suffering pubic, with doctors who live by private practice rigidly excluded except as assessors, we shall still be decimated by the vested interest of the private side of the profession in disease.'
Shaw (1957 Preface to The Doctor's Dilemma)

Chapter three discusses the historical development of medical regulation after the 1858 Medical Act up until the 2008 Health and Social Care Act. In doing do it sets the scene for the subsequent discussion of relevant sociological literature in chapter four. As chapter two discussed, under the guise of improving standards to ensure public safety, the 1858 Act did achieve its key goal of introducing a register of approved practitioners who have completed a quality assured training programme. But one thing it could not do was completely resolve existing tensions within the profession between general practitioners and physicians and surgeons. General practitioners resented the increasing importance of hospitals, particularly the teaching hospital, but they also felt that some of their colleagues were engaged in *'competitive undercutting, fee-splitting, canvassing for patients and other unethical practices'* (Titmus 1958: 172). The Act had led to the public being less clear about the various roles and relationships between the different elements of the profession. A doctor was a doctor and all that mattered was that there name was on the medical register. By the 1890s the problem of competition amongst doctors for patients had become so intense that it took the collective power of the British Medical Association – the professions trade union - the Royal Colleges and the GMC to advert a potentially *'really ugly internecine feud'* (Gould 1985: 73). It was agreed that hospital specialists would only see patients referred to them by a general practitioner for a second opinion. This created a division of labour between general practitioner – the generalist - and hospital consultant – the specialist – which remains in place today. However, this was a small (but still important) victory for the general practitioners as they were still seen to at the bottom of the medical hierarchy. Despite being the equal of their physician and surgeon peers in the eyes of the law. The Royal College of Physicians and Surgeons were the most important examining bodies. Their members' occupied key places within the teaching hospitals, universities and the GMC. It would not be until the middle of the twentieth century before general practitioners were granted their own Royal charter to create a college.

Medicine and the Establishment of the National Health Service

Aside from not resolving internal tensions between different elements of the profession and not resolving the economic insecurity faced by a large proportion of the doctors (and mostly general practitioners), the 1858 Medical Act also failed to create a formal monopoly over medical practice. It was possible to practice medicine but in doing so one must not to call oneself a registered medical practitioner (and therefore a qualified doctor). However, what the 1858 Act did do was create a formal monopoly for the registered medical practitioner in all public institutions and government medical services. This certainly placed the profession in a good position when in 1911 the state introduced the National Health Insurance Act to provide medical assistance to the working class and subsequently expanded this to include all of its citizens shortly after the Second World War. The establishment of the National Health Service (NHS) in 1948 promised universal free health care from cradle to grave (Klein 1983). Fulfilling this promise led to the state becoming more dependent up on the medical profession, which in turn gave up its economic independence from the state to secure its members future (although private practice was still allowed). By effectively placing doctors in charge of the NHS the state reinforced medicine's right to possess clinical autonomy in the workplace as well as to self regulate its educational and disciplinary activities. Indeed, the wartime coalition government's 1944 White Paper on the creation of a 'national health service' stated that *whatever the organization, the doctors taking part must remain free to direct their clinical knowledge and personal skill for the benefit of their patients in the way they feel best'* (Ministry of Health 1944: 26). Without a doubt, this was the golden age of medical power and autonomy. As Elston (1991: 67) notes, with the establishment of the NHS, medicine's *'freedom extended to include a considerable level of representation as of right on policy making bodies at all levels as well as freedom from managerial supervision over patient care'*. In return for free healthcare not only did patients have to continue to accept that 'doctor knows best', the concordat between the profession and the state was itself renewed, with the state receiving covert clinical rationing in return for granting the profession control over the day to day allocation of clinical resources (Day and Klein, 1992). There were distinct advantages for the state in doing this. By institutionalising medical autonomy in the structure of the NHS, the state in principle deflected the possibility of direct public criticism of government in regards to public health matters. For with doctors in charge, NHS clinical decision making was now directly in the hands of a group of apparently politically disinterested experts who had the public's best interests at heart. However, this golden age of medical power and autonomy was not going to last.

Changes in the GMC: Discipline, Education and Membership

By the end of the 1960's the GMC had largely remained unchanged for over a hundred years. An empire had been lost, two world wars had come and gone, women had gained the right to vote and the NHS had been born. Yet the GMC remained largely untouched by the passage of time. Although the principle of medical regulation had continued to remain unchallenged, some relatively minor changes had been made along the way concerning the two main functions entwined with maintaining the medical register: overseeing the content and quality of medical education and disciplining errant doctors. For instance, the 1968 Medical Act replaced the then traditional phrase of 'infamous conduct' with 'serious professional misconduct'. 'Serious professional misconduct' was felt to focus the GMC's disciplinary procedures on matters relating to ethical probity, such as sexual relations with patients. 'Infamous conduct' was felt by many within the profession to be associated with their Victorian forefathers somewhat obsessive concern with the regulation of self-advertisement and competition between doctors (Parry and Parry, 1976). Although advertising was still seem to be an important issue, the regulation of competition between doctors for patients was by this time less of an issue given the vast majority were by this time directly employed by the state in the NHS.

In regards to medical education, a series of Acts progressively refined the purpose and content of medical education and, in principle at least, extended the GMCs' powers in overseeing its quality (Stacey 1992). An Act in 1886 made it obligatory for new doctors to pass examinations in midwifery as well as medicine and surgery to gain access to the medical register. While the 1950 Act extended the period of university based basic medical education from five to six years by including what was called pre-registration year. A supplementary 1956 Act made this the direct responsibility of the Universities and GMC instead of teaching hospitals. Finally, the 1968 Act had formally established higher, specialist, hospital training. This was to be overseen by the Royal Colleges. It also made it clear that the purpose of basic medical education was not to produce 'the finished article', but to provide a basic grounding in medicine and prepare junior doctors for subsequent hospital based specialist training, before they finally moved onto higher vocational training in medicine, surgery or general practice. Changes in the focus of basic medical education, the addition of the pre-registration year alongside the introduction of more formal arrangements for later specialist training, were all necessary due to the rapidly expanding nature of medical knowledge and expertise. In short, changes in the organisation of medical education occurred side-by-side biomedicine's increasing reliance upon new developing forms of medical technology. The chapter will return to this issue again shortly.

In addition to these relatively small changes in regards to its disciplinary and educational responsibilities, the membership of the GMC had slightly changed since its inception in 1858. The 1886 Act had allowed five members of the GMC to be elected by the profession after many 'rank and file' doctors, especially general practitioners, made it clear that they felt the GMC was unrepresentative of the profession as a whole. By the mid-1940, and primarily in response to workload demands, the original twenty-four board members had increased to forty-two. For the first time one lay member was nominated by the Privy Council. The early critic of the medical profession George Bernard Shaw took the credit for this. Indeed, he had described the professions in general as 'conspiracies against the laity' in Act One of the Doctor's Dilemma (Shaw 1957). Subsequently, the 1950 Act increased the size of the GMC to fifty and increased its lay membership to three. They were no female members until 1951, and only one female council member until 1971, despite there being 12,596 women on the medical register at this time (Stacey 1992). In short, by the start of the 1970s the GMC remained an elitist institution, largely controlled by men, and perceived by 'rank and file' members of the profession as being detached from the realities of everyday medical practice.

It was no longer a Victorian gentleman's club as it had once been, but it was still an exclusive member's only club.

Lighting the Blue Torch Paper: The Retention Fee

'[Doctor] opposition to the GMC's elitist composition was sparked off primarily by a GMC decision in 1969 to alter the basis of its fees. Until then a doctor, on being admitted to the GMC's approved medical register, paid a life membership fee and could promptly forget about the existence of the GMC, as long as he behaved professionally.'
Moran and Wood (1993: 55)

As Moran and Wood note, the first challenge to the legitimacy of the GMC as a regulatory body came from within the profession. The fact that the council planned to introduce an annual fee for doctors to stay on the medical register ignited 'the blue torch paper'. However, the GMC also had its own problems that deserve to be mentioned. In particular, it was increasingly clashing with the Royal Colleges as it came to recognise that rapid advances in biomedicine and medical technology meant that the largely ad hoc arrangements for specialist medical education needed to be reviewed. The related question of a doctor's continued competence to practice after completing College membership exams was also becoming a real issue given the increasing rate of change in medical knowledge. The Royal Colleges did recognise this issue needed to be addressed. Indeed, in 1976 they sponsored an inquiry into doctors continued competence to practice. Perhaps unsurprisingly they concluded it was unnecessary to introduce periodic examinations to assess doctor continued competence (Ailment 1976). The GMC also did not consider it necessary at this stage for doctors to have to prove periodically their competence to retain their place on the medical register. Indeed, at this time the main source of tension between the Royal Colleges and the GMC was that the GMC felt that the medical register should be amended to include the completion of later specialist training in order to tighten up the quality of specialist medical education. This proposal would effectively place it in charge of all stages of medical education. This upset the Colleges as they felt they should retain sole control.

At the same time of this debate, the GMC had become concerned that its disciplinary procedures did not fully support doctors suffering from mental disorders or addiction to drugs or alcohol. It had no protocol for helping either the recovery or rehabilitation of such individuals. Additionally, it was under considerable financial pressures. It did not have the resources to manage a register containing far more doctors than their forefathers could ever have foreseen. Indeed, it had to cope with the registration and discipline of an influx of overseas doctors into the NHS due to an overall shortage of UK doctors (Irvine 2003). The fact that the GMC was a self-financing body, paid for by the medical profession at large, was an important element of the principle of medical self-regulation. However, it needed more money. As a statutory body, it had to have a government review to address this and its other concerns. In 1969 a Bill was placed before parliament, minus any discussion of the possibility of introducing a specialist register after lobbying from the Royal College of Physicians. At its centre was the proposal for an annual retention fee for doctors to stay on the medical register. For many of the 'rank and file' members of the profession, particularly general practitioners and junior doctors, this was the last straw. They were not represented at all on the GMC council. Why should they pay?

Articles complaining about the GMC's proposals began to appear in the medical press and then national newspapers. The disagreement became so virulent it gained the attention of parliament. Stacey (1992: 34) notes, *'[this] was the iconoclasm – the disputes got outside the 'club', indeed were taken there by defiant acts of some of the club members themselves.'* By the end of 1972, the state was faced with the very real possibility of NHS employees being unable to work because they had been removed from the medical register for no other reason than non-payment of an annual retention fee. It realised it had no option but to act. After discussions with the BMA, Royal Colleges and the GMC, it proposed a full inquiry into the organisation of the GMC. The subsequent Merrison Committee of Inquiry, chaired by Sir Alec Merrison, reported in 1975 and its recommendations informed the 1978 Medical Act.

The central issue which the government and the profession at large wanted resolving was member representation. The Merrison committee did not question the legitimacy of the principle of medical self-regulation. Indeed, Merrison fully endorsed it. He argued that *'Although it is very little in the public eye, and then only on trivial occasions, the importance to the public of the part played by the GMC cannot be overestimated. The health of the nation will be founded on the cornerstone of the wise and responsible practice of medicine and that practice is in turn founded on the wise and responsible regulation of the profession'* Merrison (1975: 7). Consequently, the GMC remained *'an example of a state-approved self-regulatory professional institution'* (Moran and Wood 1993: 56). Neither did Merrison view the issue of doctors periodically demonstrating their continued competence to practice, called variously recertification or relicensure (and in the last decade revalidation) as being part of his review.

Merrison's main recommendations concerned the council's membership, its disciplinary procedures and educational responsibilities. These led to the 1978 Act stating that the GMC's responsibility for basic medical education should be extended to include the coordination of all stages of medical education (with the Royal Colleges still responsible for later specialist professional examinations of course) as well as promoting professional standards and ethics. The 1978 Act also gave the GMC greater discretion in dealing with complaints regarding doctors suffering from health issues (nominally mental health problems or alcohol and drug addictions). It was argued that identifying sick doctors and providing them with therapy and rehabilitation rather than punishment was advantageous to the public as well as the profession. The new health procedures were linked to the GMCs disciplinary procedures and had voluntary and compulsory elements. Colleagues and patients would refer doctors, but in theory, they could refer themselves. Finally, the annual retention fee was endorsed. In return, the 'rank and file' of the profession got what they wanted – representation. The Act enlarged the council to ninety-three members, fifty of whom were directly elected from 'rank and file' members of the profession. Of the remaining forty-three, twenty-one were appointed by the Universities, thirteen by the Royal Colleges and nine by the Privy Council; seven of whom were lay members when the new council first convened. Merrison had considered providing specific places on the council for junior doctors and women. However, this idea was rejected in favour of making sure members could directly elect the majority of council members. Consequently, women remained underrepresented on the GMC despite the recognition that more female council members were needed. Indeed, between 1976 and 1989 the female percentage of council members only rose from 6.5% (n=3) of the total number of members to

13.7% (n=14) despite the fact that 23% (38,318) of the total number of registered doctors (n= 163,708) were female by 1985 (Stacey 1992: 80).

The Rise of NHS Management and the Patient Revolt

The GMC was happy with the Merrison report and the resulting Medical Act. Why should it not be? After all, it recognised the legitimacy of medical authority and autonomy by endorsing the principle of professional self-regulation (Moran and Wood, 1993). Yet at the same time the state was backing the GMC it was moving towards introducing a key variable into the NHS which would from the middle of the 1980's onwards present an increasingly significant challenge to doctor's clinical freedom – general management (Harrison and Ahmed 2000).

So what had changed? As the chapter noted earlier, on creation of the NHS the state and the medical profession entered into an agreement that was mutually beneficial. The problem was that the concordant between medicine and the state was a product of its time. During the 'consensus politics' era after the second world war the prevailing wisdom was 'experts know best'. However, by the 1970s, times had changed and the public was gradually becoming less and less willing to accept the authority of experts without question. Furthermore, when the NHS had been founded there was broad cross-party agreement that the welfare state was necessary and that steady economic growth would ensure the progressive decline of poverty and the improvement of public health. But by the late 1960's to early 1970s growing public expenditure was a very real issue, with both main political parties' instigating reviews of public services, particularly welfare and the NHS (Larkin 1995). Certainly, the 1979 Conservative administration, led by Mrs Margaret Thatcher, wished to reduce public expenditure. Thatcherism held a firm ideological commitment to 'rolling back the state' and introducing free market forces in both the public and private spheres (Riddel 1989, Dean 1999). The 1979 Conservative administrations neo-liberal commitment to the discipline of the market and the power of consumer choice meant it perceived all forms of professional self-regulation (and medical autonomy in the NHS in particular) as being opposed to choice and competition. This led to a situation where though the state was publicly supporting doctor's right to clinical freedom, it was also calling for NHS reforms to contain costs and improve efficiency. It is against this background that in 1983 the NHS Management Inquiry gave its recommendations. Roy Griffiths, who was the Managing Director of Sainsbury's Supermarket Chain, chaired this inquiry. The Griffiths report as it subsequently became known led to the replacement of the traditional hospital administrator with general managers (later known as Chief executives) tasked with ensuring the efficient use of resources. Further NHS reforms initiated by Conservative administrations throughout the 1980s and early 1990s – such as Working with Patients (Department of Health 1989a) and the Patients Charter (Department of Health 1991) – would lead to subsequent challenges to 'doctor power' under the guise of improving efficiency and empowering patients (Gabe 1994).

Increasing public concern with the principle of medical self-regulation was an interwoven theme of NHS reform and the growth of the viewpoint of patient as consumer. Certainly, public suspicion of collegiate control of doctor's discipline came to the foreground in the early 1980's as the GMCs' commitment to protecting patients' interests was increasingly questioned in the media. In 1983, Professor Ian Kennedy gave his Reith Lectures called

Unmasking Medicine (Kennedy 1983). Professor Kennedy criticised the GMC's lack of openness and public accountability. He argued that its disciplinary procedures were not transparent and protected doctors instead of patients. He also called for measures to be introduced that would ensure the continued competence of doctors. Meanwhile, programmes such as Dispatches, That's Life, World in Action and File on Four, repeatedly highlighted cases of medical malpractice and blamed the GMC for failing to ensure the doctors they investigated were trustworthy and competent. Perhaps the most important case was that of Alfie Winn. For it highlighted for many critical commentators just how out of touch with the changing needs of the public the GMC really was.

The GMC and the Case of Alfie Winn

Alfie, an eight year old boy, died after a delay in diagnosis. His parents had called their GP, a Dr Archer, after Alfie developed a temperature and started to vomit. "He arrived three hours later and asked the boy to open his mouth. The boy seemed comatose and his mother said: 'He can't hear you'. The doctor replied *'If he can't be bothered to open his bloody mouth, I shall not bloody well look at him.'* He prescribed an antibiotic. *Two hours later the family called an ambulance and Alfie was taken to hospital but died hours later of meningitis'* (Robinson 1988: 5). Subsequently Alfie's family made a formal complaint about Dr Archer and the case came before the GMC. However, the GMC dismissed the case because Dr Archer's rudeness and unwillingness to refer Alfie for hospital treatment may have been below the standard of care required by a doctor, but did not constitute "serious professional misconduct". Unsurprisingly this caused a public outcry. Alfie's case gained further media attention because he was something of a local celebrity, due to being the mascot for West Ham United football club. The GMC was actually doing what it had always done: putting its members' interests before those of the public. The problem was that increased public concern with medical malpractice had meant that the GMC was not only having to cope with an increase in disciplinary proceedings, but was also reviewing more cases like Alfie's which were directly concerned with doctor's clinical performance (Allsop and Mulcahy 1996). However, *'[though GMC was] now prepared to look at more cases bordering on the clinical, errors in practice did not rank as seriously in the [disciplinary] committee's mind as some other offences (advertising for example)'* (Stacey 1992: 183). This was because by looking at a doctor's clinical performance the GMC was effectively breaking the golden rule of the principle of clinical freedom – only the doctor in the clinical situation at hand can decide what treatment is necessary. As Stacey (1992) notes, following Larson (1977), medicine's collective belief in the need for doctors to posses clinical autonomy, due to the specialist nature of medical expertise, means it has developed an occupational culture which in technical terms is 'cognitively exclusive'. This and the previous chapter have already discussed how such exclusivity can lead to the development of elitism in relationships with outsiders and the establishment of two key internal 'club rules'. First, only club members can legitimately decide if a cause of action undertaken by another club member is appropriate. Second, club members should not punish other members for their actions towards 'outsiders', except in the most serious of instances. Primarily because it is expected that mistakes will happen and indeed 'could happen to any of us given the esoteric nature of our specialist knowledge'. This was what had happened in Alfie's case. The only problem was that the

GMC made the mistake of presuming the general public was still culturally bound to accept medical authority without question (this in itself perhaps shows just how out of touch it was by this time). Indeed, Mrs Jean Robinson, who was a lay member of the GMC in the 1980s, published a book on the GMC in 1988 in which she discussed Alfie. In her view, his case illustrated how it *'is the way doctors behave after a mistake has been made which causes most criticism and really brings the profession into disrepute'* (Robinson 1988: 35).

The Spearing Bill

Robinson was not alone in believing this. Alfie's family were supported by their local Member of Parliament, Nigel Spearing, who in 1984 proposed in parliament a two tier GMC system of "serious professional misconduct" and a lesser charge of "unacceptable medical conduct" to cover the increasingly central issue of doctors continued competence to practice. This proposal was given extra weight by the fact that Dr Archer was subsequently referred to the GMC again and identified as suffering from health issues. However, as Robinson (1988) notes, the GMC reacted angrily to Spearing's proposal because it was made by somebody outside of the medical club. It used its political connections to hold up the proposal and eventually countered it by instigating an internal review that proposed the introduction of new disciplinary procedures relating to professional performance. Importantly, the GMC now recognised it had to act because a *'notion of misconduct which marginalised the issue of clinical treatment of patients was just not sustainable in a democracy, especially in a democracy where patients were becoming daily more informed, better educated and more self-confident'* (Moran 1999: 107). Finally, but reluctantly and slowly, the rule of medical club government was giving way to the political realities of the twentieth century. The GMC proposed that it would seek statutory powers so it could suspend doctors from the medical register until they updated their skills. It would not be until 1995 before the Professional Performance Procedures Bill was enacted by Parliament. This gave the GMC statutory powers to monitor underperforming doctors. The GMC was afraid to act without full agreement from the BMA and the Royal Colleges, who in typical fashion dragged their heels on the matter. In summary, it had taken over a decade, but by the early 1990s NHS reforms and the patient revolt had led the GMC to recognise that it needed to look at doctor's continued clinical competence. It could no longer be assumed that doctors would remain competent throughout their career without periodically updating their knowledge and skills.

They can be no doubt then that the rapidly changing and expanding nature of medical knowledge meant the elite institutions of the medical profession involved in medical education, such as the Royal Colleges and the GMC, came to recognise by the end of the 1980s that they had to look at the central issue of doctor's continued competence to practice. They were coming under pressure to reform because of a substantial rise in medical litigation in the NHS (Allsop and Mulcahy 1996). Additionally, public trust in doctors was no longer a cultural given. Patients were increasingly unwilling to accept a passive role in medical care and health matters (Moran 1999). This move by the GMC towards looking at doctors continued competence to practice was progressive. Nevertheless, throughout the 1980's and into the early 1990s it remained an essentially reactive institution, providing little effective leadership to the profession at large. Indeed, it left this up to the BMA and the Royal Colleges as it historically had done. It was heavily dependent upon building consensus within the profession when deciding policy. It was representing doctors, not regulating them as it should have been, and consequently was perceived by many critical commentators to be failing as a regulatory body in its statutory duty to protect the general public (Gladstone 2000). As Slater (2000: 7) notes, *'if the profession does not fulfil its part of the bargain, then the state is obliged to reform medical regulation in order to restore public confidence'*. This is exactly what was going to happen next.

New Public Management, Medical Audit and Evidence Based Medicine

By the beginning of the 1990s, the GMC was under pressure to modernise itself. Yet, the principle of medical self-regulation had not been directly challenged. The same cannot be said for the principle of clinical autonomy in the NHS. As the previous section discussed, from the beginning of the 1980s onwards, the state increasingly adopted a more interventionist stance towards the day-to-day management of medical work in particular and the efficiency and quality of NHS care in general. This state of affairs would continue throughout the 1990s and into the first decade of the new millennium.

As noted previously, the early 1980s the Griffiths report introduced general management into the NHS. The rise of managerialism in the NHS slowly brought with it what was known as New Public Management (NPM) firmly to the foreground of the public service arena in the UK (Pollitt 1990, Hood 1991). According to Hood (1991, 1995a, 1995b), the principle components of NPM are six fold: 1) more active and accountable management. 2) A greater focus upon quality and outcomes with more explicit standards, targets and performance measures. 3) The break up of larger units into smaller ones. 4) More competition and a contract culture. 5) An increased focus on more flexible terms and conditions of employment. 6) A greater emphasis on public as consumer. The ideals of the Conservative Administration throughout the 1980s and into early 1990s were broadly in line with NPM ideas, as these in turn possessed an elective affinity with the principles espoused by Enthoven (1985). Enthoven had advocated the introduction of an internal market in the NHS and greater managerial control over medical work to ensure cost efficiency and increase service quality.

The publication of Working for Patients (Department of Health 1989) brought the internal market into the NHS through splitting purchasing and providing functions. By the end of the 1980s management had established control over hospital information systems and clinical budgets, which in themselves meant managers possessed more control over doctor's clinical activities than any 'outsider' ever had. The state's reforms further expanded managements influence to include the allocation of merit awards, the appointment of hospital consultants and annual reviews of their job descriptions. By the early 1990s Flynn noted that there had been a *'tendency during the last decade...towards an erosion of professional dominance in the face of increased...managerial power'* (Flynn 1992: 50). However, and most importantly for the purpose of this chapter, what really made the GMC, Royal Colleges and BMA sit up and take notice was that interventions such as Working for Patients revealed for the first time that state policy was undeniably following a line of reasoning which struck at the very heart of the concept of clinical freedom. Namely, given the rational and scientific basis of biomedicine, the outcomes produced by the application of medical expertise were not only open to codification and standardisation, but also surveillance and modification. This fact was vitally important for a state increasingly concerned with, on one hand, cost efficiency and the management of risk, and on the other hand, the promotion of patient involvement and choice in health care.

As the chapter has discussed, by the beginning of the 1980s medical knowledge was rapidly expanding hand in hand with new forms of medical technology that were establishing new and more costly medical interventions. It also highlighted that there was a rise of patient complaints and medical litigation in the NHS as well as a continued failure of medicine's elite institutions to meet head on the issue of underperforming doctors. This situation led the state to feel increasingly justified in developing strategies to monitor (and challenge and change) doctor's clinical activities. By the end of the 1980s, the state was arguing that it was time "to develop a comprehensive set of measures of the outcome of much of the work of...doctors" (Department of Health 1989b: 2). It had decided, *'to consider how the quality of medical care can best be improved by means of medical audit, and on the development of indicators of clinical outcome'* (Department of Health 1989b:2). First developed in the USA to track quality through analysing treatment outcomes, and endorsed by the BMA as a strategy to protect professional autonomy, medical audit seemed to be the perfect tool the state needed to place doctors under greater surveillance and control. The problem was, as a study published at the time indicated, 'rank and file' doctors may *'regard overall financial limitations as being legitimate restrictions on their autonomy...[but do]...not see a legitimate role for peer review or quality assurance'* (Harrison and Schulz 1989: 203). As the chapter has already discussed, medicine's occupational culture was based upon the 'club rule' that one doctor did not question the actions of another unless they were highly unethical or extremely out of line with accepted practice. Yet the Royal Colleges were ever aware of the turning political tide and had joined the BMA in viewing medical audit and peer review as a legitimate way of improving doctor performance while at the same time retaining medical autonomy. By the early 1990s, they were actively involved in promoting medical audit to the 'rank and file' of the profession (Hopkins 1990). The state needed such allies to make its reforms work and consequently had to accede to the view of medical audit possessed by the Royals Colleges and BMA. Namely, if medical audit was going to be used more frequently and formally, then it should follow what Pollitt (1993) called 'the medical model'. This meant that its operation remained firmly in the hands of doctors themselves who would periodically advise management on outcomes as they saw fit. However, this was not the end of the matter. As 1990s progressed, the state would move towards introducing multi-disciplinary clinical audit and proactively sought to develop risk management strategies across professional groups (NHS Executive 1994, Kogan and Redfern 1995).

At the same time that the use of medical audit and clinical audit were on the rise, evidence-based medicine was developing to address regional variations in key performance outcome areas, such as mortality rates following surgery and length of stay in hospital following admission (Ham 1988, Berg 1997). By the end of the 1980s, technological developments like the computer had become more firmly linked to existing statistical and epidemiological techniques. This had led to a rapid increase in the ability to manage and analyse clinical outcomes and establish 'low risk' guidelines and protocols for doctors to follow (Wennberg 1988). Some were worried that this would lead to the establishment of 'cook book medicine' (Ellwood 1988). Evidence-based medicine not only promised to help the state place medical work under greater surveillance, it also promised to help patients make more informed choices with regards to treatment. Nearly two hundred years had passed since the rise of biomedicine's clinical gaze and the establishment of the hospital as a site of medical authority and autonomy. Finally, a mixture of political will and modern technology was supporting changes in the nature doctor-patient power relationship. As Wennberg (1988: 34) noted at the time, *'[it] is now possible to speak of a new set of disciplines which together constitute the evaluative clinical sciences. They offer the promise of a scientific programme that can greatly improve clinical decision-making by decreasing uncertainty about the probabilities and the value to patients of the outcomes of care. They also offer new ways of communicating information to physicians and patients that can greatly increase understanding about the consequences of medical choices and thus help patients make decisions they truly want.'*

By the mid-1990s, peer and managerial surveillance of individual doctor's clinical activities had become the norm under the banner of promoting cost-efficiency, reducing risk and ensuring patient involvement in medical decision-making. The rapid development in 'clinical standards' to govern the performance of doctors and other health care staff was seen by many interested observers to be a consequence of the rise of the idea of 'patient as consumer'. For example, Allsop and Mulcahy (1996) held the increasingly common view amongst commentators that the position of medicine in the health care division of labour had changed and indeed was continuing to change. Furthermore, they held that there was an expanding web of formal rules (i.e. guidelines and protocols) as well as informal rules (i.e. norms of behaviour held by an individual health care actor's social networks) – operating both internally and externally to the medical profession itself – which were increasingly governing the day to day activities of individual doctors. This state of affairs, they felt, was a result of new relationships being forged between what they held to be the four main stakeholders involved in health care – government, citizens, managers and professionals. However, they also noted that rules and regulations to monitor medical work *'are not enforceable unless those at the service delivery level choose to implement them. A thread running through this book has been...[that the medical] profession is still in a position to determine what constitutes appropriate medical practice. Their knowledge is unique and even if guidelines and protocols were to be generally implemented, there would remain a large element of judgement in medical decision making about their application to a particular patient. Furthermore, if patients are to be involved in dealing with their own illness, advice and information often needs to be simplified, explained and filtered through the doctor. Patients, and their carers, need to remain allies of the profession if medical treatment is to be as successful as possible'* (Allsop and Mulcahy 1996: 203).

In summary, Allsop and Mulcahy held that the principle of medical autonomy in the NHS was being actively challenged. They also argued that, like other health and social care staff, 'rank and file' doctors were coming under increased surveillance and questioning from the state, management and patients. However, like Freidson (2001), they hold that the specialist nature of medical expertise means doctors need to be allowed to exercise discretion in their work and collegiate control over member straining, practice and discipline. This point will be discussed again later in this chapter. What is important to highlight here is that recognising the need for doctors to possess discretion does not mean that they should operate without transparency and accountability. As historically had been the case due to medicines 'club mentality', as legally supported by the 1858 Medical Act, and reinforced by its dominance within the NHS. Indeed, things were changing and the profession and the public now needed to forge a new relationship. As Allsop and Mulcahy (1996: 203) went on to say: *'[As] citizens and taxpayers, patients also have a right to expect accountability from the profession and a reassurance that internal forms of control, both formal and informal, are being used to maintain high standards of expert care'.*

New Labour and Clinical Governance

This trend towards the increased surveillance of medical work inside and outside of the medical profession, alongside concurrent calls for self-regulatory professional institutions like the GMC to become more transparent and accountable, did not end with the election in 1997 of New Labour. Although generally critical of many of their Conservative predecessors' health policies, under the guise of treating *'patients as equal partners in the decision making process'* (Department of Health 2000: 2), New Labour introduced measures which placed doctors under even greater surveillance and further challenged their traditional clinical freedoms. New Labour proposed a comprehensive, management-led system of clinical governance designed to set and monitor standards governing medical work. Clinical governance is officially defined as *'a framework through which the NHS organisations are accountable for continuously improving the quality of their services and safeguarding high standards of care by creating an environment in which excellence in clinical care will flourish'* (Department of Health 1998: 33). Clinical standards are set nationally by the National Institute for Clinical Excellence (NICE), which was established in 1999. This body makes recommendations on the cost effectiveness of specific treatments and disseminates clinical standards and guidelines, based upon evidence-based research, for compulsory use by doctors. It also plays a role in developing what are called National Service Frameworks (NSFs), which look at the pathways between primary (i.e. community based) to secondary (i.e. hospital based) care followed by certain patient types (i.e. those suffering from heart disease, diabetes or mental health issues) to identify activity levels and productivity figures and improve service resource allocation. The local implementation of the NSF guidelines and NICE clinical standards are monitored by what was first called the Commission for Health Improvement (also established in 1999) which has more recently been renamed the Commission for Healthcare Audit and Inspection (CHAI). CHAI is empowered to visit hospital and primary care trusts and ensure they are following good clinical governance guidelines. It awards star ratings, similar to those given to hotels, and likewise scores them based on their performance against set criteria, for example, length of time patients spend on a waiting list. As a result of the Health and Social Care Act 2008, CHAI will be integrated with the Commission for Social Care Inspection and the Mental Health Act Commission, creating a single regulator for health and social care, the Care Quality Commission (CQC). This began operating in April 2009. Originally CHAI was supported in its activities by the National Patient Safety Agency (NPSA). This was established in 2002 and focuses upon promoting good health care practice. This function will not change as a result of the creation of CQC.

The Scientific Rationality of Performance Management

Given New Labour's reforms, it is unsurprising that in his review of NHS reforms Light (1998: 431-2) stated that: 'the national framework for performance management is extensive.

The White Papers propose establishment of evidence-based patterns and levels of service, clinical guidelines, and clinical performance review, in order to ensure patients of high uniform quality throughout the service'. Furthermore, Slater (2001: 874) believes that the New Labour's NHS reforms in general, and clinical governance in particular, have established 'a rationalistic bureaucratic discourse of regulation which reveals itself through increasingly extensive rule systems, the scientific measurement of objective standards, and the minimisation of the scope of human error. Behind it lies a faith in the efficacy of surveillance as a directive force in human affairs'. This new rationalistic-bureaucratic discourse, with its focus on the surveillance and management of risk through standard setting and transparent performance monitoring, has presented a significant challenge to the principle of professional self-regulation, as it has traditionally existed within the healthcare arena in the United Kingdom (Davies 2004). Indeed, New Labour has established a Council for the Regulation of the Health Care Professions, subsequently renamed the Council for Healthcare Regulatory Excellence. This oversees the professional bodies responsible for maintaining standards in health care. It also aims to increase inter-agency consistency in the regulation of health professionals (Department of Health 2001). It is composed of the presidents of each council it oversees alongside lay members. It reviews each council annually and will refer professional misconduct decisions made by a council to the High Court (Allsop 2006). The nine councils under its remit are: General Chiropractic Council (GCC) General Dental Council (GDC) General Medical Council (GMC) General Optical Council (GOC) General Osteopathic Council (GOsC) Health Professions Council (HPC) Nursing and Midwifery Council (NMC) Pharmaceutical Society of Northern Ireland (PSNI) Royal Pharmaceutical Society of Great Britain (RPSGB).

For all these changes the principle of medical self-regulation did remain. Primarily because of the cost implications presented by the alternative of a directly state controlled regulatory body. The state made it clear that the GMC and all other professional regulatory bodies must become more open to public scrutiny, responsive to changing clinical practice and NHS service needs, as well as publicly accountable for maintaining standards (Department of Health 2000). Given this, it would be expected that some changes to the makeup of the GMC would be made. Sure enough, in 2003 its executive membership was reduced to 35 members, 14 (40%) of whom are lay members. However it was noted that *'elected and appointed medical members still form a majority on the council and the president, a doctor, is elected by the membership thus preserving a symbol of self-regulation'* (Allsop 2006:629).

What happened? New Labour's NHS reforms can be seen to be part of its 'third way' modernisation agenda. It operates somewhere between the Conservative party's rule of the market and the state socialism of the traditional Labour party. Furthermore, it is built upon the principle of ensuring partnership between stakeholders, and active patient involvement in health care delivery and reform. But most importantly, the reasons behind New Labour's reforms to medical regulation in particular, and the governance of health and social care sphere in general, can be summed up in two words: Bristol and Shipman. Certainly, they are other important medical malpractice cases, such as the Alder Hay organ retention scandal (see Irvine, 2003 for a discussion of this and other cases). Yet without a doubt, Bristol and Shipman have had the most impact on the organisation of medical regulation. These two cases will be discussed in more detail in a moment. First, it is necessary to backtrack to the beginning of the 1990s in order to outline key events leading up to them.

Reforms in Undergraduate Medical Education

As the chapter has already noted, the GMC had started the 1990s realising it had to make changes. In particular, it recognised the need to reform the content of undergraduate medical education to bring it in line with changes in the organisation and focus of the NHS. Here three key aspects of the existing course needed to be addressed. First, there was a lack of emphasis on inter-professional working practices, doctor's communication skills and the patient's perspectives of illness and disease. Second, there was a lack of integration between preclinical (i.e. classroom) education and clinical (i.e. hospital based) training, alongside an over emphasis on hospital as opposed to primary care. Third, advances in medical knowledge and technology meant that 'factual overload' was a very real issue facing the modern medical student. It also meant that school staff placed too much emphasis on assessing what students knew instead of what they could do (Nutton and Porter 1995). Yet as equally important as the need to align medical education to the changing needs of the NHS, was the recognition that the development of information technology and the knowledge based economy would place the concept of lifelong learning at the centre of Higher Education (Ransom 1994). Undergraduate medical education had to be reformed due to changes in the NHS and Higher Education and in 1993, the GMC published Tomorrows Doctors (GMC 1993). This advocated a patient centred model of medical education, focusing on multidisciplinary working and the assessment of student's clinical and communication skills. It recommended a core-plus options curriculum design, early clinical exposure in hospital and primary care settings and the use of small group teaching methods to promote self-directed learning and the development of students' lifelong learning skills. As part of this revision of undergraduate medical education, the GMC also revised its visiting policy to medical schools. Whereas previously it had largely left Universities to themselves, it now visited medical schools regularly to check on their implementation of the changes discussed in Tomorrows Doctors. Some observers highlighted that they were initial doubts over the effectiveness of these visits (i.e. Moran, 1999). However, in the last five years the GMC has substantially changed its earlier visiting policy. Due in part to reforms to the GMC itself, but also because of the developing role of the Quality Assurance Agency for Higher Education since 1997.

The Central Issue of Continuing Medical Education

The development of lifelong learning skills amongst a new generation of medical students was seen as important within the profession given the increasing political focus on doctor's continuing competence to practice. An additional factor influencing medical school reform was that by the early 1990s the state had set up an advisory committee to look at medical workforce issues, which in itself indicated that the GMC was *losing control of the agenda of medical education* (Moran 1999: 109). The reforms held in Tomorrows Doctors were undoubtedly part a reaction by the profession to the establishment of this advisory committee, as much as they was a recognition within the profession of the need to react to changes in the NHS and Higher Education. A government report in 1993 advocated reforms to junior doctor and specialist training to bring it in line with European medical training (UK training was longer). It argued for more formal arrangements for post-specialist training, called variously continuing medical education (CME) or continuing professional development

(CPD) (Calman, 1993). Calman followed this report with a further one on the topic of doctors continuing medical education. Here he argued that: *'The case for CME rests heavily on the concept of confidence: clinicians must command the confidence of the patients they treat; of the public as a whole; of the hospital managers to whom they are accountable for the quality of service to patients'* (Calman 1994: 6).

This state of affairs made it clear to members of the profession that it was the state not the professions' elite institutions which was looking seriously at doctors continuing competence to practice. A direct state attack on the principle of medical self-regulation was feared. In an editorial in the British Medical Journal (BMJ) Richard Smith (1993: 974) held that *'The government is sidelining the GMC and with it the self-regulation the profession has enjoyed since 1858'*. However, despite a global recognition amongst medicine's elite institutions of the need to act little had actually been done. This raises the question: 'What was going on?' Although the GMC and the Royal Colleges recognised the need to act on the issue of doctors continued competence to practice, the *'Royal Colleges were most interested in making sure the GMC did not stray seriously into their territory, into specialist training or CPD, or indeed act decisively on its statutory duty to co-ordinate all stages of medical education'* (Irvine 2003: 98). The Colleges had introduced more formal arrangements for CPD. They worked with the BMA and the state to establish mechanisms whereby sanctions were introduced for doctors who failed to gain CPD 'points' for completing college courses, such as exclusion from merit awards and the supervision of junior doctor training posts. However, these lacked the key sanction possessed solely by the GMC: removal from the medical register for non-completion of CPD. In summary, when medicines elites recognised something needed to be done, a tendency towards institutional inertia remained. Not least of all, because it's exclusive cognitive identity advocates a form of mutual protectionism, which frowns on 'breaking ranks' and 'whistle blowing' (Stacey 1992, 2000).

There was pressure within the profession demanding that the GMC become more proactive and take up the challenge of underperforming doctors. This is particularly amongst general practitioners, but also from powerful 'in house' commentators such as Richard Smith, who was editor of the BMJ (i.e. Smith 1992). Reformers felt the GMC was too far removed from the needs of the profession. They wanted it to provide definitive leadership to its 'rank and file' members by forging a more open and accountable relationship with the public. One of these reformers, who was heavily influenced by the sociologist and GMC lay member Margaret Stacey, as well as the medical sociologist Margot Jeffreys, was a general practitioner called Dr Donald Irvine (now Sir Donald Irvine). He would be the first leader of the GMC to be a general practitioner since its foundation one hundred and thirty seven years previously. Irvine (2005:11) noted: *'In 1995, I stood for election as President of the GMC, on a programme of reform both of professionalism in medicine and the GMC itself. There were members within the GMC, both medical and lay, who believed that such reform of the GMC had to be carried out swiftly. Otherwise public confidence in the medical profession, and in particular in the system of professional self-regulation, for which the GMC was primarily responsible, could not be sustained'*.

Medicine's New Professionalism

The foundation stone of Irvine's 'new professionalism' was the recognition that self-regulation was a privilege not an inherent right. Hence, the number of lay members of the GMC was increased to twenty-five, out of a then one hundred and four. He also advocated the establishment of clear standards that could be operationalised into outcomes for assessment. This led to the publication of 'Good Medical Practice' (GMC, 1995b), which listed the principle attributes of good medical practice under seven headings – Good clinical care, Maintaining good medical practice, Relationships with patients, Teaching and training, appraising and assessing, Working with colleagues, Probity and Health. While 'Duties of a Doctor' (GMC 1995a) placed respect for patients and the need to maintain clinical competence at the centre of medical professionalism. These documents were the first sign that the growing culture of standard setting and performance appraisal in the NHS was reaching medicine's own professional institutions. A key part of Irvine's reforms included the revision of the GMC's new performance procedures, which involved developing appraisal instruments. These operationalized Good Medical Practice into key competency 'domains' whereby assessors could mark a doctor's 'on the job' performance'. For the first time the GMC could look at the actual 'hands on' competence of underperforming doctors. The cost of this scheme, potentially between £6000 and £22000 for an individual doctor in need of remedial training and £530,000 in total per annum for the NHS, was however, an issue in some quarters (i.e. BMJ 1995). The scheme's appraisal instruments were subsequently published in the academic journal Medical Education (Southgate 2001). The scheme was linked to the final part of Irvine's reform agenda, which was the introduction of the periodic re-certification of doctor's 'fitness to practice' to stay on the medical register (known as 'revalidation'). But then Bristol happened and in the words of Richard Smith (1998), it became a situation where everything 'changed, changed utterly'.

Bristol and Shipman – 'All Changed, Changed Utterly'

The Bristol case involved the deaths twenty-nine babies and young children following elective surgery at Bristol Royal Infirmary. The three doctors involved were Mr James Wisheart, Mr Janardan Dhasmana and Mr John Roylance. Between 1990 and 1993 Mr Wisheart carried out a procedure to correct a heart deflect known as an atrio ventricular spetal defect, on fifteen patients, of whom nine died. His mortality rate was 60%. Dr Dhasmana's morality rate for this operation of 10% was far lower and within acceptable limits. His problems started when he performed a highly complex procedure called an 'arterial switch operation'. Of thirty-eight patients twenty died. The national success rate was 80-90%. Worried by the paediatric heart unit's high mortality rate, a young anaesthetist Mr Stephen Bolsin wrote about his worries to Mr Roylance, Bristol's Chief Executive. He referred the complaint to the Director of Cardiac Services, who happened to be Mr Wisheart. Mr Wisheart reprimanded Mr Bolsin for having written to Mr Roylance. Then Joshua Loveday would be operated on by Mr Dhasmana. Joshua's parents were not told of the units' high mortality rate or of the fact that the night before the operation Mr Wisheart had held a special meeting with the cardiac team, to discuss the operation. The Department of Health heard of Mr Bolson's complaint and raised concerns. It requested an external review be undertaken of the unit's morality figures. A subsequent report for the television programme Panorama contained pieces from staff saying that just before the operation they wanted to 'take the baby and run'. They did not. Nor did they officially complain or try to stop the operation. Joshua died on the operating table and his parents asked questions. Subsequently, they and other children's parents launched a local support group that complained to the GMC, which then began an investigation.

The case caught the attention of the public, doctors and government like none before it. Not only were the children's parents not informed of the units' high mortality rate but the doctors involved clearly demonstrated a lack of critical self-awareness and willingness to admit openly to mistakes and learn from them. Additionally, the case brought home to the public just what the culture of the medical club did to 'whistle blowers'. Mr Bolsin suffered for his efforts to put patients' welfare first. Indeed, he was ostracised by his peers and had to move to Australia to restart his career (Delamothe 1998). The media camped outside of the GMC headquarters for the 65-day hearing. They reported a case, which *'was a once in a lifetime drama that has held the attention of doctors and patients in a way that a White Paper can never hope to match'* (Smith 1998: 1918). The GMC found Mr Wisheart and Mr Roylance guilty of serious professional misconduct and struck them off the medical register, but not Mr Dhasmana. This was because he stopped performing the arterial switch operation when he realised his morality rate was too high. The children's parents and the media were incensed and demanded a public inquiry.

The Kennedy Report

For many, the potent image of children's gravestones made out of flowers being laid outside of the GMCs headquarters in London by anguished parents was too much to bear. Frank Dobson, the then Secretary of State for Health, made it abundantly clear on the television programme Newsnight that he felt all three doctors should have been removed from the medical register. The resulting public inquiry chaired by Professor Ian Kennedy could not reverse the GMC's decision. Between 1998 and 2001, it reported extensively on the broader failings within the management and clinical systems of the NHS to identify efficiently and effectively poor performance. A key part of this, it reported, was that NHS employees who had concerns with poorly performing colleagues must feel able to report them (Bristol Royal Infirmary Inquiry 2001). The principle of medical self-regulation as it had historically been known was under attack. In particular, the report criticised the hierarchical medical 'club culture' present in the Bristol heart unit. It noted that this was a reflection of the wider system of professional self-regulation in general. The Bristol inquiry report established the already mentioned Council for the Regulation of the Health Care Professions (subsequently renamed the Council for Healthcare Regulatory Excellence) which was empowered by the state to harmonise the work of health care regulators. It was clear to the GMC and the Royal Colleges that they had to act to remove the club culture of mutual protectionism present within medicine at large. As Stacey (2000: 39) noted *'In Britain today the balance has shifted a bit towards external governmental control, through the NHS reforms and new institutions such as NICE, but that is not all. The medical profession now seems intent upon regulating pro-actively. Both profession and government are paying more attention to the local level and its relation to national bodies such as the GMC and the Royal Colleges'.*

Revalidation

Bristol made the GMC realise its plans for revalidation needed to go ahead at pace. The consultation process started in 1998 with various stakeholders, such as the BMA and patient support groups, attending a GMC conference on the topic. The process was heated with debate raging over whether revalidation was needed, and if so, what form it should take. Members of the public wanted revalidation and voiced the need for it. Conversely, there were 'rank and file' members of the profession and members of its elite institutions, which under no circumstances wanted a periodic exam to form the basis for revalidation. The BMA's Hospital Consultants and Specialists Committee (HCSC) argued against revalidation because of the time and expense it would involve. The Royal Colleges and GMC were for it. In 1999 it was decided that *'to maintain their registration, all doctors must be able to demonstrate regularly that they continue to be fit to practice in their chosen speciality'* (GMC 1999: 1). What had to be decided would be the form that revalidation would take. A further period of consultation was entered into to decide this. The GMC wanted regional centres to undertake revalidation locally. However, this idea was dismissed by the BMA as impractical. The GMC knew it had to move quickly. As part of its reforms of the NHS and because of the problems highlighted by Bristol the Department of Health had published Supporting Doctors, Protecting Patients (Department of Heath 1999). This proposed that all doctors undergo an annual performance appraisal as part of their NHS contract. The report also proposed the establishment of a National Clinical Assessment Authority (NCAA). The purpose of NCAA was to support NHS management with doctors who are underperforming at work, providing guidance and advice as well as retraining. NCAA was established in 2001 and deals with concerns which are not serious enough to justify regulatory action and referral to the GMC. Its very existence caused a huge amount of anxiety on behalf of the GMC and 'rank and file' doctors. However, it quickly became apparent that NCAA would not replace the GMC and was supportive of doctors. Its main function is to support the implementation of clinical governance by providing accountability through employment contract, whereas the GMC provides accountability through the medical register.

The Medical Defence Union views NCAA as having a positive influence on the relationship between doctors and Trusts (BMJ 2003). NCAA certainly sees its role as being *'to ensure that the decision to suspend a doctor is taken only where it is necessary and will facilitate a resolution and to avert unnecessary or inappropriate suspension'* (NCAA 2003: 1). In an analysis of cases over a six month period it deemed that 85% of suspensions from the workplace were inappropriate and related to 'a dysfunctional clinical team' or poor Trust management. Therefore, it recommended resolution via alternative action (NCAA 2003). Yet empirical research continues to show that the inherent uncertainty present in medicine has created an anti-bureaucratic sentiment amongst doctors (i.e. Waring 2003). This, alongside a collective recognition of the inevitability of the occurrence of error, inhibits the reporting of mistakes or the expression of personal doubts about a colleague's proficiency. At least to anybody who is outside of 'the medical club'. Clearly old habits die hard.

Annual Appraisal

The proposal for doctors to undergo Annual Appraisal was similarly met with anxiety by the profession. This subsided with the publication of The NHS Plan in 2000 which highlighted that the purpose of Annual Appraisal was to support doctors to maintain 'medical excellence' (Department of Health 2000). The BMA negotiated with the state an agreement whereby Annual Appraisal (which was finally introduced nationally in 2003) would be a formative developmental educational exercise, undertaken with another doctor, and ordered in line with the principles of clinical governance and the GMCs Good Medical Practice. In other words, though in principle and practice open to managerial input and review, Annual Appraisal would be essentially doctor controlled. Furthermore, it would not lead to extreme punitive action against the doctor in question, such as removal from the medical register. Every year a doctor would maintain a portfolio of evidence of their activities and achievements. This would contain, for example, an overview of teaching and clinical duties, prescribing lists, clinical guidelines used and results of Trust clinical governance reviews (including for instance a doctors surgical success-failure ratio), certificates of attendance to Royal College CPD courses and speciality conferences, feedback from colleagues, as well as patient feedback or complaints. A Royal College trained colleague would review this portfolio evidence to identify developmental needs for the next year. In principle, the National Clinical Assessment Authority could support a doctor meet identified developmental needs.

The Shipman Case

Although not originally intended to link with revalidation it was generally agreed by 2001 that the successful completion of five Annual Appraisals, after external review by two medical and one lay GMC assessors, would in itself be enough for the purposes of revalidation (Gentleman 2001). Doctors identified as needing support would be subsequently reviewed using the new GMC performance procedures, which were discussed earlier. Though it clearly had merits, this proposed method of revalidation was 'lightweight' compared to the original intention of establishing 'revalidation centres' to undertake pass/fail tests of doctor's competence. While it never got off the ground due to the case of serial killer, Harold Shipman, a general practitioner in Hyde, Greater Manchester. Dr Shipman was a popular doctor, well respected by his patients. Between 1995 and 1998, he murdered fifteen elderly patients with lethal doses of diamorphine. Subsequently, it was discovered that between 1974 and 1998 he had murdered two hundred and fifteen patients (all elderly) and doubts remained about a further forty five (Smith 2005). The police informed the GMC they were investigating Dr Shipman in 1998 and he was subsequently convicted of murder in 2000. It was only after his conviction that he was stuck off the medical register.

Similar to the Bristol case, the Shipman case caused a public outcry. It was discovered that Shipman had previously been before the GMC's disciplinary committee in 1976 for dishonestly obtaining drugs and forging NHS prescriptions. He had been dealt with leniently and essentially 'let off' with a warning. This signalled the start of another period of intense criticism for the GMC. The state ordered a public inquiry into the Shipman case, chaired by Dame Janet Smith. As the Secretary of State, Mr Milburn, made it clear at the time: *'The*

GMC…must be truly accountable and it must be guided at all times by the welfare and safety of patients. We owe it to the relatives of Shipman's victims to prevent a repetition of what happened in Hyde' (quoted in Gladstone 2000: 10).

During the Shipman Inquiry, the GMC made changes to its membership. A new GMC was launched in 2003, just after Irvine's reign as president ended. The GMC's executive membership was reduced from one hundred and four to thirty five members, fourteen (40%) of whom were lay members. In February 2003, Professor Sir Graeme Catto took over from Irvine as president of the GMC. Like Irvine before him, Catto continued to maintain its professionally led medical regulation, based on an open and accountable partnership with patients, which best protects the public interest (Irvine 2003, Catto 2006 2007). The GMC continued with its plans for revalidation during this time. Indeed Catto wrote to doctors in 2003 telling them to 'get ready' for revalidation. However, the GMCs revalidation plans were to all intents and purposes deliberately slowed down until Dame Janet Smith published her full report in January 2005.

In her report, Smith (2005) highlighted key lessons that needed to be taken on board by the NHS and the medical profession in relation to topics such as the checking of death certificates, scrutiny of single-handed GP practices and the monitoring of death rates and medical records. About the proposal that five Annual Appraisals would equal revalidation, Smith (2005: 1048) felt that this would not have identified Shipman and did *'not offer the public protection from underperforming doctors'*. She highlighted that the formative nature of Annual Appraisal meant that it was unsuitable for use as a summative pass/fail examination tool, as required by Revalidation. She felt that instead of taking a strong stance, as required of it as a regulatory body, the GMC had essentially 'caved in' to pressure from within the profession to abandon its original idea of independent regional 'revalidation centres'. That is, the possibility of 'summative pass/fail testing' had been dropped in favour of a 'light touch' approach to revalidation that essentially involved 'rubber stamping' existing Annual Appraisals. Indeed, Smith (2005: 1174) said that the GMCs original *'proposals were unpopular with a powerful section of the profession. So the GMC retreated from its earlier vision and devised a system that it calls revalidation but which does not involve any evaluation of a doctor's fitness to practice'*. Concerned about the GMC's move away from adopting a more rigorous approach to revalidation, she actively criticised Catto's comparison of it to an MOT on a BBC radio programme. She said, *'He [Sir Catto] expressed pride in the fact that no other country in the world had a system of time-limited license dependent upon doctors demonstrating they are up to date and fit to practice. To call revalidation an MOT for doctors is a catchword. It is easy for the listener to remember. I think that many people who heard that programme would have taken away the impression that revalidation is a test for doctors, just like the MOT. That is not a true impression'* (Smith 2005: 1086).

A Culture of Medical Protectionism

About the working culture of the GMC, Smith (2005: 1176) echoed the voices of many observers in feeling that although the GMC had changed it had not changed enough: *'I would like to believe that the GMCs working culture would continue to change in the right direction by virtue of its own momentum. However, I do not feel confident it will do so. I am sure they are many people within the GMC, both members and staff, who want to see the regulation of the medical profession based upon the principles of 'patient centred' medicine and public protection. The problem seems to be that, when specific issues arise, opposing views are taken, and as in the past, the balance sometimes tips in the interests of doctors'.*

Furthermore, Smith (2005: 1176) discussed how the elected nature of medical members on the GMC made the central issue of protecting the interests of the public difficult for members: *'it seems....that one of the fundamental problems facing the GMC is the perception, shared by many doctors, that it is supposed to be 'representing' them. It is not, it is regulating them....In fact the medical profession has a very effective representative body in the BMA, it does not need – and should not have – two'*. Her recommendation was that the makeup of the GMC be changed so elected members were replaced with nominated members, selected by the Privy Council via the Public Appointees Committee after a period of 'open competition' on the basis of their ability to serve the public interest. Smith (2005: 1174) concluded that she was *'driven to the conclusion that, for the majority of GMC members, the old culture of protecting the interests of doctors lingers on'*. However, for all her criticisms of the GMC, Smith holds a similar view of medical regulation to that possessed by many doctors who, like Irvine and Catto, believe that the specialist nature of medical expertise means some form of medical self-regulation is necessary to protect the best interests of the general public.

Professionally-led Regulation and the Donaldson Report

For Irvine and Catto a key difference between the modern form of medical self-regulation, which they call professionally led medical regulation, and its traditional more paternalistic counterpart, is that it is built upon a 'new professionalism', as first advocated by the sociologist Margaret Stacey in her review of the GMC (Stacey 1992). This means it is built upon the belief that medicine's traditional 'club mentality' must be replaced with the view that self-regulation is a privilege not an inherent right, and so must be open, accountable, and undertaken in partnership with other stakeholders in the regulatory arena (Catto 2006). Such as the public, other health care professions and the state. It also means that bodies such as the GMC must possess clear standards that can be operationalized into performance outcomes against which the fitness to practice of members of the profession can be regularly checked (Irvine 1997 2003, Catto 2006 2007). Time will tell if Irvine and Catto are correct about the ability of this new professionalism to protect the public. What became clear after the publication of the Shipman report was that the criticisms regarding the GMC's working culture and proposals for revalidation meant the state had to step in and undertake a full review of medical regulation. The then Health Secretary, John Reid, commissioned the Chief Medical Officer, Liam Donaldson, to undertake the review. His subsequent report was published in July 2006 (Donaldson 2006) and informed the content of the 2008 Health and Social Care Act.

Donaldson's report contained forty-four recommendations. These boil down to the following four key points. First, it recommended that the GMC face yearly questions from a committee of MPs and that, as recommended by Smith (2005), its members should be elected independently via the Public Appointments Commission instead of the medical profession. Second, it recommended that the GMC lose control over undergraduate medical education. This being taken over by the relatively newly constituted Postgraduate Medical Education Training Board (PMETB). The PMETB board has a membership of twenty-five: seventeen medical members and eight lay members. This body was created to oversee the new two-year foundation-training programme for junior doctors, formally the pre-registration and house officer years (BMA 2005). The foundation programme is an outcomes focused competence-based curriculum, possessing explicit standards and structured supervision and assessment tools. It is designed to tackle the prevalence for poor supervision and ad hoc assessments present in traditional postgraduate training, as highlighted by Sinclair (1997). Each foundation year trainee keeps a portfolio, which includes 'on the job' peer evaluation and personal reflective elements. The implementation of the Foundation Programme under the banner of Modernising Medical Careers (MMC) forms part of current reforms of specialty and general practice training programmes, implemented in August 2007. Consequently, PMETB works very closely with the Royal Colleges and Donaldson recommended that this continue in order that clear national performance standards in each speciality can be developed for implementation.

Third, Donaldson proposed that although the GMC will still investigate complaints, it would no longer make a final decision on guilt. This will be left up to an independent tribunal. Furthermore, it is recommended the burden of proof required in fitness to practice cases will also be lessened from criminal standards – i.e. beyond all reasonable doubt – i.e. to civil standards - on the balance of probability. This was recommended by Smith to ensure the public interest. Complaints will initially be dealt with at a local level by a 'GMC affiliate' who will be appointed in each hospital and primary care trust with the most serious cases being passed up to the GMC to investigate and present the case to the tribunal. Fourth, Donaldson proposed this 'local GMC affiliate' should also be responsible for the first of what is a proposed two-strand version of revalidation. The first strand of revalidation, called re-licensing, involves the local 'GMC affiliate' via annual appraisal testing a doctor's fitness to practice so they can stay on the register of approved practitioners. Donaldson proposed the second strand of revalidation, called re-certification, should be managed by the Royal Colleges and involve the direct 'hands on' testing a doctor's fitness to practice so they can first join and subsequently remain on the specialist register. He also recommended that NHS Appraisal should be standardised and audited. Although Donaldson recommended NHS Appraisal be separate from Revalidation, he argued that like Revalidation, Appraisal should involve the collection of 360-degree feedback on a doctor's fitness to practice (i.e. feedback from medical and non-medical staff as well as patients). If a doctor fails a revalidation test then it is recommended that the NCAA support the doctor in question and work closely with the GMC to plan remedial action. Furthermore, Donaldson recommended that the NCAA develop clear protocols to help doctors with mental health and addiction problems.

'The combined effect of Donaldson's measures could be quite profound. They should result in much stronger standards based; professional self-regulation led by a revitalised GMC and the royal colleges. That would be reassuring to the public and patients, strengthen doctor's professionalism, and appeal to the huge majority of conscientious doctors who take pride in the standing of their profession. Tomorrow's doctors may well look back and wonder what all the fuss was about.'
Irvine (2006: 966)

As perhaps would be expected, Donaldson's proposals caused quite a stir amongst the medical profession. Irvine's response (as noted above) was positive, although Catto's response on behalf of the GMC would perhaps best be described as welcoming but cautious (GMC 2006). While a study of 800 rank and file doctors for the online publication doctor update (http://www.doctorupdate.net) showed that 90% of doctor's believed it is unfair to judge a doctors actions on any burden of proof less than 'beyond reasonable doubt'. Additionally, 90% thought the changes would not stop another Shipman case. 60% said the proposals would mean the end of self-regulation and only 28% thought it positive that the GMC should lose its adjudication powers. These viewpoints are similar to those expressed by the Royal Colleges and the BMA. See for instance, Royal College of Obstetricians and Gynaecologists (2006), or the Academy of Royal Medical Colleges (2006), or the Royal College of General Practitioners (2006).

Despite having some reservations, the Royal Colleges broadly welcomed the focus on developing national standards for medical education and the recommendation that poorly performing doctors will be dealt with locally with an the increased focus on rehabilitation and retraining (Bruce 2007). Revalidation is now generally accepted as being necessary by the profession and the proposal to strengthen the College's role in it is welcomed by them and the GMC. However, there was concern amongst the Colleges about the proposals regarding the removal of the GMC's responsibilities for undergraduate medical education. While the Colleges and the BMA rejected the idea that the burden of proof against a doctor in disciplinary proceedings should be less than 'beyond reasonable doubt'. There was a fear that the elimination of elected professional members from the GMC will result in the erosion of professionally led regulation (Kmietowicz 2006). This is because the proposals took away two of the four major functions of the General Medical Council: adjudication on disciplinary matters and responsibility for basic medical education. One of the remaining two - standards setting - is to be shared with PMETB. Only registration remained intact as a sole GMC function under Donaldson's proposals.

Future Unknown (For Now)

'Expert systems bracket time and space through deploying modes of technical knowledge which have validity independent of the practitioners and clients who make use of them. Such systems penetrate virtually all aspects of social life in conditions of modernity – in respect to the food we eat, the medicines we take the building we inhabit, the forms of transport we use.....[but they] depend in an essential way on trust'.
Giddens (1991: 18)

There can be no doubt Donaldson's proposals reinforce that over the last three decades there has been a cultural and organisational shift within the health and social care context toward emphasising professional accountability. The rationalistic-bureaucratic method of standard setting, surveillance and performance appraisal, which the government has implemented to support the development of clinical governance systems in the NHS, is designed to engender public confidence and trust in the service provided through the management of cost and risk (some would maintain often in that order). Furthermore, this approach shares much in common with the philosophy of accountable outcome based standard setting, operationalized into performance targets for subsequent assessment, which lies at the heart of medicines 'new professionalism'. After all, as the ex-chairman of the GMC

Irvine (2001: 1808) notes *'the essence of the new professionalism is clear professional standards'*.

Medical elites argue this signifies a 'cultural change' towards a more transparent and contractually binding regulatory relationship between medicine and the public (i.e. Irvine 1997 2003, Catto 2006 2007). Yet such approaches are often criticised in a somewhat knee jerk fashion by 'rank and file' health care professionals as providing prescriptive procedures and rules in the form of protocols and guidelines to be blindly followed without question. There is a feeling of disquiet within the medical profession with what is ultimately seen to be a politically motivated and unrealistic tendency on behalf of government to minimise clinical risk by turning medical work into a series of routine 'step by step' rules and procedures against which individual clinician performance can be measured. Because, for many, this fails to recognise the importance of the tacit and personal dimensions of medical expertise and the inherent risks present in messy 'real world' clinical practice situations. Certainly, many medical practitioners would argue that these situations are decidedly different from the sanitised world assumed by clinical guidelines and protocols. It is no wonder therefore that, regardless of their views about how it should be undertaken and by whom, many if not all doctors claim that some form of professionally led medical regulation is both necessary and in the public interest.

Freidson has repeatedly highlighted over an academic career spanning four decades that the need for doctors to exercise discretion in their work is an issue which is unlikely to disappear as long as people need and want to see a doctor to help them cope with illness and disease (Freidson 1970 1994 2001). Indeed, in his latest work Freidson (2001) has moved away from his earlier more critical view of medical autonomy (i.e. Freidson 1970). He insists that doctors must be allowed to exercise discretion in their work due to its inherently specialist nature, the tacit-indeterminate foundations of medical expertise, as well as the emphasis medicine collectively places upon providing a community service through promoting public health. He holds that non-medical external regulation of medical work is not always possible or in the public interest. He outlines three methods of regulatory control – 'Bureaucracy', characterised by managerial control, 'The Market', characterised by consumer control, and 'Professionalism', characterised by occupational self-control (Freidson 2001). He discusses how in the last two decades greater managerially led 'Bureaucracy' and a concurrent increase in the rule of 'The Market' have successfully challenged 'Professionalism', with the doctors increasingly losing the right to exercise discretion in their practice. In particular, he notes that patients are unwilling to adopt the subservient position medicine has historically accorded them. Patients nowadays frequently see themselves as active health care consumers. Additionally, there has been a rise in managerial control over clinical practice through the increased use of standardised administrative procedures, in the form of clinical guidelines and protocols. These exist under the banner of supporting greater patient choice while also improving productivity. Freidson (2001: 181) argues that *'the emphasis on consumerism and managerialism has legitimised and advanced the individual pursuit of material self-interest....the very [vice] for which professions have been criticised'*.

In summary, while previously an ardent critic of the high level of autonomy granted to medicine to control its own affairs, Freidson (2001) now emphasises the positive moral role professions such as medicine can and do play in society. Like Stacey (1992 2000) before him, he holds that the moral code of public service inherent in the concept of professionalism can act to dispel what Wilson (1990: 147) calls *'the ethical vacuum of the 'postmodern' society'*.

He argues that health practitioners themselves, not patients and managers, must ultimately control their work activities. Not least of all because the nature of their knowledge demands that society recognise professionals must possess *'independence of judgement and freedom of action'* (Freidson 2001: 122). Although he recognises that this may not be to everybody's taste, he calls for a revival of the 'ideology of service' and claims that professional monopolies are *'more than modes of exploitation or domination they are also social devices for supporting growth and refinement of disciplines and the quality of their practice'* (Freidson 2001: 203).

Sociologists like Stacey (1991 2000) and Freidson (1994 2001) echo the common view amongst professionals that it is not the principle of professional self-regulation that in itself is unjustifiable. It is only particular instances where it has been abused. Professionals must now work with the public to make sure such abuses do not happen again (Irvine 2003 2006). The advocacy by medical elites of a 'new professionalism' is an attempt to establish a new contractual relationship between the medical profession and the public against the background of increasing government intervention into the field of medical regulation (Slater 2007). Furthermore, recent attempts to change in the field of professional regulation reinforce the fact that effective medical regulation, similar to the effective delivery of health care, requires the cooperation and proactive involvement of individual medical practitioners and their elite institutions. This is because contemporary challenges to professional autonomy bring to the foreground the fact that the principle of medical self-regulation was first institutionalised in the form of the GMC as it provided a workable solution to the complex problem of *'how to [both] nurture and control occupations with complex, esoteric knowledge and skill...which provide us with critical personal services'* (Freidson 2001: 220).

The 2008 Health and Social Care Act

It is the dynamic nature of this need to both nurture and control professional expertise which has led to the Royal Colleges being allocated a significant role by Donaldson in developing national educational and practice standards, as well as the management of his proposed two-step model of revalidation. It is also why alterations and amendments to Donaldson's proposals occurred almost immediately after their publication. Indeed, by the time the government published its own discussion paper in light of Donaldson's proposals, it had already conceded, after lobbying by the GMC, that the GMC should retain control over undergraduate medical education. The GMC is currently undertaking a review of undergraduate education and it will not become clear until 2010 if there will be a national exit examination (even then it is expected a not inconsequential amount of time will lapse before such an exam is finally implemented). Again after lobbying from the GMC, it was agreed the GMC will take over the standard setting and quality assurance role of PMETB altogether (GMC 2008). Consequently, medical control over entry onto (via medical school and junior doctor training) and exit from (via appraisal of their continue competence) the legally underwritten state approved register of practitioners will continue for the foreseeable future. Not least of all because the state does not want the GMC to be completely abolished. It is, after all, a self-funding body paid for by doctors themselves. While peer assessment is still acknowledged, by both medical and non-medical observers alike, as the essential core method by which an individual doctor's clinical competence can be legitimately assessed and underperformance addressed (Irvine 2003, Catto 2006 2007, GMC 2008). Indeed, the finalised Health and Social Care Act 2008 may well propose greater managerial, patient and inter-professional involvement in revalidation, which will be implemented nationally in 2010. Yet the revalidation process will nevertheless be organized and quality assured by the royal college relevant to a particular medical speciality, operating in tandem with the GMC and NHS management. In its post-Donaldson finalized guise, revalidation is made up of two elements – relicensing and recertification – which incorporate NHS appraisal within them. Relicensing seeks to make current NHS appraisal arrangements more rigorous, with greater direct testing of a doctor's competence in regards to key day to day clinical tasks. To stay on the medical register, all doctors will now have to successfully pass the relicensing requirement that they have successfully complete five NHS annual performance appraisals. Specialist recertification will also occur every five years. It will involve a thorough 'hands on' assessment of a doctor, organized and quality assured by the royal college relevant to their chosen speciality.

The Health and Social Care Act of 2008 did however also put into place significant checks and balances to medical control over doctors activities. In line with Donaldson's proposals, the GMC will be made up of an equal number of lay and medical members, all of whom will be independently nominated by the Public Appointments Commission. While in spite of medical elite campaigning, the burden of proof required in fitness to practice cases has been lessened from criminal standards – i.e. beyond all reasonable doubt – i.e. to civil standards - on the balance of probability. Consequently, the current 'state of the field' surrounding medical regulation appears significantly different to what it was a decade ago, let alone one hundred and fifty years ago when the GMC was first established. The GMC is no longer the sole player in the medical regulatory field and now is more open and publicly accountable than it ever has been (Allsop 2006). Yet the issue of the specialist nature of professional expertise, alongside the concurrent need for professionals to exercise discretion in their work, does create a 'buffer zone' that protects doctors from outsider surveillance and control (Freidson 2001). There will no return to the 'closed shop' era of club governance. Indeed, medical elites must now increasingly advocate a transparent and inclusive governing regime under the ever-watchful eye of the state. Nevertheless, doctors still possess significant amount of freedom to control their own affairs, particularly when compared to other occupations. The current situation concerning the governance of medical expertise is therefore best summed up by Moran (1999) who argues that: '...*states are more important than ever before, either in the direct surveillance of the profession or in supervising the institutions of surveillance...[this] has not necessarily diminished the power of doctors; but it has profoundly changed the institutional landscape upon which they have to operate*' (Moran 1999: 129-30).

Yet the problem the GMC faces remains the one the historical narrative presented in this chapter shows it has persistently failed to satisfactorily address. Namely, it needs to involve the public in the governance of medical regulation as full and equal partners. To do this the current rhetoric of reform must move past its obsession with viewing the 'lay voice' solely in terms of 'the great and the good', and recognise the layered, multicultural and multifaceted nature of contemporary British society (Davies 2001). The negative reaction of the BMA and Royal Colleges to the proposal to change the level of doubt necessary for disciplinary action from 'absolute certainty' to 'on the balance of probabilities', reveals the profession still has a long way to go before it reaches this goal. The medical club is not prepared to open its doors too far. The current lack of trust between doctors and patients works both ways because there is an anticipation of risk amongst both parties: for the patient from poor medical performance and for the doctor from the threat of litigation and removal from the medical register. Despite the rhetoric of 'partnership', inherent tensions continue to exist between the stakeholders involved in medical regulation. These tensions need to be met head on, not simply ignored or brushed over as they have been in the past. Every relationship between human beings has its tensions and it *can be argued that the public will be best served by a more open debate over the areas of tension between the partners in regulation'* (Allsop 2006: 633). Only time will tell if this debate will come about as a result of the reforms to medical regulation introduced by the 2008 Health and Social Care Act. Particularly as it is arguable the necessary outcome data to ensure an informed debate will not be available until five years or more after the implementation of revalidation nationally in 2010. A point that will be returned to in chapter seven.

State and Professional Forms of Governance

This chapter has traced the historical development of the principle of medical self-regulation in the United Kingdom. The events it discussed do seem to add weight to the argument that medical autonomy has declined somewhat in the last three decades from the golden age when 'doctor knew best'. Individually and collectively, doctors have become more accountable for their actions. Yet it was also noted that doctors still possess a significant degree of control over their regulatory affairs and day to day work activities. However, a key paradox surrounding recent challenges to medical autonomy in the form of doctor's clinical freedom at the bedside and the principle of medical self-regulation is that they have occurred at a time when the success of medical knowledge and technology to promote public health is greater than it has ever been (Gabe 2004). Here it must be remembered that both this and the previous chapter have highlighted how modern medicine and the modern state are entwined entities. Certainly, the close relationship between medicine's 'club mentality' and the Victorian style of 'club governance' illustrates that the development of modern medicine and the principle of medical self-regulation is interwoven with the development of the modern state. Consequently, as Moran (1999 2004) argues, instead of signifying medicines apparent decline, it can be said that recent challenges to professional self-regulation bear witness to the fact that there has been a fundamental shift in the legitimate grounds for 'good governance' throughout all spheres of contemporary public life. Perkin (1989: 472) similarly argues that there has been a *'backlash against professional society'* as part of a profound shift in public attitudes towards institutional authority. This he holds coincided with the political and economic re-emergence of liberalism in the 1970s (Stacey 1992). Whether one agrees with Perkin or not the close relationship between medicine and the state highlights the necessity of exploring how sociologists have conceptualised the governance of medical expertise. This task is the focus of the next two chapters.

LIBRARY, UNIVERSITY OF CHESTER

Chapter 4

THE SOCIOLOGICAL ANALYSIS OF THE PRINCIPLE OF MEDICAL SELF-REGULATION

'We have always known, from sociological and general literature as well as from everyday experience that professionals and the professions act with a dual motive: to provide service and to use their knowledge for economic gain'.
Krause (1996: 9)

Chapter four provides an account of the development of the sociological analysis of professional regulation with a particular emphasis on the medical profession. As such it provides a bridge between the empirical research discussed in chapter six and the empirical and policy analysis literature relating to contemporary challenges to the principle of medical self-regulation explored in chapter five. It does this against the background of the historical narrative provided in chapters two and three. These chapters traced the unfolding trajectory of medical autonomy in the United Kingdom through detailing the changing social-political and health policy context surrounding the regulatory body which since 1858 has embodied the principle of professional self-regulation in medicine – the GMC. Here the entwined nature of medical governance with the development of the modern state was first noted. As was that a key paradox surrounding recent challenges to the principle of medical self-regulation is that they have occurred at a time when the success of medical knowledge and technology to promote public health is greater than it has been previously. These two themes are explored in this chapter and the next. But to do this the chapter must start with discussing the perspective which has dominated sociological analysis of professional regulation for the last four decades: the neo-Weberian viewpoint. This in turn requires the chapter initially focus upon delineating the development of the sociological study of the professions.

The Sociology of the Professions

'Regulating doctors is in many ways like regulating other occupations. However, doctors also have their own special features, and one reason they are special is that, almost everywhere, they are thought to belong to a distinctive category called profession. The regulation of the doctor is therefore an example of a particularly important kind of regulatory activity – professional regulation.'

Moran and Wood (1993: 24)

As the quote above notes, the sociological study of medical regulation forms an important part of the field of study in the social sciences concerned with the governance of the special category of occupations defined in the Anglo-American sociological literature as 'professions'. With particular reference to professions operating in the health and social care arena (i.e. Stacey 1992, Moran and Wood 1993, Johnson, Larkin and Saks 1995, Gladstone 2000, Allsop and Saks 2002, Davies 2004, Slater 2007). Consequently, the sociological study of medical regulation draws its conceptual and theoretical underpinnings from the sociology of the professions literature.

Two interrelated points need to be made. First, it has been said that the occupational type 'profession' is a particularly Anglo-American phenomenon. It certainly is true that in the United Kingdom and North America members of occupations traditionally categorised as professions, such as medicine and law, have been able to possess self-employed status and can be said to have enjoyed a closer relationship with the 'free market' than their mainly directly state-employed Continental cousins. In European countries, such as Germany and France, state bureaucracies have traditionally controlled arrangements relating to examination, licensing, standard setting and disciplinary procedures. All of which have historically been controlled by independent professional associations in the Anglo-American context. Here it should be noted that traditional Anglo-American professions such as law and medicine have possessed considerable privileges on the Continent despite the direct role played by the state in managing their affairs. Indeed, they have been able to secure high levels of job security and income as well as a large degree of autonomy in their work, similar to their Anglo-American counterparts (Burrage and Torstendahl, 1990). Yet it is not the aim of this book to undertake a comparative and historical analysis of the arrangements surrounding the organisation of occupational groups regarded as professions across nation-states. Consequently, the reader should be aware that the following discussion of relevant sociological literature is largely limited to the Anglo-American context and they must be careful about generalising its discussion beyond it. This leads onto the second point that needs to be noted at this stage. Namely, although this chapter discusses the sociology of the professions literature, its primary focus remains on the medical profession. It draws primarily on relevant literature pertaining to the sociological study of medicine. It takes advantage of the fact that medicine has possessed a particularly significant place in the development of the sociology of the professions literature. Medicine has played an important role in sociological analyse of the professions in the United Kingdom (i.e. Larkin 1983, Dingwall and Lewis 1983, Stacey 1992, Saks 1995, Gabe, Bury and Elston 2004). Its historical dominance in the health care division of labour over other occupations, close association with modern science and technology, as well as its claim to put its client's interests first, have all ensured it is viewed as an archetype of what a profession is (Turner 1995, Coburn and Willis 2000).

The Functionalist Perspective

'Our professional institutions are…an important stabilizing factor in our whole society'
Lynn (1963: 653)

A useful starting point from which to begin analysis of the occupational type 'profession' is the definition offered by McDonald (1995: 1) who states that a profession is an *'occupation based on advanced, or complex, or esoteric, or arcane knowledge'*. The possession of a specialist body of knowledge, which is socially valued but not possessed by all members of society, is an important element of the occupational title 'profession'. This is particularly true when new members are required to undergo a prolonged period of University-based education that includes 'on the job' training. Indeed, the Oxford dictionary (1979) defines a profession as an occupation, which *'involves knowledge and training in an advanced branch of learning'* (Hawkins 1979: 644).

Although early students of professionalism at the beginning of the twentieth century recognised the importance of the cogitative elements of the occupational type 'profession', they found the concurrent Oxford paperback dictionary definition of 'profession' meaning *'a declaration or promise'* (Hawkins 1979: 644) more important Early sociological analysis of the professions was primarily concerned with the fact that certain occupational groups in society claimed to possess high ethical standards and indeed sought to place their clients' welfare and interests before their own. This explicit moral code governs the behaviour of occupational members towards each other and society as a whole, as the Hippocratic Oath does in the case of medicine. This 'collectivity orientation' was seen by sociologists to act as a stabilising force to the excesses of the growing enterprise culture of capitalist industrial society, whose primary concern was taken to be with profit (Turner 1995). Whether or not this viewpoint regarding capitalist society was correct, early sociologies focus on the altruistic connotations associated with the concept of professionalism reflected the concern of functionalist sociology with how social consensus and social order are maintained.

Durkheim, Professionalism and Laissez Faire Capitalism

Indeed, a founding father of functionalist sociology, Emile Durkheim (1957), viewed professional groups as important preconditions to the generation of social stability and consensus in society. Durkheim's concern with the professions as a stabilising force to the excessive individualism of *laissez faire* capitalism stems from his view of society as an organism constantly striving for equilibrium. He argued that individuals within pre-industrial societies possessed shared values and beliefs that generated a social consensus called 'mechanical solidarity'. However, he argued that traditional forms of moral authority, which generated collective norms and values, were being undermined by a growing specialisation within the division of labour. This was due to the increasingly complex nature of industrial society as the eighteenth and nineteenth centuries progressed. This produced a state of affairs, which was causing alienation and *anomie* (i.e. anti-social individualism) amongst the general populace. This worried Durkheim. He believed that when collective norms and values declined, social restraints similarly decayed. This could lead to a situation where *'nothing remains but individual appetites, and since they are by nature boundless and insatiable, if there is nothing to control them, they will not be able to control themselves'* (Durkheim 1957: 11). All was not lost. Durkheim argued that a new form of *'organic solidarity'* was emerging. This was based upon the recognition of the need for cooperation between individuals due to their growing functional interdependence within the social sphere as society became more complex. He held that the professions formed moral communities, which promoted values such as selflessness that engendered social consensus and *'organic solidarity'*.

This viewpoint informed much of the subsequent sociological analysis of the professions until the 1960s. For instance, Tawney (1921) held that the economic individualism of capitalism was inherently destructive to the community interest and that the morality of professionalism could be used to counter its excesses. He stated that *'the difference between industry as it exists today, and profession is, then, simple and unmistakeable. The essence of the former is that its only criterion is the financial return, which it offers its shareholders. The essence of the later is that though men enter it for the sake of livelihood the measure of their success is the service which they perform, not the gains which they amass'* (Tawney 1921: 94 -95). Similarly, Parsons (1949) emphasised the social altruism of professional groups by arguing they possessed a 'collectivity-orientation'. While Carr-Saunders and Wilson (1933: 497) held that the professions: *'inherent, preserve and pass on a tradition...they engender modes of life, habits of thought and standards of judgement which render them centres of resistance to crude forces which threaten steady and peaceful evolution...The family, the church and the universities, certain associations of intellectuals, and above all the great professions, stand like rocks against which the waves raised by these forces beat in vain'*.

The early functionalist hegemony regarding the sociological study of the professions also revealed itself in the work of authors who were concerned with identifying characteristics which taken together denote that an occupation is a profession. For example, Etzioni (1969) classified occupations into 'professions' and 'semi-professions' based upon characteristics such as length of training. Barber (1963: 671) held that professions possessed four essential attributes – a high degree of generalised and systematic knowledge, an orientation towards the interest of the community instead of individual self-interest, a high degree of self-control exercised by practitioners over behaviour through the possession of a code of ethics internalised during a prolonged period of education and training, and finally, a reward system of monetary and status rewards that are symbolic of work achievement not self-interested gain.

To this day occupations such as medicine protest that they possess a 'service ideal' when they seek to justify collective privileges. Such as the principle of self-regulation and the individual social and economic rewards which come with the possession of professional status. The previous chapter discussed how contemporary changes in the governance of medical expertise have led commentators to re-emphasize the positive social role played by the professions in society (i.e. Freidson, 2001). Yet the core problem with the early functionalist approach to the sociological analysis of the concept of professionalism is that it takes uncritically the altruistic claims of occupations calling themselves professions at face value, while it also views the task of sociology as being to quantify and measure the concept, 'professionalism'. Furthermore, the functionalist approach to the analysis of professionalism was criticised for being largely ahistorical. It lacked consideration of the process by which occupations utilised their cognitive and altruistic resources to exercise power in order to initially gain and subsequently maintain the social and economic rewards associated with the possession of professional status (Johnson 1972). Sociologists were coming to realise that they were starting their analysis of the professions with the wrong question. As Hughes (1963: 656) wrote *'in my studies I passed from the false question 'Is this occupation a profession?' to the more fundamental one 'What are the circumstances in which people in an occupation attempt to turn it into a profession and themselves into professional people?'*.

Hughes was highlighting that classifying an occupation as a profession was what society did and it was not the task of sociology to do it in more scientific terms. Rather, its focus should be on investigating the socio-economic and political circumstances out of which the concept of professionalism arose. This signalled the beginning of a more critical turn in the sociological study of the professions. In contrast to the Functionalist viewpoint, this focused upon the material and symbolic benefits gained from the possession of an occupational monopoly over license to practice (McDonald 1995). According to this more critical viewpoint *'professionalism is not a set of traits which jobs have in common, nor a distinct ethic, but a mode of occupational control'* (Moran and Wood 1993: 25)

Critiquing the Altruistic Foundations of Medical Privilege

'The professional rhetoric relating to community service and altruism may be in many cases a significant factor in moulding the practices of individual professionals, but it also clearly functions as a legitimation of professional privilege'.
Johnson (1972: 25)

As the above quote illustrates, by the start of the 1970s sociologists were turning away from the viewpoint that the professions transcended the unbridled self-interest they held to be symptomatic of modern society (McDonald 1995). Functionalist sociologists mostly accepted the altruistic claims to public service espoused by professions such as medicine. Indeed, they often endorsed the fact that this separated them from other occupational groups. However, the 1970s saw social scientists question increasingly the legitimacy of the self-espoused altruistic tendencies and 'value-neutral' knowledge claims of occupational groups, which possessed professional status. In the context of the medical profession, they began to focus upon how medical professionalism has operated ideologically as an exclusive form of occupational control. This was seen to operate both at the micro-level of everyday interaction through the concept of clinical freedom at the bedside and the macro-institutional level through the principle of state-licensed self-regulation. They highlighted how poorly performing doctors, and in some cases even criminals, were being shielded from public accountability by the 'club rule' of mutual protectionism inherent within medicine's self-regulatory system.

A focus upon professional self-interest as opposed to professional altruism lay at the heart of the growing Symbolic Interactionist critique of the early Functionalist view of the professions in American sociology. The Interactionist viewpoint assumes reality is socially constructed in and through everyday social interaction. Consequently, it viewed professionalism as *'an ascribed symbolic, socially negotiated status based on day-to-day interaction'* (Allsop and Saks 2002: 5). Studies of the medical profession inspired by this viewpoint, such as Becker's *Boys in White* (1961) highlighted that *'[the] professional principles of altruism, service and high ethical standards were...less than perfect human social constructs rather than...abstract standards which characterized a formal collectivity'* (McDonald 1995: 4). Yet, instead of focusing on the micro-individual level of the individual professional interacting within his or her work-sphere, the growing critique of the professions in the Anglo-American literature primarily focused on the macro-organisational and societal level. This was largely informed by neo-Weberian sociology, as the next section of the chapter will now demonstrate.

The Neo-Weberian Perspective

'[No] summer's bloom lies ahead of us, but rather a polar night of icy darkness and hardness'.
Weber (1946: 128)

The 1970s saw the growth of the neo-Weberian critique of the professions in general and medical dominance and power in particular. Weber focused upon trying to understand emerging new social patterns in the nineteenth century caused by the rise of industrial technology, the growth of scientific knowledge and the greater potential than ever before for participation by the general populace within the political sphere. Weber was a polymath interested in law, economics, politics, science, religion as well as sociology. A key unifying theme in his writing is the idea that the progressive rationalisation of life was the main directional trend in western civilisation (Whimster and Lask 1989). By rationalization, Weber meant a process by which explicit, abstract, calculable rules and procedures (what he called 'formal rationality') increasingly replaced more traditional and personal, social values and ways of life (what he called 'substantive rationality') at the organisational and institutional levels which govern social life (Gerth and Wright Mills 1946). Rationalisation leads to the displacement of religion by specialised rationalistic knowledge and scientific expertise. It also leads to the replacement of the skilled worker and artisan with the factory production line and machine technology. It demystifies and instrumentalities life, and *'means that…there are no mysterious incalculable forces that come into play, but rather that one can, in principle, master all things by calculation'* (Weber 1946: 139).

Though Weber did not specifically address the issue of the growth of the professions his concept of rationalisation is clearly tied to the development of modern scientific forms of expertise, of which modern medicine is a part. As Murphy (1988: 246) notes *'[the] process of formal rationalization has generated a new type of knowledge, the systematic, codified, generalized (which implies abstract) knowledge of the means of control (of nature and of humans)'*. This is a point the chapter will return to in a moment. However, it is important to note here that sociologists with a historical bent, such as Parry and Parry (1976), Berlant (1975) and Larkin (1983), primarily drew upon Weber's economic theory of monopolisation when analysing the initial growth and subsequent development of professions such as medicine (Weber 1978). In doing so, they highlighted collective preoccupations with pecuniary interests, securing economic and technical domains, as well as consolidating positions of high social status and power within the socio-political arena. This was to be expected as Weber views professionals as a privileged commercial class, alongside bankers and merchants. He holds that they seek to exclude competitors and reap economic and social rewards through pursuing strategies that enable them to monopolise the marketplace for their services by controlling market entry and supply. By engaging in collective social mobility (i.e. the formation of group organisations and political pressure groups) occupational groups such as medicine seek to obtain privileges from the political community, to become what Weber (1978: 342) calls a legally privileged group, and ensure *'the closure of social and economic opportunities to outsiders'*.

Freidson and Medical Power

Two key early proponents of the neo-Weberian 'social closure' model of the professions were Freidson (1970) and Larson (1977). As his work came chronologically first, the chapter will discuss Freidson before moving on to Larson. In 1970, Freidson published his landmark study of the American medical profession, *Profession of Medicine*. In line with Weber's 'social closure' perspective, Freidson held that medicine was a particularly powerful example of how professionalism operated ideologically as a form of occupational control to ensure control of the market for services. Freidson (1970: 137) highlighted that the professions possessed three powerful interlocking arguments on which they justified their privileged status: *'Professional people have the special privilege of freedom from the control of outsiders. Their privilege is justified by three claims. First, the claim is that there is such an unusual degree of skill and knowledge involved in professional work that non-professionals are not equipped to evaluate or regulate it. Second, it is claimed that professionals are responsible – that they may be trusted to work conscientiously without supervision. Third, the claim is that the profession itself may be trusted to undertake the proper regulatory action on those rare occasions when an individual does not perform his work competently or ethically'.*

Freidson recognised that medical autonomy must be viewed as having limits as the state was involved in the organisation and delivery of health care. Occupations must submit to its 'protective custody' to reap the social and economic rewards associated with being a profession. Nevertheless, the state largely left doctors alone to control the technical aspects of their work. This made it for him such a good example of what a profession is. He argued that *'so long as a profession is free of the technical evaluation and control of other occupations in the division of labour, its lack of ultimate freedom from the state, and even the lack of control over the socio-economic terms of work, do not significantly change its essential character as profession'* (Freidson 1970: 20).

Freidson discussed how medical professionalism operated ideologically as a form of occupational control at the micro-level of everyday interaction through the concept of clinical freedom at the bedside, as well as at the macro-institutional level through the principle of state-licensed, self-regulation. The common link between the micro and macro aspects of medical autonomy for Freidson was the need for a doctor to exercise personal judgment and discretion in her work due to it's inherently specialist nature (Freidson 1970 1994 and 2001). This state of affairs was legitimised by the scientific basis of modern medical expertise and public acceptance of medicine's altruistic claim that it put patient need first. Furthermore, Freidson argued that medicine's freedom to control the technical evaluation of its own work had led to it possessing a high level of dominance and control not only over patients but also over the work of other health care occupations, such as nursing for example. Freidson (1970: 137) stated that medicine *'has the authority to direct and evaluate the work of others without in turn being subject for formal direction and evaluation by them. Paradoxically its autonomy is sustained by the dominance of its expertise in the division of labour'.*

In *Profession of Medicine* and his other major study, *Professional Dominance* (1970), Freidson was concerned with mapping out the negative consequences of medical autonomy in the Anglo-American context. He concluded that the dominance of medicine in the health care arena had a negative effect on the quality of health care patients received. For Freidson medicine was failing to self-manage satisfactorily its affairs and ensure that adequate quality control mechanisms to govern doctor's day-to-day activities were in place. Freidson (1970:

370) believed that the development of unaccountable, self-governing institutions surrounding medical training and work had led to the profession of medicine to possess *'a self-deceiving vision of the objectivity and reliability of its knowledge and the virtues of its members....[Medicine's] very autonomy had led to insularity and a mistaken arrogance about its mission in the world'.*

Larson and the Indeterminate and Determinate Cognitive Dimensions of Professional Privilege

There can be no doubt that Freidson argued forcefully that medicine was a powerful example of how professionalism operated ideologically as a form of occupational control. For him it was a publicly mandated state supported supplier of a valued service, exercising autonomy in the workplace. This included dominance over other occupations in the health care division of labour as well as collegiate control over recruitment, training and the regulation of members conduct. Regardless of Freidson's critical insights, his work lacked a thorough historical dimension. Aware of this, Larson undertook an historical analysis of the rise of professionalism as a legitimate form of occupational control in her work *'Rise of Professionalism'* (McDonald 1995). She discusses how by engaging in a 'professional project' occupations such as medicine sought to become professions by obtaining a monopoly over the market for their services and enhancing the standing of group members within the social and political spheres: *'My intention....is to examine how the occupations we call professions organized themselves to attain market power...Professionalization is thus an attempt to translate one order of scare resources – special knowledge and skills – into another – social and economic rewards. To maintain scarcity implies a tendency to monopoly: monopoly of expertise in the market, monopoly of status in the system of stratification'* (Larson 1977: xii and xvii).

As chapter two noted, the rise of the clinical gaze of modern medicine in the eighteenth century changed the nature of the doctor-patient power relationship in favour of the medical profession (Jewson 1974 1976). Bound up with this was a growing focus upon gaining direct personal experience of clinical phenomena on which to build 'craft expertise' and justify clinical decisions. This is not to say that the increasingly formal and scientific aspects of medical expertise did not play a vitally important role in medicines successful claim to professional status. Clearly they did. But as Larson (1977) notes, in addition to the possession of a formal knowledge base, it requires the presence of a high level of 'indetermination' in the exercise of expert judgment and technique for the monopolistic claims of the 'professional project' to succeed. Larson (1977: 31) specifies that an occupation's knowledge base must be *'formalized or codified enough to allow standardization...and yet ...must not be so clearly codified that it does not allow a principle of exclusion [or discretion] to operate"* Furthermore, Larson (1977: 41) observes that *"the leaders of the professional project will define the areas that are not amenable to standardisation; they will define the place of unique individual genius and the criteria of talent that cannot be taught'.*

Larson is indebted to the work of Jamous and Peloille (1973). Following Weber's insights into the nature of modernity these authors recognised that the abstract, scientific, nature of modern expert knowledge meant it was open to a process of rationalisation and codification into standardised rules and procedures. They argued that this was offset by the fact that uncertainty is ever present in the application of such knowledge, and they put forward the notion that occupations possess an 'indetermination' and 'technicality' ratio (an I/T ratio). Those occupations classified as professions, possess a high level of indetermination at the basis of their expertise. Similar to Larson they held that the outcomes of the application of expert knowledge are more dependent on the *potentialities and talent of the practitioner than techniques and transmissible rules'* (Jamous and Peloille 1973: 140). This leads to an emphasis in professional education and training on *'individual and social potentialities, experience, talent, intuition etc'* (Jamous and Peloille 1973: 139). In short, it is the "I" in the I/T ratio that creates the basis for social prestige and distance between the expert and the client. This was illustrated in chapter two in the context of the development of the modern medical profession and the principle of professional self-regulation through the 'birth of the clinic' (Foucault 1989).

In examining the process by which occupations originally claim and subsequently maintain professional status, Larson (1977: 6) acknowledges that *'the goals and strategies pursued by a given group are not entirely clear or deliberate for all the members'*. This is an important point. Larson's reliance on historical documentary evidence means the concept of 'professional project' does not refer to the day-to-day actions of individual 'rank and file' members. Rather it refers to a generalised course of collective action initiated by organisational and institutional professional elites over a particular historical period. The value of Larson's analysis is that it highlights the key role in obtaining and sustaining a market monopoly played by the establishment of occupational control over the educational credentials associated with entry into a profession. This includes the important role the 'indeterminate' aspects of a profession's expertise play in establishing this control as legitimate. As chapter two discussed in some detail, the establishment of occupational control over educational credentials is a vitally important element of historical accounts of the development of the professions. Particularly for understanding how professionalism operates ideologically as a methodology of occupational control. The possession of exclusive control over the dissemination of its knowledge base to new members means a profession's elite organisations possess substantial bargaining power from which to negotiate a 'regulative bargain' with the state. As Allsop and Saks (2002: 6) state: *'access to formally accredited education and training is...a crucial portal on which exclusory closure is based that generates definitions of insiders and outsiders'* For example, in his analysis of the legal profession Burrage (1988: 228) states that: *'In my judgement four goals have been constant and pre-eminent in the history of the legal profession...First, lawyers have sought to control admission to, and training for, legal practice. Second, they have tried to demarcate and protect jurisdiction within which they alone are entitled to practice. Third, they have tried to impose their own rules of etiquette, ethics or practice on one another. Finally, they have tried to defend and if possible enhance their status'.*

The Exclusive Cognitive Identity of the Medical Club and the Clinical Mentality

The work of authors such as Burrage, Larson and Freidson calls attention to the fact that a professions' possession of a monopoly over the market for its services is not a neutral and straightforward consequence of its possession of esoteric expertise or a code of conduct which appears to regulate member's behaviour so their actions place clients' interests first and foremost. The neo-Weberian 'social closure' model of professionalization became increasingly popular amongst sociologists as it focused upon the role of professional self-interest, instead of alleged altruistic tendencies, in the initial formation and subsequent development of professions such as medicine. As shown in chapter three, a continued series of high profile medical malpractice cases throughout the 70s' 80s and 90s revealed the tensions between public and professional interest. As reflected in the early work of Freidson (1970). While the sociologist and GMC lay member Margaret Stacey (1992) used insights of Larson and Freidson to show that medical control of the GMC had led to a similar tension between medicine's concern with maintaining its professional privileges and the GMC's role in protecting the public interest.

The neo-Weberian perspective places a heavy emphasis upon undertaking an historical analysis of the development of modern medicine and the regulation of medical training and work. As chapters two and three noted, this reinforces the need to recognise how the 'closed shop' nature of the culture of the medical club is tied up with its epistemological foundations in modern science in general and the biomedical model in particular. This has led to a particular form of reasoning, known as 'the clinical mentality' being placed at the centre of the occupational structure and culture of the modern medical profession. Following Larson (1977: 17) it can be argued that medicine has long possessed an *'exclusive cognitive identity'*. As noted earlier, the development of an exclusive 'members only' occupational identity, based upon the esoteric cognitive expertise shared by group members, formed a key part of the process by which the fledging medical profession initially sought to convert its increasingly scientific credentials into social and economic rewards during the nineteenth century.

Sociological accounts of medical knowledge, work and training highlight how doctors collectively and individually possess a 'cognitive exclusiveness' towards outsiders, given the specialist nature of medical work and the lengthy period of time it takes to train a new member of the medical club. These also reveal that a key characteristic of the culture of the medical club is a mutual respect amongst group members for each other's clinical experience and expertise. This is reinforced by the hierarchical nature of the career structure of the medical profession in general and the organisation of local medical teams in particular. This leads to the general refusal, on behalf of juniors, to criticise publicly seniors in all but the most extreme cases, particularly if they want to work their way up the career ladder (Seabrook 2004).

Sociological studies of medical training and work have repeatedly highlighted that the development of 'clinical acumen' by trainees must be accomplished through the application of a characteristic mode of reasoning that is bound up with this feeling of exclusiveness, namely 'the clinical mentality'. This often transcends and takes precedence over the more formal scientific basis of medical expertise that is frequently presumed to lie at the basis of medical power. In his now classic elucidation of the clinical mentality Freidson (1970) notes that an individual doctor's knowledge and expertise is personally acquired through direct first-hand experience over the course of her professional career. Freidson (1970: 170) holds that at the basis of the clinical mentality lies a *'kind of ontological and epistemological individualism'*. He argues that the nature of her work makes the medical practitioner a pragmatist. She is driven to draw upon her experience of previous similar concrete clinical cases when making her professional judgments, instead of utilising more formal resources such as clinical protocols or statistical evidence. Freidson holds that this pragmatism comes about from a doctor's need to take action and make clinical decisions in complex practice situations so she can make a positive difference (or at least do no further harm) to the lives of the patients she is professionally responsible for. Indeed, Freidson (1970: 170) says that: *'In having to rely so heavily upon his personal, clinical experience with concrete, individual cases…the practitioner comes essentially to rely on the authority of his own sense, independently of the general authority of tradition or science. After all, he can only act on the basis of what he himself experiences, and if his own activity seems to get results, or at least no untoward results, he is resistant to changing it on the basis of statistical or abstract consideration. He is likely to need to see or feel the case himself'.*

Freidson (1970) is not alone in making the point that the expertise of the medical profession is made up of formal-determinate and tacit-indeterminate dimensions (i.e. Allsop and Mulcahy 1996, Stacey 1992 2000) as well as holding that it is the latter, rather than the former, that is often ultimately used by doctors to justify clinical decisions (i.e. Armstrong, 2002). Bosk (1979: 91-94) in his discussion of the management of surgical errors argues that doctors possess two distinct 'warrants for action': 'the academic' and 'the personal'. He describes how a doctor's personal 'clinical acumen' or 'clinical expertise' is often used to 'trump' academic knowledge. As I have discussed earlier, Becker's (1961), Atkinson's (1983) and Sinclair's (1995) studies of medical education similarly show that during clinical training personal experience is often rhetorically contrasted by clinical teachers with the more formal medical knowledge trainees find enshrined in course textbooks. For example, Becker (1961: 225) notes that: *'even though it substitutes for scientifically verified knowledge, it [experience] can be used to legitimate a choice of procedures for a patients treatment and can even be used to rule out use of some procedures that have been scientifically established'.*

The veneration by members of the medical fraternity of the autonomy of the individual practitioner and the existence of clinical judgment and expertise, accounts for the presence of variation in clinical diagnosis and treatment, as well as the fact that medical practitioners can be collectively and individually resistant to innovation and change. However, it also leads to a shared belief amongst medical club members that they can legitimately exclude outsiders from judging members of the club. For there is a mutual recognition between club members that the inherent uncertainty at the basis of their expertise means that it is a case of 'there but for the grace of god go I' when medical errors occur. They therefore collectively 'close ranks' to ensure club members are protected. The highly personal but mutually shared nature of the clinical mentality, alongside the inherently insular nature of medicine's 'members only' regulatory club, leads to a natural reluctance on behalf of individual members to report any concerns they may have about other club member's competence. Not least of all because club members fear of being ostracised by their peers and their careers consequently blighted. Furthermore, this situation has led to tendency within medical training for 'teaching by humiliation', particularly when trainees make common clinical errors (Sinclair 1995). A growing body of sociological literature reporting medical students' experiences of being bullied, shouted at and publicly humiliated (Silver and Glicken 1990, Schuchert 1998, Seabrook 2004). This is in spite of the fact that medicine's elite institutions have recognised that they must promote an occupational culture that is more open and accountable and encourages individual practitioners to learn from their mistakes (Catto 2006 2007). For medicine's 'new professionalism' requires doctors report medical errors, whether or not they are made by themselves or their peers, and actively admit to mistakes and learn from them (Irvine 1997 2003 2006).

The Dominance of the 'Social Closure' Model

Given the previous discussion, it is not surprising to learn then that the neo-Weberian viewpoint has dominated the sociological study of professional regulation in the UK for the last four decades. In addition to the important insights its offers into the nature of the 'clinical mentality' and the fundamentally exclusory nature of 'club governance', it encapsulates the socio-legal and political realities of the regulatory context with regards to the professions in general and medicine in particular (Stacey 1992, Moran and Wood 1993, Johnson Larkin and Saks 1995, Allsop and Saks 2002, Davies 2004, Allsop 2006, Slater 2000 2003 2007). The interrelated concepts of 'professional project', 'occupational monopoly' and 'social closure' reflect the reality of 'state licensure', as achieved by professions such as medicine, in the Anglo-American context (McDonald 1995, Elston 2004). Additionally, although the exact process by which an occupation becomes a profession (i.e. professionalization) differs between nations and occupations, the general form of state licensing of professional groups in the Anglo-American context has historically been based upon *'the model of the medical profession of the nineteenth century...In this respect, all the health professions are licensed by statute, and the terms of the licence may be modified by parliament'* (Allsop and Saks 2002: 7). Furthermore, it can be argued that the neo-Weberian viewpoint will continue to encapsulate the medical regulatory context for the foreseeable future. For whatever the outcomes of the current White Paper may be, medical control of the GMC will remain in some form, and medical elites such as the Royal Colleges will continue to take the lead in controlling entry onto and exit from the register of approved medical practitioners (see chapter two).

However, the neo-Weberian perspective is not beyond criticism. It can be accused of being as one sided as early Functionalist accounts when they uncritically accepted the altruistic claims made by occupational groups such as medicine. For the neo-Weberian viewpoint does highlight how professions sought to obtain, protect and promote their self-interest over the interest of their clients. Nevertheless, it can be argued that it does so by neglecting that the day-to-day activities of a large number of health care practitioners demonstrate that they possess a strong personal commitment to their work. Indeed, they often place their personal needs second to their professional commitments in order to ensure that patients receive the best quality of care possible. It could equally be argued, however, that the value of the neo-Weberian analysis lies in the fact that it reinforces the need for the general public and state to recognise that doctors need to be able to exercise discretion in their work, and indeed can by and large be trusted to place their clients interests before their own. While at the same time reinforcing to doctors that the possession of a distinctive mixture of cognitive and altruistic characteristics, does not in itself justify the extent to which they have traditionally been left alone to manage their own affairs.

The Feminist Critique

By the end of the 1970s, there was a growing Feminist critique of how the professions sustained gender inequalities in society. A 'gender blindness' existed in the neo-Weberian view of the professions. For example, Spencer and Podmore (1986) argued that sociological accounts of the legal profession ignored that female solicitors were marginalised by their male colleagues, and discussed how this was related to broader social expectations regarding appropriate male and female roles and relationships. Their empirical research found that discrimination against women within the legal profession occurred primarily because the confrontational nature of court hearings meant law was held to be a masculine, aggressive, occupation. Female solicitors were defined by their male colleagues as 'the other' through engaging in gender laden discourses that variously categorised them as 'sex objects', 'different beings' 'over emotional' or 'basically not tough enough'. This situation enabled the allocation of female solicitors into what were seen as gender appropriate careers, such as family law, and actively excluded them from elite occupational positions within the profession. At the time of Spencer and Podmore's study in the mid 1980s, only 2% of judges were women while they were no women law lords. This was preventing them from becoming a part of the legal professions self-regulatory elite (Dingwall and Lewis 1983). As noted earlier a similar situation was found by Stacey (1992) in her study of the GMC. The first female member of the GMC was not elected until the 1950s. That is nearly one hundred years after the foundation of the GMC in 1858. There were only three female members of the GMC throughout the 1970s and early 1980s (two of whom were non-medical, including Stacey herself). While there was an over-representation of female doctors in what were seen within the profession as being 'female friendly' specialties, such as general practice. As in the case of the legal profession, 'female friendly' specialties were not conducive to obtaining access to the higher echelons of the professions elite training and regulatory institutions.

Feminism is a not a unitary social theory. It incorporates authors operating from Liberal, Radical, neo-Marxist, Black and Postmodern viewpoints, to name a few (Anthias and Yuval-Davies 1993). The concept of patriarchy has traditionally been at the centre of feminist viewpoints, with its claim that there is an all-pervasive 'male gaze', which directly oppresses women and possesses institutionalised power within the apparatus of the state. This has been criticised by feminists and postmodern thinkers who hold an anti-essentialist view of the self, and so reject the idea that there is a universal female subject or a common 'feminine' experience and identity (Barrett and Phillips 1992). Authors working in the field of 'men's studies' extend these views further and use the notion of 'hegemonic masculinity' to explore the oppressive features of the rational, domineering, aggressive and exploitative white Anglo-Saxon Protestant male (Connell 1995).

Throughout the 1970s and 1980s a growing number of authors interested in the social role of medicine and working from a Feminist perspective, focused upon the fact that the history of modern medicine and its treatment of women was tied up with a broader narrative of subordination of 'the female' to 'the male' (Butler 1993). Women were socially constructed as 'the other' and assigned normative social roles belonging to the private sphere. For example, studies by Barker-Penfield (1979) and Holmes (1980) traced the historical development of the medical discipline of obstetrics and gynaecology. They highlighted how this was tied up with a socio-economic need to manage the female body to locate its biological destiny within the social roles of mother and housewife. The work of Pfeffer

(1985) shows that the form of language used in medical textbooks to describe common 'female conditions' construct the female body as being a poor second to its healthier male counterpart. Pfeffer's work discusses how a women's experience of her body is mediated through medical categories and conditions that possess fundamentally negative gender images, as 'infantile' uterus, 'failed' labour, placental 'insufficiency', 'irregular' menstrual cycles and hormonal 'imbalances'.

Underlying the critique of the Feminist perspective was the belief that the structure of medical knowledge was in many ways sexist and patriarchal due to medicines close relationship to science (Fox-Keller 1985). The Feminist perspective holds that the rationality of 'the Enlightenment', which spawned modern scientific thought, was inherently masculine (Butler 1993). Women were perceived as 'the other' and held to be illogical or irrational. Women were fundamentally flawed and emotional creatures inextricably bound to their reproductive role (Ehrenreich and English 1979). As Fox-Keller (1985: 78) maintains, the Feminist perspective held that *'in characterising scientific and objective thought as masculine, the very activity by which the knower can acquire knowledge is genderised'.* Ehrenreich and English (1979) documented how women were socially defined by society as fragile creatures that were prone to hysteria. The development of scientific medicine over the course of the nineteenth century allowed the source of this problem to be increasingly located within the female reproductive system. This explanation was seen as socially acceptable as it precluded men from the possibility of becoming 'hysterics'. To this day female patients more than male patients are likely to be viewed as 'unhappy', 'depressive' and 'anxious' by general practitioners and psychiatrists. Furthermore, they are more likely to receive pharmacological treatments such as Valium and Prozac and Seratoxat (Prior 1999).

The critique of the Feminist perspective of medical knowledge and practice extended into the very organisation of the medical profession. Witz (1992) argued in line with the neo-Weberian thesis that the medical profession obtained its market monopoly in the United Kingdom through using its educational credentials as a 'bargaining chip' from which to negotiate with state control over its regulatory arrangements. She also held that medicine's achievement of 'social closure' in the nineteenth century succeeded because the strategy of closing off medical training and practice to all but an elite few was in line with boarder social norms of the time. Medicine actively sought to keep women in the private not public sphere. It excluded women and to a lesser extent working class men from practicing medicine due to its historically close association with the gentry. She argues that medicine's elite institutions used, firstly, 'exclusionary strategies' to deny women entry into medical school and so the medical register, and secondly, 'demarcatory strategies' where medical control was firmly established over other health care occupations dominated by women, such as nursing and midwifery. As chapter earlier discussed, medicine's professionalization process was certainly dominated by men and involved the appropriation of healing and caring domains that had traditionally belonged to women. Far from being a neutral science medicine reflected the patriarchal and class based nature of society at the time.

By the mid 1980s the work of Feminist authors such as Ann Oakley (1984) had made a significant contribution to the growing recognition that the practice of modern medicine was largely socially and culturally bounded. Authors working within neo-Weberian and Feminist positions shared a common view of medical practice, which was diametrically opposed to medicine's self-image as scientific, value-free and morally neutral (Elston 2004). However, despite of the important contribution of the Feminist perspective, the neo-Weberian continued to dominate sociological analysis of professionalism and the principle of professional self-regulation in the Anglo-American literature. The Feminist perspective tended to be held by sociologists concerned with the sociological analysis of the professions to supplement and expand the neo-Weberian perspective, not necessarily replace it (Lupton 1994). The was because there was an ongoing debate within sociology about the extent to which the clinical gaze of modern medicine was a social construct and therefore could be seen as inherently 'gendered' (Williams and Calman 1996). Some commentators held the view that although a human undertaking, and therefore open to a range of intervening socio-economic and cultural factors, medical science does reflect a reality that exists 'out there' independently of the observer (Kelly and Field 1994). Modern medical expertise and technology consequently was seen to exist beyond the particular circumstances surrounding their creation and application. Both Elston (1991) and Ahmed and Harrison (2000) note that medical judgments are likely to be seen as valid and true because modern medicine possesses a considerable amount of 'cultural authority' over definitions of reality. This is due to the predictive power of the randomised clinical trial. However, other social commentators held that it is impossible to trust the objectivity and neutrality of the seeing-knowing subject whose gaze extracts knowledge from the world, whether they are a scientist, a doctor or a philosopher (Hoy 1986). The growing 'social constructionist' influence of postmodernism in sociology gave weight to the view that human knowledge of the world is limited by language. Indeed, this asserts that it is impossible to apprehend reality outside of the arbitrary linguistic conventions and metaphoric imperatives belonging to the 'language games' used to describe it (Drolet 2004). Most sociologists, like Turner (1995) for example, held onto the middle ground within this debate. He argued that some aspects of modern medical knowledge and expertise, such as for example the diagnosis and treatment of Hyperactivity in children, are more clearly socially constructed than others, such as for example cirrhosis of the liver, as these possess a structural and biochemical origin within the human body.

Adopting a somewhat pragmatic position in this manner has meant that to this day it is possible to detect, as Riska (2001) discusses, three possible stances towards the question of whether or not medical knowledge and work are too gendered. First is the view that medicine is a gender-neutral activity and the creation and application of medical knowledge and expertise is a value-free affair. As Riska notes, this viewpoint is not so much held by feminist authors themselves but by members of the public as well as many doctors themselves. Second is the view that medicine is an inherently masculine activity, which promotes a negative view of women and the female body. It relegates women to the private sphere and the role of mother and wife due to their reproductive role and biological difference to the 'alpha male'. Riska notes that the third position operates somewhere in the middle of these two extremes. This view holds that the creation and application of modern scientific medical knowledge does appear to mirror the nature of the world in which human beings live. Furthermore, it does enable them to access and actively manipulate the biological realties of their existence. This position also asserts the practice of medicine is nevertheless an inherently social activity; it reflects the broader cultural values of the society within which it operates. Therefore, medicine possesses gendered processes and practices. Riska (2001) provides cross-national evidence to show that although more women today than ever before are pursing medicine as a career, a 'glass ceiling' still operates inside the medical club that stops female doctors accessing certain prestigious surgical sub-fields.

There are two key interrelated reasons why sociological analysis of professionalism has continued to be dominated by the neo-Weberian viewpoint. First, the neo-Weberian viewpoint by and large reflects that nature of the regulatory context in the United Kingdom in regards to health and social care professions in general and the medical profession in particular (Stacey 1992, Moran and Wood 1993, Johnson Larkin and Saks 1995, Allsop and Saks 2002, Davies 2004, Allsop 2006, Slater 2007). Indeed, although the GMC is under threat in its current format, it will continue to exist. Furthermore, medical control over admission onto and exit from a state approved register of practitioners will undoubtedly continue (Bruce 2007, GMC 2008). It is precisely because of this fact that feminist authors working within the UK context, such as Elston (1991, 1997, 2004), Stacey (1992, 2000) and Witz (1992), used the framework provided by neo-Weberian viewpoint when analysing how medicine as a profession is regulated.

Second, the growing Feminist critique of medicine remained focused upon forms of medical knowledge and technology that were experienced mainly by women, such as reproductive technology (Lupton 1994, Elston 1997). Although this focus was justifiable, it nevertheless limited the ability of the Feminist perspective to contribute to broader sociological debates regarding the regulatory arrangements concerning occupational groups categorised as professions. Because its research focus was 'gender exclusive', the contribution of the Feminist perspective lies within the broader field of the sociology of health and illness and not within the sociological study analyse of professional self-regulation (Nettleton 1995, Coburn and Willis 2000). Particularly as this is restricted to the analysis of occupational groups which claim to possess not just esoteric specialist knowledge but also an ethical code of conduct that requires they place their clients' interests before their own (McDonald 1995). This code of conduct is used to obtain not only social and economic rewards but also exclusive occupational control over members training, practice and discipline (Freidson 1970 1994 2001). This includes traditionally female dominated occupations such as nursing (Stacey 1988). The history of the professionalization of nursing in the UK shows how broader social norms alongside the restrictive actions of a male dominated medical profession initially blocked nurse's claim to professional status. That is until a mixture of NHS service needs and continued political activism on behalf of nurses throughout the 1950s and 1960s eventually lead the establishment of a General Nursing Council in 1979 (Riska and Wegar 1993). Yet historical narrative shows that throughout this time nursing sought proactively to exclude third party evaluation of practitioners' activities as a key part of its quest for professional status. Indeed, like the medical profession before it, nursing eventually acquired a legal statute through parliament that enshrined in law its right to possess exclusive occupational control over a register of member's entry into and exit from the nursing profession, as well as the standards governing members training, practice and discipline (Davies and Beach 2000). Furthermore, similar to other occupations categorised as professions (e.g. medicine, law, psychiatry and social work) nursing's self-regulatory body has in the last two decades been accused of being elitist, inherently inward looking and 'protectionist', as a result of high profile malpractice cases in the media. This has led to calls for greater lay involvement in nurse regulation and a more open and multi-disciplinary approach towards nurse training and discipline.

Medicine and the State: The Invasion of Capital into the House of Medicine

Despite its dominance in the sociological study of professional regulation, the neo-Weberian perspective was criticised by authors operating from a neo-Marxist viewpoint for failing to account for the entwined nature of the development of the modern state and professions such as medicine, as was touched upon earlier when discussing 'club governance' (Moran 1999 2004). Indeed, although his *Profession of Medicine* was (and still is) regarded as a sociological classic, Freidson was criticised by neo-Marxist commentators for ignoring the political economy and under theorising the relationship between medical and state power. As Larson (1977: xiv) notes, Freidson's work does tend to assume that the professions are *'independent from or at least neutral vis-à-vis the class structure'*. In contrast, the neo-Marxist perspective of the professions argued that medical dominance in the health care division of labour played a central role in the surveillance and reproduction of working class labour on behalf of capital (Johnson 1977). As Johnson (1977: 106) notes: *'the professionalism of medicine – those institutions sustaining its autonomy – is directly related to its monopolization of 'official' definitions of illness and health. The doctor's certificate defines and legitimates the withdrawal of labour. Credentialism, involving monopolistic practices and occupational closure, fulfils ideological functions in relation to capital and reflects the extent to which medicine in its role of surveillance and the reproduction of labour power is able to draw upon powerful ideological symbols'.*

McKinley is typical of the neo-Marxist viewpoint when he states, 'the House of Medicine under capitalism will never contribute to improvements in health unless such improvements facilitate an acceptable level of profit' (McKinley 1977: 462). According to neo-Marxists, there is no difference between the production of taken for granted capitalist commodities such as cars, fridges and clothes, and the practice of the surgical techniques of modern medicine; such as open-heart surgery (Navarro, 1976). Both involve the search for profit. Large corporations involved in the production of medical supplies, particularly pharmaceutical therapies, profit from individual experiences of illness and disease (Navarro 1986). Neo-Marxist commentators may agree with their neo-Weberian counterparts that medicine possessed substantial control over other health care occupations and patients. Nevertheless, they also held that medical work was increasingly coming under direct bureaucratic-managerial surveillance and control operating on behalf of capital (McKinley 1977). A point that will be returned to in chapter five when the proletarianization thesis is discussed.

The neo-Marxist sociologist Navarro (1976 1986) argued that medical autonomy is tied to the needs of capital. He held that it only emerged because the increasingly scientific foundations to medical expertise were congruent with the interests and needs of nineteenth century industrialists, who were using the apparently neutral concept of science to justify the introduction of new factory-based mass production methods. Navarro (1976: 31) argued that there had been an *'invasion of the house of medicine by capital'* and consequently medical knowledge and technology could not be seen as separate from capitalism but rather was part of it. Medical knowledge was not overlain onto capital ideology but rather modern medicine under capitalism is capitalist medicine (Navarro 1980). Navarro views medicine's essentially mechanistic view of the human body as being tied up with the capitalist mode of production. Neo-Marxists argue that medicine plays a key role in supporting the status quo in the capitalist system by reinforcing the idea that 'lifestyle choices' as well as 'natural processes' are responsible for personal and collective experiences of illness and disease. They hold that in adopting this approach medicine camouflages alternative social and economic factors relating to worker exploitation under the capitalist system (McKinley 1977). They follow Marx's colleague, Fredrick Engels, who in his key text *The Condition of the Working Class in England* (1974) held that an individual's personal experience of for example alcoholism, was an outcome of the impoverished life chances available to low paid workers living in the slums of industrialised cities. For Engels dependence on alcohol was a result of an attempt to 'blot out' the harsh reality of the working and living conditions present in nineteenth century society. It was not due to some inherent biological tendency towards addiction. Waitzkin's (1989) work on how doctor-patient interaction reinforces class inequalities focuses upon this point. Waitzkin (1989: 223) argues that during the doctor-patient encounter *'technical statements help direct patients' responses to objectified symptoms, signs and treatment. This reification shifts attention away from the totality of social relations and the social issues that are often causes of personal troubles'*.

A key criticism of the neo-Marxist viewpoint is that similar to Functionalism it seeks to explain medicine's position in society as stemming from the important social role it plays in maintaining the established social order. The main difference between the two perspectives is that neo-Marxists regarded this order as exploitative and ultimately offering no benefit to the individual worker. This is an overly simplistic viewpoint. In contrast, authors operating from the Foucauldian Governmentality perspective may like their neo-Marxist counterparts focus upon how health and social care professions such as medicine are deeply bound up with the process of governing populations. So much so that Governmentality authors such as Johnson (1995: 13) hold that, *'the expert is not sheltered by the environing state, but shares in the autonomy of the state'.* Yet the key difference between the respective neo-Marxist and Foucauldian perspectives is that while the neo-Marxist viewpoint sees this state of affairs as fundamentally repressive, by arguing it sustains class-based inequalities, in contrast a Foucauldian viewpoint considers its productive affects. It does this by focusing upon the role professional expertise plays in promoting and sustaining an individuals' capacity for engaging in self-surveillance and self-regulation (i.e. through acting on advice provided by their local general practitioner and other public health experts regarding appropriate dietary and exercise regimes) (Peterson and Bunton 1997). For the Governmentality perspective sees this as being part of the ability of expertise to render *'the complexities of modern social and economic life knowable, practicable and amenable to governing'* (Johnson 1995: 23). The chapter will now turn to discussing the Governmentality perspective and its contribution to the sociological study of the professions and professional regulation.

Governmentality and the Revival of Liberalism

As chapter two noted, the 1970s and 1980s saw the renewal of liberalism as an economic and political ideology, with its emphasis on individualism, advocacy of 'rolling back the state', and belief in the ability of the discipline of the market to promote consumer choice, improve service quality and minimise risk. Classical liberalism emerged in the seventeenth and eighteenth centuries, through the works of a variety of writers, such as Thomas Hobbes, John Stuart Mills, Adam Smith, Thomas Locke, Jeremy Bentham and Herbert Spencer. It is possible to identify at the centre of classical liberalism the underlying concept of 'possessive individualism' (Macpherson 1962). Macpherson (1962) argues that for these thinkers the individual and her capabilities 'pre-figure' the circumstance into which she is born. In short, her talents and who she is owes nothing to society, rather she owns herself, and she is morally and legally responsible for herself and herself alone. She is naturally self-reliant and free from dependence on others. She need only enter into relationships with others because they help her pursue her self-interests. According to this viewpoint, society is seen as a series of market-based relations made between self-interested subjects who are actively pursuing their own interests. Only by recognising and supporting this position politically and economically will the greatest happiness for the greatest number be achieved. Classical liberalism is a critique of state reason, which seeks to set limits on state power.

It is against this background of the re-emergence of liberalism that sociologists concerned with the role and governance of expertise within society have recognised the importance of the work of Foucault and his concept of Governmentality in the analysis of the relationship between the professions and the state (Peterson and Bunton 1997). The work of Foucault (1965, 1970, 1972, 1977, 1979, 1982, 1985a, 1985b, 1986, 1989, 1991a, 1991b) highlights how individual subjectivities are neither fixed nor stable, but rather are constituted in and through a spiral of power-knowledge discourses. These are generated by political objectives, institutional regimes and expert disciplines, whose primary aim is to produce governable individuals (Deleuze 1988 Peters 2001).

At the end of eighteenth century onwards there was a steady growth in "the dubious sciences", what Foucault calls the human sciences, particularly new scientific disciplines, such as psychiatry. Foucault holds that a key outcome of the rise of these new sciences was the more intensive use of 'dividing practices' to objectify an individual and their body via systems of notation, classification and standardisation (Turner 1992). Foucault argues that through their examination and assessment techniques experts produce normative classifications for subjective positions (normal, mad, sexually deviant etc) which increasingly became inscribed within the disciplinary regimes of society's organisational and institutional structures. There regimes spread throughout society as a whole as the dominance of the 'pastoral power' of Christianity started to decline and a more secular concern with 'the conduct of conduct', Governmentality, emerged from the sixteenth century onwards (Foucault 1991).

Foucault first published his study of Governmentality in 1979 (Foucault 1991b) and further developed it as a concept within a series of lectures given at *the College de France* (Burchell 1991). Foucault discusses that from around the sixteenth century onwards an ever growing number of treatises were published on the governance of the soul and the self, the family and the state. These were published against an increasingly complex background of technological development, rapid social change and political and intellectual upheaval. It should not be surprising to learn that events such as the enlightenment, the reformation, the rise of modern science and development of industrial capitalism, collectively led to a growth in the writing of treatises which sought to answer fundamental problems of rule: *'how strictly, by whom, to what end, by what methods etc'* (Foucault 1991b: 88). Foucault notes that these treatises focused more and more upon the idea that good governance entailed 'the right disposition of things' and had as its aim 'the common welfare and salvation of all'. Governance came to involve securing the security, health, welfare and happiness of the population. The *"population comes to appear above all else as the ultimate end of government'* (Foucault, 1991b: 100). Over time, governance would become increasingly tied into a liberalist conception of economics. Good government was economical, both fiscally and in its use of power. Furthermore, the development of new forms of expertise, Foucault's dubious 'human sciences' such as psychology, medicine and sociology, are tied up with this need to govern the population to ensure its betterment. This was because at an increasingly complex administrative and bureaucratic level the population was seen as possessing its *'own regularities, its own rate of deaths and diseases, its cycles of scarcity, etc'* (Foucault 1991b: 90). Consequently, *'novel forms of expertise in the fields of public health hygiene, mental health and mass surveillance emerged in concert with developing government policies and programmes...and were intimately involved in the construction of governable realms of social reality'* (Johnson, 1994: 142). The modern professions and their associated training and regulatory arrangements are emergent as an aspect of the formation of a liberal form of Governmentality that has as its target the population and its welfare, and which itself was emergent with the growth of capitalist industrial economies across Europe during the nineteenth century.

Foucault notes that two other forms of power, Sovereignty and Discipline, are tied up with the development of the power of a population-focused form of Governance, with its concern for 'the conduct of conduct', to enable the promotion of the security, health, wealth and happiness of individual subject-citizens. Sovereign 'command' power is exercised over subjects through the juridical and executive arms of government. Historically, sovereign power is related to monarchical rule, with its executive mechanisms of constitutions, laws and parliaments. Over time, these were made into more representative institutions through the development of democratic ideals, with allegiance to the monarch becoming transformed into allegiance to the rule of law (Foucault 1991b). The power of Discipline goes back to ancient religious, military and educational practices. As Foucault noted in *Discipline and Punish* (1977) its expansion over the population during the seventeenth and eighteenth centuries is tied up with a growing administrative and institutional need to survey and make docile individual and collective bodies. Disciplined individuals have acquired habits of action and thought which enable them to act in appropriate and expected ways and to do so through the exercise of self-control (Foucault 1977). 'Good governance' is about how to best align the Sovereign power of command and productive Disciplinary power in order to achieve the primary object of securing the health, wealth and happiness of the population. This is why Foucault argues that the power of Governance does not replace the power of Discipline or Sovereignty. Rather it recruits them. Indeed Foucault (1991b: 102) argues that *'we need to see things not in terms of the replacement of a society of sovereignty by a disciplinary society and the subsequent replacement of a disciplinary society by a society of government; in reality one has a triangle, sovereignty-discipline-government, which has as its primary target the population'*.

In short, the power of Governance is where *'technologies of domination of individuals over one another have recourse to processes by which the individual acts upon himself and , conversely...where techniques of the self are integrated into structures of coercion'* (Foucault 1980: 2). Governance *'retains and utilizes the techniques, rationalities and institutions characteristic of both sovereignty and discipline... [but it also]...departs from them and seeks to reinscribe them. The object of sovereign power is the exercise of authority over the subjects of the state within a defined territory, e.g. the deductive practices of levying taxes, of meting out punishments. The objects of disciplinary power is the regulation and ordering of the numbers of people within that territory e.g. in practices of schooling, military training or the organisation of work. The new object of government, by contrast, regards these subjects and the forces and capacities of living individuals, as members of a population, as resources to be fostered, to be used and to be optimized'* (Dean 1999: 12).

Liberal Government: Club Governance as the 'Natural State' of Things

The institutionalisation of professionalism as a self-regulatory strategy was ensured by liberalism's focus upon what is natural and what is not. The development of modern, rational and scientific expertise is entwined with the growth of the view that personal freedom is the 'natural state' of humankind and minimal forms of government are the 'natural way of things' (Rose 1999). Governmentality seeks the optimum method by which to affect 'at a distance' the way individuals conduct themselves without recourse to direct forms of repression or intervention unless it is absolutely necessary (Barry, Osborne and Rose 1996). This is because the effectiveness of liberal 'mentalities of rule' lies in their ability to align *'the objectives of authorities wishing to govern and the personal projects of those organisations, groups and individuals who are the subjects of government'* (Rose 1999: 48). A key method by which this goal was achieved from the nineteenth century onwards (and still today) was by harnessing the expertise of doctors, lawyers, and teachers etc *'into the process of governing, but it did so in the institionalized forms of independent, neutral colleague associations, controlling recruitment and training, providing codes of conduct and procedures of discipline...underwritten by government in the form of official recognition of license'* (Johnson 1994: 144). The restrictive practices of professionalisms exclusive 'club mentality' may seem on the surface to be oppositional to liberalisms 'free market' political philosophy. In reality, 'club governance' formed an essential part of the emergence of liberal Governmentality. Indeed, the gentleman's club was a 'hot bed' of commerce in Victorian society and similar to the 'professional club' it had clear ideas about who should get through the front door (Moran 2004). Consequently, the establishment of state-sanctioned jurisdictions for emergent professions such as medicine over the surveillance, classification and care of poor-rich, sick-healthy and mad-sane subjects, was not solely the result of successful occupational strategies of advancement based upon claims to possess esoteric expertise and an altruistic code of conduct. Rather, class and gender inequalities influenced the 'club rule' form that professional self-regulatory institutions such as the GMC took. While the establishment of the jurisdictions of emergent professions over particular elements of the general population was an outcome of programmes and policies that sought the legitimate expansion of the ability of government to shape and enhance the self-regulating capabilities of individuals along predetermined lines (Rose 1992 1999, Barry, Osborne and Rose 1996). This was because *'this form of power cannot be exercised without knowing the inside of people's minds, without exploring their souls, without making them reveal their innermost secrets. It implies a knowledge of the conscience and an ability to direct it'* (Foucault, 1982: 783). For example, over the last century, the medical profession has significantly contributed to an intensitification in the surveillance and control of the body and the self of the individual subject under the banner of maintaining the health of the population. As Armstrong (1983: 112) notes: *'[in] the twentieth century the human body has been subjected to a more complex, yet perhaps more efficient, machinery of power which, from the moment of birth (or, more correctly, from the time of registration at an ante-natal clinic) to death, has constructed a web of investigation, observation and recording around individual bodies,, their relationships and their subjectivity, in the name of health'.*

The "Enterprise Self" of Neo-Liberal Governmentality

The focus of Governmentality is upon the role of professional expertise as a 'socio-technical' device through which the self-regulating subjectivity of citizens is surveyed and managed 'at a distance'. It does not view contemporary challenges to professional privilege, such as reforms to the GMC, as being only concerned with reducing the high level of freedom from outside control that the professions have historically possessed (Johnson 1994 1995). It highlights how they are also concerned with the ultimate object of Governmentality: the population in general and the individual subject-citizen in particular. Indeed, as Johnson (1994: 149) notes, *'government-initiated change has, in recent reforms, been securely linked with the political commitment to the 'sovereign consumer'. In the case of reform in the National Health Service, this translates...[to a] stress on prevention, the obligation to care for the self by adopting a healthy lifestyle, the commitment – shared with the new GP – to community care'.*

From a Foucauldian perspective, contemporary sociological analyses of the professions and the governance of professional expertise must be set against a background of the re-emergence of liberalisms' 'possessive individualism' in the last three decades in form of the 'enterprise self' of neo-liberalist Governmentality (Rose 1996a 1999). Here, as Rose (1999: 87) notes: *'a new relation of individuals to expertise is established, based not upon welfare bureaucracies, social obligations and the inculcation of authoritatively established norms, but upon the mechanisms of the market and the imperatives of self-realization'.*

Rhodes (1994) notes that the attitude of UK government towards professionals since the 1980s has been dominated by a concern for the '3 Es': economy, efficiency and effectiveness. This is demonstrated by the rise of New Public Managerialism in the public sector (Pollitt 1990 1993). The growth of a rationalistic-bureaucratic managerial discourse of outcomes based transparent standard setting and performance appraisal in the health and social care arena is bound up with this. Indeed, it is often argued that a *'new commercialised professionalism'* (Hanlon 1998: 54) has emerged which stresses the need for professionals to develop managerial and entrepreneurial skills (Hanlon 1994 1998). This is a result of government attempts to improve trust in public sector services by seeking to redefine professionalism so that it becomes more commercially aware, target focused and managerially accountable. In this regard, the Foucauldian viewpoint shares much in common with neo-Weberian accounts of the contemporary situation faced by the medical profession. Both hold that there has been an increase in government intervention in the public sector and in turn the work of health and social care professionals. As part of this, doctors have increasingly become entwined in a particular system of governance, namely 'clinical governance', which requires the medical profession work alongside management to align clinical authority with economic viability (Flynn 2002). However, authors working from a Governmentality viewpoint also see the emergence of a more economically aware form of professionalism as taking place against a background of a profound shift in *'the nature of the present'* (Rose 1992: 161) and the way *'[we] come to recognise ourselves and act upon ourselves as certain kinds of subject"* (Rose 1992: 161). For in this way *"a person's relation to all his or her activities, and indeed his or her self, is...given 'the ethos and structure of the enterprise form'* (Rose 1999: 138). Indeed, from a Governmentality perspective, challenges to medical autonomy in the NHS and the principle of medical self-regulation in the form of the GMC form part of a broader shift in the grounds under which the legitimate governance of the population is practiced (Rose 1999). This is due in no small part to the ascendancy of 'the enterprise self' throughout all spheres of modern social life. As Burchell (1993: 275) argues: *'One might want to say that the generalization of an "enterprise form" to all forms of conduct – to the conduct of organisations hitherto seen as being non-economic, to the conduct of government, and to the conduct of individuals themselves – constitutes the essential characteristic of this style of government: the promotion of an enterprise culture'.*

The emergence of neo-liberalism in the 1970's re-activated classical liberalism's concern with the liberty of the individual, advocacy of free markets and call for less direct government. It emphasised the entrepreneurial individual, endowed with freedom and autonomy, and a self-reliant ability to care for herself; driven by the desire to optimise the worth of her own existence (Rose 1993 1996a 1999). For example, the conservative home secretary, Douglas Hurd, stated in 1989 *'the idea of active citizenship is a necessary complement to that of the enterprise culture'* (Hurd 1989, quoted in Barnett 1991: 9). Neo-liberal forms of Governmentality seek to govern through the autonomy of the governed. Citizens should be active, not passive, and democratic government must engage the self-regulating capabilities of individuals. Neo-liberal government focuses upon the use of the 'technologies of the self' because the *'citizens of liberal democracy are to regulate themselves; government mechanisms construe them as active participants in their lives...Such a citizen subject is not to be dominated in the interests of power, but to be educated and solicited into a kind of alliance between personal objectives and ambitions and institutionally or socially prized goals or activities. Citizens shape their lives through the choices they make about family life, work, leisure, lifestyle, and personality and its expression. Government works by 'acting at a distance' upon these choices, forging a symmetry between the attempts of individuals to make life worthwhile for themselves, and the political values of consumption, profitability, efficiency and social order'* (Rose 1990: 10).

Burchell (1996: 28-29) argues that neo-liberalisms dual advocacy of the self-regulating free individual and the free market have led to *'the generalisation of an 'enterprise form' to all forms of conduct'*.. Similarly, du Guy (1996a, 1996b) argues that 'enterprise', with its focus upon energy, drive, initiative, self-reliance and personal responsibility, has assumed a near-hegemonic position in the construction of individual identities as well as in the government of organisational and everyday life. Enterprise, he argues, has assumed *'an ontological priority'* (du Guy 1996a: 181). du Guy holds that *'a discourse of enterprise makes up the individual as a particular sort of person – as an 'entrepreneur of the self'* (du Guy 1996b: 11) so *'every individual life is, in effect, structured as an enterprise of the self which each person must take responsibility for managing to their own best advantage'* (du Guy 1996b: 14) . The concept of the self as enterprise requires that the possession of an essential core self is taken as the central feature of personal identity. How else could individuals be expected to become responsible for themselves and the care of their bodies and not a burden on the state? The very notion of the enterprise self requires a political commitment to the idea that all individuals are capable of self-fulfilment. This is the core mechanism by which the self-regulatory capabilities of the individual can be enhanced and entwined with the key objectives of governance: the security, health, wealth and happiness of the general population.

Consequently, failure to achieve the goal of self-fulfilment is not associated with the possession of a false idea of what it means to be human, or that individuals do not possess an essential core self which is the 'real' and 'true' them for all eternity. Rather, it is the fault of poor choices, a lack of education or the 'dependency culture' created by the welfare state. It is the result of 'learned helplessness', which in itself can be resolved with *'programmes of empowerment to enable [the individual] to assume their rightful place as self-actualizing and demanding subjects of an 'advanced' liberal democracy'* (Rose 1996a: 60)

Expert Enclosures and Technologies of Performance and Agency

The ascendancy of the enterprise self has increasingly led, as Rose (1993: 285) notes, expertise being increasingly *'governed by the rationalities of competition, accountability and consumer demand'* Rose (1993 1996a 1999) argues that the increasing institutionalisation of expertise during the nineteenth and twentieth centuries led to expert knowledge becoming integral to the exercise of political authority. Experts gained *'the capacity to generate 'enclosures', relatively bounded locales or fields of judgement within which their authority [was] concentrated, intensified and rendered difficult to countermand'* (Rose 1996a: 50). However, as a result of the rise of the enterprise self the enclosures are now being *'penetrated by a range of new techniques for exercising critical scrutiny over authority – budget disciplines, accountancy and audit being the three most salient'* (Rose 1996a: 54). As Osborne (1993) discusses, ever since the re-emergence of liberalism in the 1970s there has been a gradual reformulation of health care governance so that 'the field of medicine' is, to a greater degree than ever before, simultaneously both governed and self-governing. In an attempt to promote public trust in public sector reforms, the state becomes increasingly involved in medical governance and seeks to promote greater accountability and transparency within professional systems of self-governance. To achieve these goals it adopts a strategy whereby professional expertise is increasingly subjected to an additional layer of management and new formal 'calculative regimes' (Rose and Miller 1992), including the setting of performance indicators, competency frameworks and indicative budget targets. Rose (1996a 1999) emphasises the enormous impact of the trend in all spheres of contemporary social life towards 'audit' in all its guises, with its economic concern with transparent accountability and standardisation, particularly for judging the activities of experts. This is because two technologies are central to the promotion of the enterprise self at the organisational and individual levels. A 'technology of agency' which seeks to promote the agency, liberty and choices of the individual as they strive for personal fulfilment, and a 'technology of performance' which seeks to set norms, standards, benchmarks, performance indicators, quality controls and best practice standards. These help to survey, measure and render calculable the performance of individuals and organisational structures. Dean (1999: 173) notes:

'From the perspective of advanced liberal regimes of government, we witness the utilisation of two distinct, yet entwined technologies: technologies of agency, which seek to enhance and improve our capabilities for participation, agreement and action, and technologies of performance, in which these capabilities are made calculable and comparable so that they might be optimised. If the former allow the transmission of flows of

information from the bottom, and the formation of more or less durable identities, agencies and wills, the later make possible the indirect regulation and surveillance of these entities. These two technologies are part of a strategy in which our moral and political conduct is put into play within systems of governmental purposes'.

Bound up with the technologies of agency and performance of the enterprise culture is what can be called a progressive and insipid process of 'contractualization'. Institutional roles and social relations between individuals are increasingly defined in terms of explicit contract, or at the very least, 'in a contract like way'. The promotion of the enterprise form involves the creation of processes where subjects and their activities are *'reconceptualized along economic lines'* (Rose 1999: 141) Indeed, Gordon (1991: 43) argues that entrepreneurial forms of governance rely on contractualization as they seek *'the progressive enlargement of the territory of economic theory by a series of redefinitions of its object'*. Entrepreneurial forms of governance 're-imagine' the social sphere as a form of economic activity by contractually: a) reducing individual and institutional relationships, functions and activities to distinct units, b) assigning clear standards and lines of accountability for the efficient performance of these units, and c) demanding individual actors assume active responsibility for meeting performance goals, primarily by using tools such as audit, performance appraisal and 'performance-related pay' (du Guy 1996c). Here judgement and calculation are increasingly undertaken in economic 'cost-benefit' terms, which give rise to what Lyotard (1984: 46) terms the 'performativity principle': the performances of individual subjects and organisations serve as measures of productivity or output, or displays of 'quality' and *'an equation between wealth, efficacy and truth is thus established'* (Lyotard 1984: 46).

Neo-liberal Governmentality is concerned with 'the conduct of conduct' and seeks to govern through the autonomy of the governed. It is concerned with ''the practices of liberty' i.e. it is concerned with practices which structure, shape, predict and make calculable the operation of freedom. This is also why the traditional 'closed shop' form of professionalism as a self-regulatory strategy for institutionalising expertise has been challenged by the rise of the enterprise self but self-regulatory privileges have not been completely erased. For in a very real and practical way government depends upon expertise to render social realities governable - whether it is in the field of health, education or law - through shaping the self-regulating capacity of subjectivity among all citizens, *including* that belonging to professionals themselves. The effectiveness of neo-liberal 'mentalities of rule' lies in their ability to align *'the objectives of authorities wishing to govern and the personal projects of those organizations, groups and individuals who are the subjects of government'* (Rose 1999: 48). The 'diagnostic truths' and 'recommendations for action' provided by experts such doctors play a vital role in fostering such alignments. Consequently, from this viewpoint, the emergence of a 'new professionalism' within professions such as medicine is inextricably bound up with a broader shift in the nature and scope of legitimate authority and forms of governance within modern democratic liberal society. Certainly the apparent re-appropriation of rationalistic-bureaucratic 'technologies of performance' by occupational elites within professions such as medicine appear to belong to a particular 'mentality of rule' which recognises that *'[rule] 'at a distance' [only] becomes possible when each [agent] can translate the values of others into its own terms [so] that they promote norms and standards for their own ambitions, judgements and conduct'* Rose (1999: 50). For example, a recent study of the 'Governmentality of clinical governance' in primary care by Sheaff (2004) found that there had been a shift towards more formal networks of collective peer review of individual doctors work practice. Primarily through the contractual use of rationalistic-bureaucratic 'technologies of performance' such as medical audit and evidence based medicine. Greater peer surveillance of clinical practice is justified by doctors themselves because they sought to reduce unnecessary variations in the quality of clinical care as well as minimise economic costs. This is in addition to forestalling a perceived growing threat of managerial control over medical work. The overarching outcome of this shift towards greater surveillance and control of individual doctor's activities was an increase in the view that individual doctors could and indeed should be placed under peer surveillance and control. Hence, governing objectives for greater cost and risk containment existed alongside an increase in professional accountability, and were aligned with the medical professions self-image of itself as an independent and yet morally and socially responsible occupation.

The Contribution of the Governmentality Perspective

The Governmentality perspective makes a significant contribution to the sociological study of the professions and professional regulation. It highlights the key role professions, such as medicine, have played in the governance of the population. In doing so, it adopts a similar critical view of the emergence of professionalism as a form of regulatory control as the neo-Weberian perspective. Importantly, it reinforces the need for current debate surrounding recent challenges to the principle of professional self-regulation, to also consider the changing nature of the relationship between subject-citizens and the state, as a result of the political and economic re-emergence of liberalism since the mid to late-1970s. For the Governmentality perspective notes the ascendancy of the concept of the 'enterprise self' into all spheres of contemporary life. In doing so it highlights how challenges to the principle of professional self regulation and concurrent calls to reform the GMC can be seen to be directed towards the object of Governmentality - the population in general and the individual subject-citizen in particular – as much as they are the medical profession. For medicine, and indeed the health and social care professions as a whole, form but one part of a complex array of governing calculations, strategies and tactics which seek to promote the security, wealth, health and happiness of the population (Rose and Miller 1992). It is important for social scientists to recognise this. As in terms of Isaiah Berlin's (1969) famous dichotomy of 'positive' and 'negative' liberty, although liberal mentalities may appear at first to promote 'negative liberty' (i.e. the personal freedom of the individual subject to decide who they are and discover what they want to be) they in reality promote 'positive liberty' (i.e. that is a view of who and what a citizen-subject is and should be). This carries with it the very real danger of authoritarianism (Dumm 1996).

A Critical Assessment of the Governmentality Perspective

The Governmentality perspective highlights how it is theoretically useful to collapse the 'common sense' dichotomy of state-profession, which often exists in sociological accounts of the professions and the governance of expertise. For neo-liberal 'mentalities of rule' are concerned with 'the conduct of conduct' as they seek to promote the autonomous self-actualised enterprising subject, who as an active citizen of a modern democracy recognises they are responsible for themselves. This means that modern government must seek to govern through the freedom and aspirations of their citizen-subjects so that they come to recognise and self-regulate their activities in such a way that they 'naturally' align with broader social, economic and political objectives. This requirement has led to a critical re-configuration of the legitimate grounds on which 'good governance' can be practiced. With the 'field of medicine' becoming more than ever before simultaneously 'governed' and 'self-governing' as a consequence (Osborne 1993). As illustrated by the re-appropriation by medical elites of an emergent rationalistic-bureaucratic discourse of outcomes based standard setting and performance appraisal in the face of its increasing use by 'outsiders', such as hospital management, to monitor the activities of doctors.

However, the Governmentality perspective suffers from two key interrelated weaknesses. First, it possesses a tendency to over state the dominance of the 'enterprise form' in the social, economic and political spheres, as well as the construction of human subjectivity, and so an individual's sense of personal identity. As the chapter has noted, authors such as Gordon (1987), Burchell (1993) and du Guy (1996a) hold that reforms in the public sector since the 1980s have been bound up with a political programme that is primarily concerned with the promotion of the enterprise self as an 'ontological priority'. This is because *the discourse of enterprise brooks no opposition between the mode of self-presentation required of consumers, managers and employees and the ethics of the personal self* (du Guy 1996a: 64). Thus, public sector reforms have sought to challenge the traditional work identities of public sector workers, including that of professionals. Primarily through undertaking a 'cultural crusade' concerned with changing *the attitudes, values and forms of self-understanding embedded in both individual and institutional activities* (du Guy, 1996a: 151). For the world of enterprise valorises the autonomous, productive, self-regulating individual and requires that all workers *come to identify themselves and conceive of their interests in terms of these new words and images* (du Gay, 1996a: 53). There does seem to be an element of truth in this viewpoint. However, the enterprise self, with its 'bundle of characteristics' such as energy, initiative, ambition, calculation, self-sufficiency and personal responsibility, is just one of an array of competing discourses and associated bundles within society. These operate within the public and private spheres on individual subjects, constructing subjective positions for them to occupy, and influence their sense of personal identity. People perform a range of identities in different places, with different people, and at different times, over the duration of their life course (Bauman 1996). As Hall (1996: 4) notes *identities are never unified…never singular but….constructed across different, often intersecting and antagonistic discourses, practices and positions*. In short, the discourse of enterprise is not all consuming. Rather, it exists amongst a plethora of already existing, overlapping and frequently competing discourses. These often relate to key social categories such as gender, age, and ethnicity and so on, which act upon an individual, influence how they come to understand themselves as a particular type of subject, and consequently self-regulate their actions to produce personally desired effects (Fournier and Grey 1999). du Guy (1996a: 150) admits as much when saying *although enterprise prefers a tabula rasa on which to write it compositions, it actually seeks to produce its effects under circumstances not of its own choosing*. One example of a competing discourse on which the discourse of enterprise must seek to write itself with varying degrees of success is of course the discourse of professionalism. Regardless of whether or not it is called 'old' or 'new', it emphasises independence of thought and action in the name of service to others. For its sense of affiliation has not traditionally lain with bureaucratic procedures or managerial imperatives, but rather with a particular body of esoteric knowledge and specialist expertise, which belongs to a somewhat exclusive community of practitioners who possess a shared ethical code of conduct. Furthermore, the ability of professional practitioner's 'new professionalism' to resist or subvert the predominately economic focus of the enterprise culture, is itself a matter for sustained empirical investigation that must include all public sector occupational groups. Kuhlmann (2006a: 222) for one believes that doctors have been able to *"amalgamate managerialism and professionalism.....and [been able to] outflank tighter public control and [attempts] to create a comprehensive system of accountability"*. Although she acknowledges that her work is primarily focused on health care reforms in Germany, and argues that further cross-national research is needed before any firm conclusions are drawn.

The second key weakness of the Governmentality perspective is that in a practical sense professional groups and the state are different entities. It arguable that they should be treated as such if sociological understanding is furthered regarding the role institutionalised forms of expertise such as medicine play in the governance of the population. Certainly, it is often necessary for practical reasons to demarcate professional expertise from the governing apparatus of the state. Particularly when analysing empirically the affect of contemporary reforms on the principle of professional self-regulation in the eyes of professional practitioners themselves. It is the neo-Weberian 'social closure' perspective that is most useful here. For its account of the historical development of medicine's 'exclusive cognitive identity', which underpins its 'members only' stance concerning the issue of who should regulate doctors, reflects the nature of the regulatory context and the form of the occupational culture of the medical profession in the Anglo-American context. As illustrated by the continued insistence by medical elites that whatever changes to the current system are introduced, they should be heavily involved in deciding if a doctor is indeed 'fit to practice' and should remain on the state-approved register of practitioners

Synthesising the Neo-Weberian and Governmentality Perspectives: The Restratification Thesis

Despite these two weaknesses, the value of the Governmentality perspective lies in the fact that it reinforces the need to view recent internal reforms within the professions, alongside greater external surveillance of their actions by the state, as being linked with broader changes in how 'good governance' is viewed and practiced within modern liberal democratic society. While as the previous discussion has illustrated, the Governmentality viewpoint shares much in common with the dominant neo-Weberian perspective in terms of how it views the regulatory arrangements surrounding the health and social care professions. Given that the neo-Weberian perspective reflects the reality of the regulatory context, as well as offers important insights into the occupational culture of the medical profession, I would argue that the Governmentality viewpoint could be used to supplement and expand upon the neo-Weberian perspective. Indeed, I would argue that synthesising these two viewpoints is a fruitful approach to adopt when analysing the regulation of medical expertise. Both argue that it is necessary to adopt a critical and historical approach when studying how professionalism operates as a regulatory strategy, as well as when exploring the reasons behind current reforms in the regulation of professional expertise. Importantly, both hold that recent challenges to the principle of professional regulation have caused professional elites to place 'rank and file' practitioners under greater surveillance and control, as they seek to maintain collective self-regulatory privileges. The chapter noted how the Governmentality perspective argues that the 'field of medicine' has become more than ever before simultaneously 'governed' and 'self-governing' (Osborne 1993). This is a state of affairs conceptualised by the neo-Weberian perspective under the banner of the restratification thesis (Freidson 1985 1994 2001). The next chapter discusses the development of the restratification thesis to illustrate the value of recognising this point of agreement between the neo-Weberian and Governmentality perspectives.

Chapter 5

THE RESTRATIFICATION THESIS AND CHALLENGES TO MEDICAL AUTONOMY IN THE UK

Chapter five discusses the development of the restratification thesis to illustrate the value of recognising points of agreement between the neo-Weberian and Governmentality perspectives. It achieves this through exploring how sociologists conceptualised social changes that were held to be challenging medical autonomy, in the form of clinical freedom 'at the bedside' and the principle of self-regulation, from the 1980s onwards. As will become clear, this opens up an important line for empirical inquiry that is examined further in chapter six.

Challenging Medicine

The restratification thesis first emerged in the mid 1980s, in response to the growing recognition within sociology that something was happening to medical autonomy. It was conceptualised as being in decline by what are respectively called the proletarianization and deprofessionalization theses (Freidson 1985). Writing at the beginning of the 1970s, Haug (1973), the originator of the deprofessionalization thesis, argued that medical autonomy was being challenged due to a process of rationalisation and codification of medical knowledge and expertise into standardised rules and procedures. She focused on the role this played in reducing 'the knowledge gap' between patient and doctor, as well as in supporting the rejection of professional paternalism, as a more informed and critical general public became less inclined to act deferentially toward experts. Haug (1973:206-7) noted that this process was only just starting: *'[The] tension between the public demand for accountability and the professionals insistence on final authority has not yet erupted into general warfare...But there have been skirmishes'.*

Haug (1973) argued that a 'tipping point' had been reached, with medicine starting to lose its prestigious social-political position. She cited five interrelated factors to support her viewpoint. First, while medical knowledge was rapidly expanding it was undergoing a process of codification at a general level. This, Haug argued, was leading to medicine losing its control over its defined body of knowledge due to a rise in automated retrieval systems, such as computer algorithms, for symptom assessment. Second, the public were becoming more educated, better informed about health matters, and more likely to challenge physician authority than ever before. Third, as medical knowledge expanded, medicine as a profession was increasingly fragmenting into specialities and sub-specialties, with individual doctors becoming ever more dependent upon each other for expert advice, as well as ever more dependent upon non-medical expertise. One physician no longer held all the power over a patient. This reduced even further individual and collective autonomy. Fourth, there had been a growth in the patient self-help groups and a rise in alternative medicine as public trust and belief in medical expertise declined. It became ever clearer through high profile media cases, that in reality medicine's cognitive and altruistic claims did not live up to expectation. Fifth, increases in medical care costs meant the public were demanding doctors be held more accountable for their actions. Indeed, in some cases, they wanted the principle of medical self-regulation to be abolished.

The deprofessionalization thesis tends to focus on topics that indicate that there has been a decline in public trust of medicine and the threat this poses to the principle of professional self-regulation. The growth of media coverage of gross medical malpractice cases like Harold Shipman is a good example. It focuses upon the fact that attitudes to traditional forms of authority are changing and highlights that the public increasingly expects their governing institutions to operate in a transparent and accountable manner. In contrast, the proletarianization thesis highlights the existence of the potential for expert work in general, and medical work in particular, to become subject to rationalisation and routinization. Today's 'indeterminacy' becoming tomorrows 'technicality'. It focuses upon how this causes medical work to become subject to managerial bureaucratic control in the name of controlling costs and promoting consumer choice.

Writing at the same time as Haug (1973), the originator of the proletarianization thesis, Oppenheimer (1973), held that the work of professionals was becoming subject to a process of rationalisation in the name of economy and efficacy. This had happened in the factory at the beginning of the industrial revolution over a hundred and fifty years earlier. Like Haug (1973), Oppenheimer held that the scientific nature of modern specialist knowledge and expertise meant it was open to communication as a set of rules, procedures and operational imperatives where passed on to others who had not received any formal training. Work tasks could be broken down into parts so that, on one hand, workers performed one or a handful of tasks from a whole process, and on other hand, administrative and bureaucratic authorities could determine overall working conditions and priorities. Furthermore, Oppenheimer focused upon the fact that professionals were operating in large organisational settings (such as modern hospitals) as salaried employees, where he held the growth of bureaucratic rules, procedures and authority was undermining professional autonomy.

'The bureaucratised workplace....[tends to replace]...in the professionals' workplace factory-like conditions – there are fixed jurisdictions, ordered by rules established by others; there is a hierarchical command system; jobs are entered and mobility exists on the basis of performance in uniform tasks, examinations, or the achievement of certification, or "degrees"...The gap between what the worker does and the end product, increases'.
Oppenheimer (1973: 214)

For Oppenheimer a process began whereby administrative routines, measures and targets controlled professional work. His central thesis was that the work of professionals was increasingly becoming subordinated within bureaucratic structures to the control of administrative elites operating under fixed rules and procedures, which the professions had no control over. McKinlay (1977), McKinlay and Arches (1985) and McKinlay and Stoeckle (1988) noticed this theme from an explicit neo-Marxist perspective, and in the context of medicine. They held that as medicine had advanced and entered large scale corporate and bureaucratic settings, physicians lost several professional prerogatives associated with the principle of self-regulation, such as control over entrance criteria, training context and content, workplace autonomy and the object, tools and means and remuneration of their labour. They discussed how the American federal government and managerial 'corporate rationalizers' were affecting the content of medical work and medical school curricula. Medicine was becoming fragmented into sub-specialisms, as medical knowledge expanded. Non-medical staff that operated largely outside of direct medical control were also intervening in the doctor-patient relationship as medical techniques became ever more reliant on new technologies. Patients were increasingly the clients of the organisations doctors worked within, instead of being the direct responsibility of an individual doctor. Under these circumstances, they felt medicine as an occupation could no longer be held to be professionally dominant. Contrasting the position of self-employed physicians at the turn of the twentieth century with their modern day counterparts McKinlay and Stoeckle (1988: 201) concluded that: *[Every] single prerogative listed has changed, many changes occurring over the last decade. The net effect of the erosion of these prerogatives is the reduction of the members of a professional group to some common level in the service of the broader interests of capital accumulation'.*

They argued that while the proletariat possess a 'false consciousness' regarding their true exploited position in capitalist society, doctors similarly possessed a 'false consciousness' with regards to their 'true' social position: *'For doctors who are increasingly subject to this process, it is masked by their false consciousness concerning the significance of their everyday activities and by an elitist conception of their role so that even if the process is recognised, doctors are quite reluctant to admit it'* McKinlay and Stoeckle (1988: 201). McKinlay and Stoeckle's discussion of the proletarianization thesis fails to recognise that doctors are not quite like other workers. It is highly questionable that by the 1980s the entire labour force in the Anglo-American context had been progressively proletarianized under advanced capitalism. Regardless of their salaried status and managerial inroads into controlling medical work, doctors retained the power to direct and supervise the work of others and maintain a range of specialist skills, which enabled them to collectively bargain for positions of high social privilege, status and power.

Neo-Marxists like Navarro (1988) who are critical of Freidson admit he is correct in maintaining that medical autonomy is essentially a collective not individual property. Furthermore, relative to other health care occupations, medicine occupies a prominent position in the health care arena as no other occupation has the capacity to dominate it. This being said, by the mid-1980s Freidson (1994) recognised that medicine was, first, coming under pressure from the state to reform its regulatory and training institutions, second, was being placed under third-party greater surveillance and control by the rise of managerialism, and third, was no longer as dominant over other occupations in the health care arena as it once had been. Nursing, for example, was establishing its independence from traditional medical control as the state started to emphasise multidisciplinary working patterns in its attempts to reduce costs, maximise efficiency and respond to a rise of consumerist calls for increased patient choice.

Medical Autonomy in Decline?

In the 1970s, critical commentators shared a common emphasis on viewing professionalism ideologically as an exclusionary self-regulatory strategy for organising the performance of professional work. As chapter four discussed, this revolves around the principle that members of a profession must exercise control over their work, and the standards by which work outcomes are judged, due to the specialist nature of their expertise. Occupational control over members training and discipline forms a logical part of this viewpoint. Yet, by the mid-1980s, the changes posited by the respective deprofessionalization and proletarianization theses were acknowledged as actually starting to occur by sociologists (Saks 1995, Corburn and Willis 2000). It was beginning to look like medical dominance and autonomy was going into long-term decline, just as the deprofessionalization and proletarianization theses had predicted. Rapid advances in medical knowledge made it apparent that medicine was becoming less homogenous and fragmenting into sub-specialities, as new diagnostic and therapeutic technologies developed due to the advent of the computer age and advances in pharmacology, molecular biology, genetics and immunology (Gabe, Kelleher and Williams 1994). This caused medicine to become ever more dependent upon non-medical occupations operating outside of its direct jurisdiction to treat illness and disease (Elston 1997). Concurrent with the rapid growth in medical expertise and the growing internal fragmentation of the profession was a rise in managerial attempts to control medical work. There was the ascendancy of managers or 'corporate rationalizers' as the state sought to contain burgeoning health care costs (Coburn and Willis 2000). The invasion of the state via management into 'medical turf' was also related to growing public concern with the risks involved in modern medical treatment. High profile media cases engendered doubts in the consciousness of the public concerning the ability of medicine to ensure individual doctors possessed high ethical standards (Stacey 1992). They also contributed further to an already burgeoning consumerist demand for greater patient choice and control over medical encounters as well as health care organisation and delivery (Stevens 1986). This was reflected in the growth of alternative medicine, an increase in the threat of patient complaints and medical litigation, as well as the presence of a high level of dissatisfaction amongst patients with the doctor's communication and information sharing skills (Fitzpatrick 1984, Stacey 1988, Dingwall 1991).

Not Decline, But Restratisfication

Despite these broad changes the proletarianization and deprofessionalization theses and their applicability outside the United States of America was questioned (Gabe 1991). By the end of the 1980s, many commentators agreed that although clear differences between the American and UK health care systems remained *'[both] countries are moving towards greater third-party control of both global health care budgets and clinical decisions'* (Harrison and Shutz 1989). Yet as Elston (1991) pointed out, although there had been a rise in managerialism on both side of the Atlantic, after the establishment of the NHS in 1948 the majority for UK doctors had become salaried state employees. This meant greater potential existed for direct state interference with regards to medical autonomy in the NHS, as well as medical school admission numbers and curricula content to meet NHS workforce planning needs (Larkin 1983). Elston (1991: 66) highlighted that, under the conditions assumed by McKinlay and Arches (1985), *'the proletarianization of the British medical profession was virtually completed forty years ago'*. Rather than showing that UK medicine had been proletarianized earlier than American medicine, Elston (1991: 66) argued that this demonstrated the importance of *'disaggregating components of autonomy in analysis'*. Following Starr (1982), Elston (1991: 61) defined 'Medical Dominance' as medicines authority over others and subdivided it into 1) 'Social Authority', which related to medical control over the actions of others, and 2) 'Cultural Authority', which related to the acceptance of medical definitions of reality and therefore medical judgments being accepted as valid and true. She divided 'Medical Autonomy' into three main categories: 1) 'Economic Autonomy' (the right of doctors to determine their remuneration), 2) 'Political Autonomy' (the right of doctors to make policy decisions as the legitimate experts on health matters) and 3) 'Clinical or Technical Autonomy' (the right of the profession to set its own standards and control clinical performance, as exercised through clinical freedom at the bedside and collegial control over recruitment, training and discipline) (Elston 1991:61).

Elston argued that it was possible for the different components of medical autonomy to operate independently from each other. She held that her historical and comparative analysis of UK and American medicine showed that for much of the twentieth century American doctors enjoyed a considerably higher level of 'Economic Autonomy' compared to their UK counterparts. The reduction of UK doctors 'Economic Autonomy' because of their employment in the NHS after its inception in 1948 had not affected their other professional privileges. The profession's prominent position within the NHS meant it possessed considerable 'Social Authority' over other occupations operating in the NHS. Likewise, its 'Clinical Autonomy' and 'Political Autonomy' were enhanced, as it exerted a powerful influence over the shaping of health care policy and practice. Approximately 80% of all health expenditure was determined by decisions made by doctors with the government leaving medicine effectively in charge of the NHS during this 'golden age' of medical power (Klein 1983).

Elston (1991) was equally critical of the deprofessionalization thesis. Focusing on doctor's right to self-regulate their activities, she acknowledged that there had been challenges to the principle of medical self-regulation, as embodied by the GMC. Nevertheless, she argued, *'the modifications of professional self-regulation appear as a series of incremental adjustments to contain criticism rather than substantial diminution of collegiate control'* (Elston 1991: 81). Furthermore, she recognised that patients demanded to be given greater informed choice and this was tied up with the dominance of neo-liberal economic ideology within the health care arena, and specifically NHS reforms emphasising *'the discipline of the market and consumer power'* (Elston 1991: 78). However, she found little hard evidence to support the viewpoint that the public was rejecting the validity of medical science's 'Cultural Authority'. She acknowledged that the potential power of medical knowledge and expertise to cure all ills was increasingly questioned. But she argued that *'[the] growth of the women's self-help movement and holistic well-women centres and the apparently increasing use of alternative practitioners suggests some of the disillusioned are exiting the system, but only partially and on a small scale... [furthermore there]... is little baseline data against which changes in the level of public confidence in and valuation of medicine can be tested'* (Elston 1991: 82)

Additionally, sociologists could not agree if the proletarianization and deprofessionalization theses were applicable within the American context, where they were first generated. Freidson was a key critic (i.e. Freidson 1985 1994). He agreed that changes were occurring in medicine's relationship with the public, and acknowledged that this was due to medical knowledge and expertise expanding, as well as becoming formalised into rules and procedures with the advent of computer technology and the information and communication revolutions. However, he argued that: *'The professions…continue to possess a monopoly over at least some important segment of formal knowledge that does not shrink over time, even though both competitors and rising levels of lay knowledge may nibble away at the edges. New knowledge is constantly acquired that takes the place of what has been lost and thereby maintains the knowledge gap. Similarly, while the power of computer technology in storing codified knowledge cannot be ignored, it is the members of each profession who determine what is to be stored and how it is to be done, and who are equipped to interpret and employ what is retrieved effectively. With a continual knowledge gap, potentially universal access to stored data is meaningless. In sum, while the events highlighted by proponents of the deprofessionalization thesis are important, the argument that members of the professions are losing their relative prestige and respect, their special expertise, or their monopoly over the exercise of that expertise over time are not persuasive'.*
Freidson (1994: 134-5)

Although he recognised that medical paternalism had been rejected and the public were more active health care consumers, Freidson dismissed the idea of deprofessionalization as he held that medicine was not losing control of its monopoly over its expertise. He believed that the development of new techniques to monitor the efficiency of performance and the allocation of resources did not in itself reduce medical autonomy. What matters is whose criteria for evaluation are used and who controls any ensuing action This is an important point, for as the chapter has repeatedly highlighted, to function ideologically as a method of occupational control, professionalism requires that occupational members control the technical evaluation of work activities. In the context of the proletarianization thesis, the growing threat of bureaucratic-managerial control over medical work does challenge medical professionalism as it can, for example, introduce non-medical criteria from which to judge work performance. Freidson recognised this. Furthermore, he held that many of the changes that neo-Marxist authors such as McKinlay and Stoeckle (1988) identified have indeed occurred. It was true for instance that in America a large number of doctors had moved from possessing self-employed to employed status. Concurrent with this shift were moves towards subjecting the work of individual doctors to performance evaluation and management control (Coburn and Willis 2000). This was because the spread of 'managed care' across America to control costs and improve efficiency had created strong pressures to reduce medical autonomy in clinical decision-making. However, Freidson retorted that while the individual autonomy of doctors was affected by this state of affairs the collective institutional autonomy of the profession as a whole remained intact (Freidson 1994). This was because concurrent with these changes to the health care system in America had been the growth in co-opted medically qualified managers controlling the surveillance and evaluation of medical work. Freidson argued that the rise of medically qualified mangers illustrated that medicine was not undergoing a process of proletarianization, but rather was dividing into more pronounced 'elite' and 'rank and file' segments. For him, it became internally fragmented due to advances in medical knowledge as well as the threat played by the rise of managerialism on one hand and the consumerist 'patient choice' movement on the other: *'Professionalism is being reborn in a hierarchical form in which everyday practitioners become subject to the control of professional elites who continue to exercise the considerable technical, administrative, and cultural authority that the professions have had in the past'* (Freidson 1994: 9).

Freidson believed that the loyalties of these co-opted doctors ultimately lay with their clinical colleagues not their 'corporate masters'. He held that the purpose of 'elite' placing the 'rank and file' under ever more formal surveillance and control was to maintain collective privileges and sustain medical professionalism as a methodology of occupational control: *'[These] changes do not affect the position of the profession as a corporate body…so much as they affect the internal organisation of the profession in the relation amongst physicians. In essence, I suggest, they are creating more distinct and formal patterns of stratification within the profession than have existed in the past, with the position of the rank and file practitioner changing most markedly'* (Freidson 1985: 6).

For Freidson the rise of peer review mechanisms brought about by the increased use of surveillance tools such as medical audit were not a sign of the proletarianization of medicine. Rather they were an essential part of the process of restratification, which he held was occurring within medicine. Audit and peer review were well-established surveillance mechanisms in America by the late 1970s, unlike in the UK (Harrison and Schulz, 1989). Furthermore, Freidson (1994: 145) went on to argue that *'there is little evidence that the special status of rank and file professionals will deteriorate so much that they will find themselves in the same position as other workers. Even though they will be subject to more formal controls than in the past…[in] all likelihood, they will also exercise considerably more discretion than other workers in performing their work, and will be able to participate in formulating standards and evaluating their own performance through some type of peer review. Finally they will still enjoy at least occupational kinship with their superiors'*.

Freidson's arguments for the existence of restratification within medicine feel like good common sense. This because any attempt to raise standards and cut costs clearly requires the cooperation of the medical profession (Gray and Harrison, 2004). Also, it is somewhat ironic that at the same time sociologists were arguing about a possible decline in the status and power of the medical profession, modern medical technology and expertise were making significant improvements to people's lives. As Kelly and Field (1994: 36) note: *'To deny the effectiveness of modern medical procedures such as coronary artery bypass, renal dialysis, hip replacement, cataract surgery, blood transfusion, the pharmacology of pain relief and the routine control of physical symptoms in restoring or improving the quality of life for those suffering from chronic illness is to deny the validity of the everyday experiences of the lay public in modern Britain. In stressing the limitations and costs of medical interventions, the physical and social contributions of modern medicine are all too frequently ignored'.*

Support for the Restratification Thesis in the UK context

Taking up this point Elston (1991) argued following Freidson (1994) that medicine in the UK was undergoing a process of restratification. She noted that the fact it was already embedded within the managerial and bureaucratic structures of the NHS facilitated this process. She agreed that managerial 'corporate rationalizers' were in ascendancy. Not least of all because state reforms to health care throughout the 1980s had introduced performance surveillance mechanisms into the NHS, such as indicative clinical budgets, prescribing lists and medical audit. However, she argued that the embedded nature of medical expertise in the NHS, as well as the political bargaining of professional elites such as the Royal Colleges, meant that these mechanisms were largely placed in the hands of co-opted medical-managers (Exworthy 1998).

Elston's advocacy of Freidson's restratification thesis is supported by empirical work conducted with clinical directors in the UK by Kitchener (2000) between 1991 and 1997. The role of clinical director was created because of the introduction of an internal market in the NHS in the early 1990s. This separated purchasing and providing functions in order to improve efficiency by introducing an element of open market competition into service provision, in line with neo-liberal conservative economic policy (Elston 1991). Clinical directors operate as part of a clinical directorate, which is under the control of a medical director who sits on the hospital board. They are responsible within particular clinical areas for overall budgets, the recruitment of staff and monitoring service quality. Kitchener (2000) interviewed a number of clinical directors over time as well as non-medical administrative hospital staff. Kitchener (2000: 149) concluded that *little evidence emerged from this study to indicate any significant appropriation of clinical tasks or decisions by other groups....[indeed clinical directors have]...proved successful in protecting medical autonomy and resisting the increased managerial control...The result is that peer review is still widely perceived to be the primary means of quality control in UK hospitals...This position remains far removed from a managerial process of quality assurance that the reformers hoped would allow externally driven performance analysis to reduce clinical autonomy and costs'.*

Elston (1991) argued that in the UK context the 'Cultural Authority' (i.e. the belief that medical definitions of reality are valid and true) of medical judgments had remained and would remain intact. In line with Freidson's (1994) restratification thesis, she recognised that individual doctor's 'Clinical Autonomy' would slowly decline, and at the same time there would be an increase in the formalisation of the methods by which the profession's own elite institution controlled their members. Indeed, Elston (1991: 96) argued, *'it may turn out that it is the 'corporate rationalizers' within the profession who are in the ascendant in Britain'.* Alongside Kitchener's (2000) empirical work with clinical directors Elston's restratification arguments concerning the possible ascendancy of 'corporate rationalizers' *within* UK medicine are also supported by Armstrong (2002). Armstrong argued that what he called a medical 'administrative elite' had emerged, grouped around 'the academy' and the 'professional colleges'. They were concerned with standardising the everyday clinical decisions of 'rank and file' doctors using evidence-based medicine. This focused upon standardising clinical judgments by disseminating the results of randomised controlled clinical trails through *'formalised tools such as audits, clinical guidelines and protocols'* (Armstrong 2002: 1772). Random control clinical trials were used because they represent the pinnacle of medicine's 'Cultural Authority' due to their objective and 'value-neutral' scientific methodology.

Elston's (1991) ideas about medicine's 'Cultural Authority' were also endorsed by Harrison and Ahmad (2000) whose analysis of medical autonomy in the UK was undertaken at three different levels. They held that four strands operate at the micro-level of medical autonomy: 1) 'Control over Diagnosis and Treatment' i.e. decisions regarding what tests and examinations are in order and what drugs and procedures to prescribe or who to refer a patient too, 2) 'Control over Evaluation of Care' i.e. judgments concerning the appropriateness of treatment, 3) 'Control over the Nature and Volume of Medical Tasks' i.e. the ability to self-manage workloads and priorities, 4) 'Contractual Independence' i.e. the right to engage in private practice. At the meso-level is the relationship between the state and the profession, including the legal basis of the right to self-regulation and state recognition of the British Medical Association as medicine's 'peak association'. Finally, at the macro-level is the 'Bio-Medical' model. This is akin to Elston's (1991) concept of 'Cultural Authority' as it relates to the social and intellectual prominence possessed by medical knowledge. It holds that the authority of medical judgments lies ultimately in their apparently scientific, objective and value-neutral nature (Mishler 1989).

Harrison and Ahmad reviewed developments in the health care arena between 1975 and 2000. With particular attention to the rise of managerialism and greater state intervention into the principle of medical self-regulation through the establishment of 'clinical governance' bodies such as NICE. Harrison and Ahmad (2000:138) concluded that *'a not insignificant decline in the autonomy and dominance of British medicine has occurred over the last twenty-five years...The decline is clearest at the micro-level of clinical autonomy and at the meso-level of corporatist relations with government even though at the time of writing the Labour institutions of clinical governance and primary care organisation are only just coming into existence'.* From the perspective of individual doctors, medical autonomy was in decline. They also argued, contra Elston, that the principle of medical regulation was being successfully challenged. This was because of incidents such as the Bristol case. Yet they held like Elston that *'the dominance of the 'biomedical model' at the macro level remains largely intact'* (Harrison and Ahmad 2000: 137). Furthermore, they discussed the rise of 'administrative elites' within medicine, with Royal College members and medical academics being engaged in what they called 'the guideline industry'. They also noted that the biomedical model was being re-appropriated by non-medical management and the state as they sought to curtail medical autonomy in order to control health care costs. Indeed, *'many of the manifestations of managerialism outlined...depend upon it: observation of medical practice variation, clinical performance indicators, the quasi-market and clinical guidelines are examples'* (Harrison and Ahmed 2000: 138).

In summary, for Harrison and Ahmed, managerial 'corporate rationalizers' were seeking to curtail the autonomy of doctors using the outcomes generated by medicines own 'corporate rationalizers' working in the 'guideline industry'. While the state was adopting a rationalistic-bureaucratic discourse of performance management to justify policy changes regarding the governance of medical work in particular and the delivery of health care in general. For example, the National Institute for Clinical Excellence (NICE) now approves clinical guidelines prepared by professional and academic institutional elites in order to establish National Service Frameworks (NSF). The Commission for Health Improvement (CHI) subsequently inspects local compliance. Here Harrison and Ahmed (2000: 138) argue that there has been a rise in what they call "scientific-bureaucratic' medicine which is *'scientific in the sense that its prescriptions for treatment are drawn from an externally generated body of research knowledge, and bureaucratic in the sense that it is implemented through bureaucratic rules (albeit of a very specialised kind), namely, clinical guidelines'.*

Harrison and Ahmed (2000) agree with Elston (1991) that medicine's 'Cultural Authority' has largely remained intact while individual doctor's clinical autonomy has declined. Because of the process of restratification, an 'administrative elite' within medicine has developed. This is due in no small part to their increasing presence within NHS management structures and growing participation within 'the guideline industry'. However, they also point out that since the publication of Elston's arguments in the early 1990s, the state has sought to re-appropriate medicine's 'Cultural Authority' for its own ends. It is placing the 'Biomedical Model' at the heart of its own reform program to manage rising health care costs, promote patient choice and respond to increasing public awareness of potential risk. Harrison and Ahmed (2000) hold that state support for the development of scientific-bureaucratic medicine within the NHS, with its reliance upon biomedical research evidence and promotion of clinical guidelines, is leading to the replacement of the 'tacit' dimensions of medical expertise with algorithmic rules to be followed in a step by step sequence, regardless of particular situational contingencies (Berg 1997). This process forms a key part of the strategy by which the state is seeking to engender public trust in new systems of professional accountability. Empirical work conducted by Harrison and Dowswell (2002) concerning GPs prescribing behaviour and case note reporting endorses this viewpoint. They examined case-note recording behaviour in respect to angina and asthmas sufferers over a nine month period and concluded that the general practitioners in the study had become more 'bureaucratically accountable' for recording their clinical decisions and key data relating to patient cases, such as smoking habits, blood pressure results, inhaler techniques and prescriptions. There was a reduction in their autonomy to *'determine their own clinical practices and evaluate their own performance without normally having to account to others'* (Harrison and Dowswell 2002: 221). The study concluded that the doctors interviewed were engaging in self-surveillance as they changed their behaviour and acted as if their patient records would be inspected because there was greater potential for them to be inspected. This was because Primary Care Trusts were, in turn, being placed under the threat of greater surveillance and control by state the establishment of the NSFs and NICE. In contrast to this, Armstrong's (2002) empirical research showed that the general practitioners maintained their autonomy from clinical guidelines and protocols through justifying variations as responses to 'situational contingencies', such as patient calls for shared decision making during doctor-patient encounters. Armstrong agrees with Harrison and Ahmed (2000) and Harrison and Dowswell (2002) that state-backed administrative systems are utilising medical elites to reduce clinical variation, and so eliminate the 'postcode lottery' by promoting 'technicality' and reducing 'indeterminacy', through the generation of clinical guidelines and protocols via the biomedical research model. However, unlike them he cites the work of Jamous and Peloille (1970). This was discussed earlier in chapter four. He and concludes that *'in effect, GPs can be seen as attempting to maintain 'indeterminacy' in their everyday work – the traditional basis for professional status – in the face of a new forms of 'technicality' promoted, ironically, by their colleagues in the medical elite'* (Armstrong 2002: 1776).

The contradictions that exist between the conceptual viewpoints of Elston (1991) and Harrison and Ahmed (2000), as well as the empirical work of Armstrong (2002) and Harrison and Dowswell (2002), about the restratification thesis, are not resolved when other empirical studies relating to the UK context are examined. For example, empirical work conducted in the UK with general practitioners by Weiss and Fitzpatrick (1997) found that GPs did not feel that the expanding role of 'prescribing guidance advisers' was threatening their clinical autonomy. They could still exercise their discretionary rights to choose what to prescribe. On the other hand, Calman and Williams (1995) found that some doctors they interviewed welcomed the new opportunities for career advancement that were occurring through assuming greater managerial and administrative duties. However, others felt threatened by patients becoming better informed and more demanding during doctor-patient encounters. In short, there was a perceived increase in the threat of greater bureaucratic control over their actions due to the rise of clinical guidelines and prescribing lists.

Highlighting Current Gaps in the Sociological Literature

There seems to have been a cultural and organisational shift within the health and social care arena from emphasising 'professional autonomy' to promoting 'professional accountability', as a result of broader social changes within society over the last several decades. This has led to medicine becoming more internally divided into elite and 'rank and file' roles (Davies 2004). A state of affairs recognised by both the neo-Weberian and Governmentality perspectives (Grey and Harrison 2004). Yet it cannot be denied that contemporary sociological analysis of the medical profession in the UK suffers from the fact that *'systematic empirical studies are not numerous'* (Harrison and Ahmed 2000: 130). Furthermore, comparative analysis across nation-states is equally unsatisfactory. The UK is not alone in seeing the rise of a rationalistic-bureaucratic discourse of performance appraisal within health care arena; which sees medical practitioners increasing being co-opted into the surveillance of medical work and non-medical criteria being included into the evaluation of the appropriateness of doctor's clinical judgments (Coburn and Willis 2000). In the American context, and contra Freidson (1994), McKinlay and Stoeckle (1988) argue that the interests of their organisational masters dictate co-opted medical managers' actions. This is because American medicine operates primarily within for-profit organisations, which have a compelling interest in micro-managing medical work (i.e. to maximise profit). Similarly, Coburn (1997) argues that in the Canadian context the state partially controls medicine because of a process of restratification. Barnett (1998) does the same when analysing challenges to medical autonomy in New Zealand. The work of these authors reminds us that the previously dominant position of medicine in health care arena has been challenged internationally by a more interventionist state intent on subjecting medicine to the surveillance and control of health care management. However, none of these authors relies on systematic empirical data to make their arguments (Coburn and Willis 2000). Consequently, their work reinforces the fact that research that is more empirical is urgently needed, particularly from the perspective of doctors themselves (Lupton 1997, Elston 2004).

Additionally, the primary focus of sociological studies concerning the possible decline of medical autonomy has remained the health care system in which clinical judgments are made. This is to be expected. The principle of professional self-regulation has historically been justified as a legitimate regulatory strategy by professions such as medicine through a mixture of claims to altruism and the need to exercise discretion in their work due to its esoteric and specialist nature (Allsop and Saks 2002). It must be remembered, however, that the neo-Weberian critique of the professions reinforced the need to recognise the important role played by educational credentials in ensuring the legitimacy of control over regulatory and disciplinary arrangements surrounding group members (Johnson 1977, McDonald 1995, Elston 2004). The 'shoring up' of professional training and disciplinary procedures (due to the presence of external threats to occupational control over these regulatory functions) logically forms an important part of the restratification thesis. It would be reasonable to assume that elite members within professional groups attempt to retain control of the use and interpretation of their specialist knowledge through submitting 'rank and file' members to formalistic methods of surveillance and control within the educational as well as the clinical context (Freidson 1985 1994 2001, Grey and Harrison 2004).

Chapter three noted the increasing advocacy by the Royal Colleges of workforce surveillance tools such as medical audit and continuing profession development (Irvine 2003). It also discussed concurrent changes in the content of undergraduate medical education and the GMC's visiting and inspection policy towards medical school (Bateman 2000). Such reforms serve to show that medicine's elite institutions have increasingly found themselves in the position of having to subject 'rank and file' members to more formalistic control. They have had to adapt to changing social-political circumstances that require they become more open and accountable for their actions than they were previously (Stacey 2000). In short, recent changes in medical training and regulation appear to support the validity of the restratification thesis. Furthermore, medical elites have increasingly used 'learning portfolios' to support a new, open and accountable governing regime as they seek to maintain collectively held self-regulatory privileges (Challis 1999, Wilkinson 2002). Today's medical students will encounter portfolio based professional development planning and performance appraisal throughout their professional careers (Davis 2001). Paper-based and electronic portfolios are used throughout medical school and junior doctor training, in later specialist training and to support the Annual Appraisal of doctors as part of their NHS contract (BMA 2005). This is because portfolios support the implementation of outcome based performance appraisal (Snadden 1998, Searle 2000, Wilkinson 2002). Not least of all because many materials can be called a portfolio, including log books of activity, observational 'check lists', records of critical incidents and collections of personal reflective narratives (Redman 1995, Morrision 1996).

The increasing use of portfolios within medicine is primarily due to their ability to act as a concrete record of an individual doctor's competence and career development. They are completed in an apparently inclusive manner under the banner of promoting individual and institutional transparency and accountability, as required by medicines 'new professionalism' and predicted by the restratification thesis (Freidson 1994). Portfolios are not value-neutral educational tools. Under medicine's new governing regime, they are workforce surveillance and disciplinary tools, used by medical elites to promote quality control and ensure individual and institutional transparency and accountability. The true utility of portfolio learning as a regulatory tool lies in the fact that 'portfolio keepers' must define their own needs through self-assessing their performance in order to identify future learning goals. Portfolio based performance appraisal requires 'portfolio keepers' admit to areas of poor performance, and previous mistakes and errors of judgment (Gilbert 2001). Furthermore, they need to write these down and keep a somewhat personal record of attempts to improve their performance (Redman 1995). In short, portfolios seek to work on the subjectivity of individual users 'at a distance' through requiring 'portfolio keepers' engage in self-surveillance by promoting a sense of personal responsibility for meeting performance criteria governing the successful completion of designated work tasks (Wilkinson 2002). This is tied up with the aim of engendering real cultural change within the medical club while maintaining the legitimacy of the principle of professional self-regulation, albeit in its new more inclusive, transparent and accountable form (Davies 2004). Portfolio based performance appraisal undoubtedly possesses a dual focus upon 'technologies of agency' and 'technologies of performance', supported by a process of 'contractualization', which sees the establishment of mutually binding outcome based performance criteria governing the relationship between trainee and trainer, in addition to the relationship between these individuals and their training organisation (Dean 1999). However, perhaps most importantly, the relationship between a training organisation and its 'watchdog' body is also 'quality assured' by this method (Bateman 2000). This shows how portfolios act as medicine's new *"visible markers' of trust [which as]...tools of bureaucratic regulation fulfil [a] function as signifiers of quality'* (Kuhlmann 2006b: 617). In conclusion, the political utility of portfolio learning as a governing strategy that supports the renewal of principle of self-regulation operates at two levels. First, its confessional narratives, lists of activities and checklists of key occupational competences, can all be used as a personalised bureaucratic surveillance record of key events and 'turning points' in the career biography of individual workers. Second, at the same time as this they act as an organisational bureaucratic surveillance record that provides clear evidence of institutional transparency and accountability (Gilbert 2001). As recognised by the restratification thesis and required under the conditions of 'regulated autonomy' imposed by neo-liberal 'mentalities of rule' (Rose 1999).

Conclusion: Proposing an Empirical Investigation into Portfolio based Performance Appraisal within the Medical Club

Despite this move towards a structured competence focused outcome based approach to training and career progression by means of formal appraisal, very little has changed since the beginning of the 1990s, when in her review of the possible decline of the medical profession Elston (1991: 84) stated: *'[In] preparing this paper, I have been forcibly reminded of the paucity of recent detailed empirical studies by medical sociologists of the major institutions of British medicine. Research into the professional organisations and institutions of medical education and collegiate control has been conspicuous by their absence in recent years. As we seem certain to be facing a period of continued public and internal scrutiny of doctor's power and performance, such research is needed more than ever now'.*

In conclusion, as this chapter has discussed, despite ongoing debate amongst sociologists surrounding what the future holds for professional self-regulation, only a relatively small number of empirical studies in peer-reviewed academic journals discuss explicitly doctors own perceptions of recent changes (Ahmed and Harrison 2000, Elston 2004). Examining how portfolio based performance appraisal is undertaken within the medical club by 'rank and file' doctors provides an opportunity to empirically analyse if a process of real cultural change is underway within medicine from the perspective of doctors themselves. It fills a recognised gap in the current sociological literature regarding the contemporary governance of medical expertise. Focusing upon self-imposed and modernising changes within medical training which aim to promote institutional transparency and accountability certainly warrants the serious attention of social scientists (Davies 2004). Particularly given ongoing debate regarding what possible future role medically dominated institutional bodies currently involved in medical training should possess within the governance of medical expertise. Consequently, the next chapter proposes three interrelated research questions to guide an empirical investigation in relation to the implementation of portfolio based performance appraisal within the medical club.

Chapter 6

PERFORMANCE APPRAISAL INSIDE THE MEDICAL CLUB

The previous chapter concluded by arguing for the need to investigate the implementation of portfolio based performance appraisal within the medical profession. Chapter six outlines the findings of research conducted to fill this gap within the academic literature. The process of data collection and analysis occurred between 2007 and 2008. Revalidation was an unknown quantity when the research started, so the decision was made to focus upon exploring the introduction of appraisal within medicine through discussing with doctors their experience of annual appraisal as well as conducting trainee appraisal during clinical training placements. The following three research questions to guide the research:

1. What are the perceptions of 'rank and file' doctors involved in supervising and assessing medical students and junior doctors during workplace clinical placements concerning the recent introduction of portfolio based Annual Appraisal for them as part of their NHS contract?
2. What are the perceptions of 'rank and file' doctors involved in supervising and assessing medical students and junior doctors during workplace clinical placements concerning the introduction of portfolio based performance appraisal for trainees as part of recent broader reforms in the training of medical students and junior doctors?
3. Do 'rank and file' doctors involved in supervising medical students and junior doctors during workplace clinical placements think that the introduction of portfolio based performance appraisal has made them more personally accountable for their educational activities? Including for how they keep up to date and 'fit to practice' in their chosen medical specialty, as well as for how they themselves judge medical students and junior doctors as 'fit to practice'? If not why not? If they do think they are more accountable, in what way do they think they are more accountable. What are their attitudes towards this self-reported increase in accountability?

The conduct of the research was determined by the British Sociological Association guidelines on ethical research practice. To protect their right to anonymity study participants have been given pseudonyms (see appendix 1). The location the study took place in is referred to as 'Blue Town' and its medical school as 'Blue School'. In order to answer the research questions a sample population had to be defined theoretically on the basis that to be included a doctor in Blue Town had to be subject to annual appraisal as part of their NHS employment contract, and therefore was either a consultant or general practitioner. Furthermore, they had to be involved in supervising and assessing medical students and junior doctors during their clinical training placements, and therefore had to have used a trainee's portfolio to track and assess their progress. Not all doctors can become consultants and general practitioners. Not all consultants and general practitioners are involved in medical education. Those involved in the training of medical students are not necessarily involved in the training of junior doctors (and vice versa). 189 doctors in the Blue Town area are involved in supervising and assessing medical students and junior doctors during clinical placements. Each was contacted and asked if they would agree to participate in the research. 103 did.

The decision was made to use interviews to collect data. Primarily due to their utility as a research tool for exploring in detail with a social actor their points of view regarding a topic of mutual interest to both them and an interviewer. Good research practice dictates that data typically needs to be collected from between 30 and 50 interviewees before theoretical saturation is reached, with emergent themes fully explored and generalizable to comparable settings (Bryman 2006). 46 doctors from a range of specialities were eventually interviewed. Interviews ranged between 45 and 90 minutes in length. They were tape-recorded, transcribed in full, and securely stored. Although initially selected on the basis of their gender, age, ethnicity and medical speciality, interviewees were increasingly selected at random from the list of volunteers as key themes emerged over time and these variables were discounted as core explanatory factors concerning the ritualistic nature of the conduct of appraisal.

Data collection and analysis was divided into three overlapping stages typical to the conduct of qualitative research (Strauss and Corbin 1990). Stage one was the 'open coding' stage. It lasted for 15 interviews and focused upon asking open-ended questions, related to interviewee's personal experience of appraisal. A key part of this first stage was the quantification of the rich qualitative data being generated. Counting reoccurring words and phrases is useful for categorizing informant's experiences into themes, as well as exploring whether textual data can be safely generalized (Bryman 2006).

Stage two was the 'axial coding' stage and lasted for 16 interviews. Throughout this stage the research deliberately sought to disprove its developing understanding of the conduct of appraisal by framing interview questions in such a way that informants used their own personal experience to answer them in a either a positive, 'supporting', or negative, 'disproving', sense. To further ensure the validity, reliability and generalization of research data, emergent themes were thoroughly triangulated using informant characteristics.

Stage three, the 'selective coding' stage, lasted for 15 interviews. During this stage data is collected for confirmatory reasons. This ensured the two emergent key themes were fully saturated (i.e. no new or contradictory data was collected) and linked to an explanatory core theme, or 'central storyline', which as the chapter will discuss later, was defined as 'paperwork compliance' (Strauss and Corbin 1990).

Setting the Scene: Recent Changes in Medical Training

'Things have changed a lot around here recently'
Dr White (General Practitioner)

As chapter three discussed, the last two decades have seen undergraduate and postgraduate medical training undergo a period of intensive reform (Bligh 2001). All forty-six interviewees recognised this fact. As the following comments from Dr Red (Surgeon) illustrate:

'I would say I first noticed that the way we train students and juniors was beginning to change around the mid-90s. You see, the system really hadn't changed since, well, I think you could reasonably argue that nothing much had changed since the 1940s (laughs)....I certainly remember starting to really notice changes after (Blue School) changed its course in 1996....For one thing students started to have better basic clinical and communication skills. They could really talk to patients, take a history and perform an initial (physical) examination, and in a far more advanced way than your average student could in my day...But then we never really got formally taught communication skills at medical school. We just got thrown in the deep-end when we were juniors...I also started to notice that I was being asked to do more and more formal teaching for students and juniors, that is on top of the more traditional ward round teaching. You could tell things were getting more structured and formal training-wise...There is more bureaucracy and a greater administrative workload involved in providing (clinical) placements for trainees these days....More and more paperwork keeps coming my way from the medical school and the (postgraduate) deanery...'.

Dr Red is directly and indirectly touching three important themes that emerged from discussion of recent reforms in medical training with research informants. First, interviewees recognised the need for changes in medical training and were supportive of recent changes to undergraduate and postgraduate training. Second, they felt that because of recent reforms clinical placements had become more structured than they had been previously. The introduction of portfolio based performance appraisal was bound up with this. Third, it was possible to identify from their accounts that although recent changes in medical training placed doctors under greater collegiate surveillance and control, their accountability to medical elites nevertheless possesses a 'ritual quality' (Pym 1973). Furthermore, it was possible to identify a mixture of 'structural' and 'ideological' factors which were directly affecting the implementation of portfolio based performance appraisal. This chapter will now start to explore these three themes.

A Different Type of Medical Trainee

'I think as a clinical teacher you have to accept that today's trainee is different to yesterdays'.
Dr Orange (Physician)

All interviewees held that 'new curriculum' medical students and junior doctors possess a different set of skills than their predecessors. They were quick to note that today's medical curricula are very different to the ones they themselves completed as trainees.

'The old and new curricula are very different. You really are comparing a competency and skills based curriculum to, in a sense, a knowledge-based curriculum, which did not necessarily equip students with the skills and competence needed to be a good house officer.'
Dr Lilac (General Practitioner)

As Dr Lilac notes, medical training is becoming increasingly focused upon ensuring today's young doctors possess key communication, study and practice skills relevant to the work tasks they will be required to complete when they begin their medical careers. Dr Yellow (Surgeon) concurs:

'I think one of the strengths of the new system for medical students is that the students are much more able to go out and find things out for themselves, and do projects and research...You ask them to find out something and they are able and motivated to go and find it out...They also have very good communication skills. I think that overall the course does make a good job of preparing them for postgraduate training by focusing upon key practice skills'.

Given this increased focus upon preparing medical students for the job they will take up when they graduate, it should be no surprise to learn that interviewees' held that today's medical students are far better prepared for the role of junior doctor than their predecessors were:

'Today's trainees are far better prepared for their future jobs. I think a large reason why is because in final year they 'shadow' the house officer whose job they will take over when they graduate'.
Dr Green (General Practitioner)

The production of a 'different type' of junior doctor because of recent reforms in medical training is to be expected. When first published *Tomorrows Doctors* (GMC 1993 2002 2003) required medical schools change substantially the content of the undergraduate medical curricula and focus upon producing medical graduates who were prepared for their immediate junior house officer job (Bligh 1998). First, it required that medical schools remove the traditional preclinical-clinical training divide. Traditionally medical students had no contact with patients and learned the basic sciences in years one and two of the undergraduate course, before embarking upon 'hands on' clinical training during years three, four and five (GMC 1993 2002 2003). *Tomorrows Doctors* replaced this with a 'core-plus-options' model with earlier clinical contact with patients (in year one in most medical schools). As part of this, less emphasis was placed upon ensuring students memorised large amounts of basic science knowledge (Bligh 1995). Second, it required medical schools to establish 'clinical skill training centres' which focused upon developing core clinical and communication skills (Bradley and Bligh 1999). Third, it required medical schools to increase community-based training in the general practice setting (Parsell and Bligh 1995) Fourth, it required medical schools to develop student's potential for independent learning and critical thinking (Bullimore 1998). This was seen as essential given the rapidly changing and expanding nature of professional knowledge, exponential growth of new medical technologies and a concurrent focus upon using 'evidence based medicine' to inform clinical practice (BMJ 1999).

In the context of junior doctor training, it was recognised from the 1990s onwards that junior doctors working hours and overnight 'on-call' duty in hospitals (with 100 hour working weeks being all too common) not only endangered patients, but also affected trainees' well-being, educational achievements and career progression (McKee and Black 1993). The *New Deal* (Department of Health 1991) limited junior doctors to a maximum of 72 hours 'on duty' and 56 hours actual work in light of growing concern over the quality of medical practice, training and regulation (Stacey 1992). The Calman report of postgraduate training recommended more formal supervision for junior doctors as well as the introduction of protected teaching and learning time (Calman 1993). This started a process of formalisation within postgraduate training that eventually over the next decade would lead to the development of the Foundation Programme (BMA 2005). The two year foundation programme for junior doctors (introduced in August 2005) aims to provide trainees with a structured competency based, outcome focused, training programme, utilising nationally agreed clinical performance standards in specialty-specific 'key skill' domains (BMA 2005). These practice benchmarks are provided by the Royal Colleges. The implementation of the foundation programme locally, by the regional postgraduate deaneries responsible for junior doctor training, is supported by a regular quality assurance surveillance and inspection programme run jointly by PMETB and the GMC. This is to meet the contemporary requirement for transparent and accountable medical governance (Bruce 2007).

The Problem with Problem Based Learning

In summary, from the 1990s onwards it was accepted within the medical profession at large that how medical students and junior doctors were trained required modernisation (Bligh 1998). It should come as no surprise to learn that all the doctors interviewed recognised that recent reforms to undergraduate and junior doctor training were needed, as the following comments from Dr Red (Surgeon) and Dr White (General Practitioner) illustrate:

'Oh yes, the changes were definitely needed, you have to keep up with the times, and I remember what it was like for me as a junior doctor...Under the old system you were very much thrown in at the deep end from day one...Often you were so tired towards the end of your shift that you could actually fall asleep standing up'.
Dr Red

'I think it goes without saying that everybody recognised that it was about time the undergraduate course changed. I certainly had wanted things to change for a long time'.
Dr White

Although broadly supportive of recent reforms in medical training, concerns were expressed by all interviewees regarding the use of Problem Based Learning (PBL) by Blue School. PBL is a specific type of small group learning technique, first applied in the medical training context in the 1960s at McMaster medical school in Ontario. Post-*Tomorrows Doctors* it was adopted by many UK medical schools, such as Manchester, Glasgow, St Bartholomew's, St Georges, Liverpool, Birmingham and Newcastle to name but a few (Maudsley 1999). The PBL method dates back to the American Pragmatist Philosopher, John Dewy, who advocated an educational method known as 'multiple working hypothesis' (Chamberlain 1965). Students are presented with real-life problem in the form of a written case scenario. In the context of medical education, the scenario is typically a 'presenting patient' who possesses certain clinical symptoms (for example, breathlessness, lack of appetite and night sweats). A group must solve the 'problem' and decide upon an appropriate course of patient treatment, through proactively identifying and accessing learning resources (Dolmans and Schmidt 1996). Although widely held to develop students' self-directed and critical thinking skills, PBL has had a mixed reception within medical education (Norman 1988). It is seen by some to reduce the acquisition of basic science knowledge, due to its focus upon acquiring knowledge that is only of direct relevance to the immediate 'problem case' (Vernon and Blake 1993, Finucane 1998). The introduction of PBL by Blue School was held by research informants to have a direct affect upon 'new curriculum' medical students' basic science knowledge base. This related to the depth of their understanding of anatomy, physiology and pharmacology. As Dr Orange (Physician) explains:

'They do possess good clinical and communication skills but they lack a solid grounding in the key basic sciences. I am thinking of anatomy and physiology here. I know that there is a general philosophy nowadays of 'you need to know what you need to know', but I would argue that you have to build your general competence as a doctor upon a solid foundation of core basic science knowledge'.

As discussed in chapter two, subjects such as anatomy and physiology have been at the heart of medical training since the rise of the biomedical model in the nineteenth century. It is not surprising to learn that their reduced presence within undergraduate curricula caused some comment amongst the doctors interviewed. Despite their concerns, interviewees did argue that the old system of undergraduate training tried to instil too much knowledge into medical students. They certainly did not want a return to *'(the) old days of digesting bucket loads of facts, the vast majority of which you never really needed again once you left medical school'* Dr Lilac (General Practitioner). They recognised that a key goal of *Tomorrows Doctors* had been to reduce the 'factual burden' that medical education had long placed upon a medical student (GMC 1993 2002 2003). They also acknowledged that 'new curriculum' students had the necessary learning and critical thinking skills so they could 'fill in' gaps in their knowledge. They maintained that a typical final year medical student's knowledge was an adequate level to work as a junior doctor. Nevertheless, they believed that Blue School should adopt more traditional didactic teaching methods in addition to using PBL. This reflected current argument within medical education circles that a 'hybrid' mixture of PBL and didactic teaching is the best way to train medical students, given the need to ensure they possess a core amount of basic science knowledge (Finucane, 1998). Interviewees argued that *'(you) need to make sure that they have the core knowledge in anatomy that you will always need as a doctor, regardless of if you work in A&E or general practice, and the traditional lecture is a key way of getting that across'* Dr White (General Practitioner).

Further discussion revealed that informants argued this point because they were concerned with the possible negative impact a 'PBL-heavy and lecture-light' course could have upon a students' future career progression. Trainees need to pass Royal College examinations once they finished junior doctor training, which as Dr Lilac (General Practitioner) pointed out are heavily *"knowledge intensive"*. In summary, interviewees recognised that their own medical training had been too focused upon memorizing 'facts and figures', but they nevertheless felt it provided them with an essential core knowledge base that they could draw upon throughout their medical career. They argued that this was missing from the new 'lecture-light' PBL course at Blue School, as the following comments from Dr Black (Physician) and Dr Purple (Surgeon) serve to illustrate:

'I know that we must not focus on knowledge of the basic sciences too much these days but I do think they should have more depth to their knowledge than they typically have at the moment...(They) can't answer some quite key basic anatomical and physiological questions. OK, they can go and find out the answers, but that is not the point, the course teachers at (Blue School) need to make sure the fundamentals are in place really'.
Dr Black

'They (Blue School) need to provide students with more formal teaching in key areas like anatomy, physiology and pharmacology....You have to have the building blocks in place so trainees have a fighting chance when they hit the (royal) college exams'.
Dr Purple

Exploration of doctors concerns over the use of PBL by Blue School revealed two issues highly relevant to analysis of the introduction of portfolio-based performance appraisal within the medical club. Although doctors were quite happy to discuss their concerns in interviews, their accounts showed a mixture of apathy and ambivalence when raising the topic with Blue School. It should be stressed that this was not because they felt they could not complain to Blue School out of fear of reprisal. Rather, two interrelated factors seemed to be at work here. First, they are not medical school or postgraduate deanery employees. Indeed, they felt a sense of distance between themselves and the medical school (a fact I will touch upon again later). Consequently, they may agree that changes to medical training were necessary to modernise it in the face of NHS reform, but as the following comments from Dr Yellow (Surgeon) highlight, they did not feel directly and personally responsible for something they saw as being a consequence of Blue Schools' own choice to use PBL i.e. a reduction in students' core basic science knowledge:

'Yes, I did mention it in passing once at some meeting or other. I was told that the reduction in core knowledge was a consequence of the changes being made, and that was that really...It's really down to them, not me, to do something about it. That is if they want things to be different of course, and I don't get the impression that they do;.

Second, their accounts reinforced the fact that there is a natural tendency within the medical club for doctors to respect each others 'turf' and right to autonomous practice, regardless of if they are working in medical education or clinical practice (Stacey 1992 2000). As the following comments from Dr Green (General Practitioner) serve to illustrate:

'Did I mention my concerns to (Blue School)? Look, when you have been doing this for as long as I have you realise that whatever happens at the medical school or the (postgraduate) deanery happens there, and whatever happens here in the hospital happens here, and never the twain shall meet. I mean, obviously we both want to turn people into good competent doctors. But do you really think the medical school or (postgraduate) deanery cares what we think or do past a certain level? No, we leave each other alone to get on with out jobs....(so) what matters to them most is making sure they are enough (clinical) placements for trainees...(and) that all the necessary paperwork is filled in and returned to them on time'.

Dr Green's comments reinforce the importance of the need to pay close attention to 'rank and file' medical practitioners perceptions of the relationship between doctors responsible for providing trainees with clinical placements and assessing their clinical performance, and the medical elites responsible for the content, governance and quality assurance of medical training. In the context of the restratification thesis, it is important to identify how accountable they feel to medical elites for what they do educationally, given the contemporary move toward a 'standards driven' open, transparent and accountable form of governance within the medical club. Not least of all because this strategy is being used by medical elites to sustain professional autonomy, in the form of the principle of medical self-regulation, in the face of growing calls for lay, managerial and inter-professional involvement in medical regulation. The next section of this chapter will discuss this point in relation to the implementation of portfolio based performance appraisal within medicine.

Portfolio Based Performance Appraisal and Medicines New Professionalism

'(Governance is) a form of activity aiming to shape, guide or affect the conduct of some person or persons'.
Gordon (1991:2).

Portfolios can be said to act as one of medicines key new 'visible markers' of trust within the contemporary governing context (Allsop 2006, Kuhlmann 2006b). As chapter three discussed, the introduction of portfolio based performance appraisal within the medical club has played a key role in reforming the governance of medical training and regulation over the last decade (Challis 1999, Southgate 2001, Wilkinson 2002, Irvine 2003). It modernises how medical governance systems operate. The 'fitness to practice' of medical trainees and experienced 'rank and file' doctors is now more than ever before monitored in an open, transparent and accountable fashion, utilising 'best evidenced' minimum performance standards devised by medical elites themselves (Stacey 2000, Southgate 2001, Irvine 1997 2003 2006, Catto 2006 2007). As the ex-chairman of the GMC Sir Donald Irvine (2001: 1808) notes *'the essence of the new professionalism is clear professional standards'*. Chapter five argued that the growing use of portfolios within the medical training and regulatory context is bound up with the emergence within the medical club of a rationalistic-bureaucratic discourse of outcome based standard setting and performance appraisal (Irvine 2003, Slater 2000 2003 2007). Certainly, at the centre of portfolio based performance appraisal lies an administrative rationalistic-bureaucratic process of standard setting and outcomes management (Harrison and Ahmed 2000, Grey and Harrison 2004). This relies upon the functional analysis of an occupational role in order to break it down into its constitutive parts and translate key competencies into specific measurable outcomes and minimum performance requirements (Searle 2000, Harrison 2004). Although their exact content may change depending upon the context of their application, portfolios tend to come with outcome-based performance standards and targets attached (Dean 1999, Searle 2000, Southgate 2001). For example, in the context of NHS Annual Appraisal, consultants and general practitioners must keep a portfolio of their continuing professional development which contains information relating to prescribing patterns, the outcomes of case note analysis, the results of clinical audit, as well as patient complaint case outcomes and even surgical operation success rates (Black 2002, Bruce 2007). Similarly, in the Foundation Programme for junior doctors, trainees must maintain a portfolio which contains evidence of their ability to perform key clinical skills within a range of medical and surgical specialties, as well as their ability to use clinical protocols and 'best evidence' practice guidelines when providing patient treatment and care (BMA 2005).

Portfolio based performance appraisal does possess a certain value as a 'learning tool' that must be recognised (Redman 1995, Gilbert 2001). In line with vocational and professional education in general, a portfolio is typically defined within medicine as a *'dossier of evidence collected over time that demonstrate a doctor's education and practice achievements* (Wilkinson 2002: 371). It is argued by educationalists that portfolios help portfolio keepers to develop their study and critical thinking skills by requiring they 'take charge' of their learning and professional development in order achieve personal career aspirations. Portfolio keepers are encouraged to identify their own learning needs, set learning goals in light of these, and subsequently record activities and achievements for later peer review (Gilbert 2001). This is done under the guise of promoting 'reflective practice' (Long 1986) within the professional training context. (i.e. Snadden and Thomas 1998, Challis 1999, Wilkinson 2002). For here, 'being reflective' of one's performance, and admitting mistakes and learning from them, is held to represent 'good professionalism'. Not least of all because it is taken to signify willingness to place one's client's needs and interests above one's own. This why portfolio based performance appraisal requires individuals to provide written statements concerning their learning needs and work performance in light of minimum performance standards governing an occupational task (Fletcher 1997, Southgate 2001, Wilkinson 2002). Yet recognising the educational value of portfolio based performance appraisal simply reinforces the need to focus on the political role portfolios play as governance tools. For their usefulness as educational tools reflects and reinforces their political value as an administrative and managerial tool that ultimately protects the principle of professional self-regulation. They may well act as a personalizable biographical career record containing information relating to a practitioner's continued professional competence (Snadden and Thomas 1998). The adoption of clear standards governing the performance of work tasks certainly does allow individual practitioner's competence to be judged and recorded. However, most importantly, in doing so they enable an organisations' ability to monitor the achievement of these standards to in turn be assessed and verified by an independent third party. Consequently, whatever its educational value as a tool for ensuring an individual's professional competence and professionalism, portfolio appraisal's political value lies in its ability to function as an individually productive peer review exercise that also serves to protect professional autonomy at the institutional level in the form of the principle of professional self-regulation (Gilbert 2001). After all, who other than a professional's peers possesses the necessary expertise to set the standards judging the quality of their work? This is an invaluable state of affairs if you happen to be a member of an organisation subject to overarching regulatory 'watchdog bodies'. As medicine is with regards to the Council for the Regulation of The Health Care Professions.

Doctors under Surveillance?

The political utility of portfolio based performance appraisal reinforces the need to answer several interrelated questions regarding their practical application within the medical club. Does portfolio based performance appraisal survey what it intends to survey and produce the effects that it intends to produce? Does it survey and record a medical trainee's or doctor's clinical performance and competence, including their self-monitoring inspections of their learning needs and professional practice achievements? Does it encourage its user to engage in self-inspection and practice self-discipline? Does it ensure organisational transparency and accountability through producing an accurate administrative account of professional competence and career development?

Taking to doctors indicates that they feel they are coming under greater collegiate surveillance and control. They are becoming more accountable for what they do educationally, in terms of how they supervise and assess the 'fitness to practice' of trainees, as well as how they maintain their own continued professional competence. Informants believed, first, that a key effect of recent reforms in medical education had been the introduction of more structured clinical placements for trainees, and second, that as part of this change the clinical performance of trainees was coming under greater formal surveillance and testing than previously had been the case. Both at medical school and during their 'off site' clinical placements. The follow comments from Dr Red (Surgeon) and Dr Yellow (Surgeon) illustrate these points.

'Yes, I do think that we are placing students under more surveillance these days. As medical teachers, we have always been concerned with knowing how students perform. But I do think things have intensified as a result of recent reforms in the (undergraduate) curriculum..(and that) they are also being more intensively monitored in areas you weren't so formally assessed in in my day, such as communication skills...There certainly was much more freedom to explore clinical areas when I was at medical school. You see, when they first come here they get a structured timetable and their attendance is monitored...they now have allotted teaching time in clinic as well as ward teaching sessions with me and my colleagues...before, well, things were much more flexible, you really just had to turn up for ward rounds, and you had a bit of clinical teaching here and there on top, and the rest of the time was yours to use as you wanted. And I think that approach did help me as a medical student as I could follow up areas that I wanted too explore further out of personal interest, and I don't think today's students and juniors have that freedom, as everything is moving towards becoming much more regulated and structured in medical education these days.'
Dr Red

'The introduction of the foundation programme does mean that juniors now have a much more structured training experience...they have a formal timetable of clinical teaching relating to different specialty areas... (and) they get a lot more formal testing of their 'hands on' ability to do the job...so yes, I would say that they definitely are under more surveillance, and certainly a lot more than we were as juniors I can tell you!'
Dr Yellow

Interviewees also held that the use of portfolio based performance appraisal was bound up with a more general increase in the surveillance of doctor's clinical activities:

'The portfolio is a tool for monitoring their competence to perform to minimum practice standards within a given clinical area. That is a given. But I do think that like many things these days in medicine it is also about keeping track of what you are doing and recording it to cover your arse, and the portfolio system introduces students to that fact of life early on'.
Dr Purple (Surgeon)

Interviewees also reported that its introduction in medical training had had some affect on how they personally went about supervising trainees during clinical placements:

'If you look at the portfolio for final year (medical students) and the one for the foundation programme, well, they ask the same of you as a supervisor really, they both require you have a series of one on one meetings with a trainee, and the both ask you to fill in certain forms when you assess them...The upshot of all this change I think is that you really have to keep a closer eye on what you are doing as their supervisor.'
Dr Pink (Physician)

Interviewees' held that recent reforms in medical training had led to the academic and clinical performance of students and junior doctors being placed under greater surveillance than previously. They also argued that the growing use of portfolio based performance appraisal within medicine was bound up with the introduction of a more formal educational structure in clinical placements. They noted how this state of affairs contrasted to the traditional organisation of clinical placements for junior doctors and medical students. It is often held that the vast majority of clinical teaching and supervision within medicine has been undertaken traditionally in an opportunistic 'ad hoc' basis (Stacey 1992, Bridgens 2003). Until recently much of the clinical teaching that occurred at the bedside during ward rounds, as well as in hospital clinics, surgical theatre and GP surgeries for that matter, was undertaken at the personal behest and whim of the attending senior doctor (Atkinson 1995, Leinster 2003). The nature, quantity and standard of clinical teaching trainees receive was viewed by social scientists and medical educationalists to suffer from considerable variation in quality (i.e. Atkinson 1981, Sinclair 1997, Bligh 2001). That the quality of clinical education is inconsistent, and required greater direct medical school and postgraduate deanery intervention to ensure consistency, has been well known to sociologists since Becker (1961) first undertook his study of medical education in the late 1950s. Longitudinal studies of doctor's careers throughout the latter part of the last century, as well as the early part of this one, have highlighted that senior doctors possess a high level of dissatisfaction with the organisation of the clinical training they received as medical students and junior doctors. In particular, they have concerns over the consistency of educational provision and general standard of clinical teaching offered to trainees (i.e. Allen 1995, Carvel 2002). This in itself may explain why the doctors interviewed were supportive of recent attempts to reform undergraduate and postgraduate medical education. However, the continued reliance of juniors on seniors for job references to enable career advancement has led to a certain amount of despotic patronage within the clinical training and practice context (Stacey 1992, Allsop 2002). This has helped inoculate it from calls for reform. That is until relatively recently, when medical elites have recognised that they have to reform medical training and regulation. Consequently, they initiated a process of change that will take time to take affect (Stacey 2000). Nevertheless, as the chapter will discuss, in spite of positive attitudes concerning the need for change, interviewees reported educational practices congruent with a traditional view of the roles between clinical teacher and trainee (Bligh 2001). They also possessed attitudes towards the reporting of underperformance that were in line with the 'patronage system' medicine has operated traditionally under (Gladstone 2000). They reinforced the need for trainees 'to keep their heads down' and do as they are told, if they want to 'get on' and pass a clinical placement as well as get a good reference.

Interviewees' accounts revealed that this move towards more structured clinical placements for trainees was linked with the introduction of different set of expectations of them as educational supervisors who were responsible for the assessment of a trainees' clinical competence. They were quick to highlight that portfolio based performance appraisal required two key things from them. First, they should meet with trainees in a structured manner during clinical placements, agree a trainee's learning goals in light of pre-defined clinical performance standards (at the beginning of a placement), monitor progress towards them (typically halfway through a placement), and assess their achievement (at the end of a placement). Second, they should provide a formal written record in the trainee's portfolio of these meetings, their assessment of whether or not a trainee has met the minimum standard required of them, and include in this record the reasons for their decision. This would be reviewed by the medical school or postgraduate deanery staff. As Dr Orange (Physician) notes:

'The portfolio the students use requires you undertake assessments of their progress. Now that of course used to happen but it is now much more directed by the medical school through the portfolio... It's the same with the foundation programme portfolio too. What it all boils down to is the distribution of more and more pieces of paper to complete ...and it is expected that I read them all, and use them when I make my own assessment of a student, before I tick and sign yet another piece of paper to say they are competent...the amount of paperwork involved makes it a very bureaucratic process really.'

Bureaucratic Accountability and the Restratification Thesis

Interviewee's accounts of the use of portfolio based performance appraisal within the medical club indicated that 'rank and file' doctors involved in the supervision and assessment of trainees during clinical placements are being subject to greater collegiate surveillance and control. They were becoming more 'bureaucratically accountable' to medical elites (in this case to their local medical school and the postgraduate deanery) for how they supervise and assess medical students and junior doctors. The concept of 'bureaucratic accountability' was first developed by Harrison and Dowswell (2002), who undertook an analysis of doctor's clinical autonomy. They looked at case record reporting and clinical guideline adherence by general practitioners with respect to angina and asthma patients. Their study highlighted that there was greater collegiate emphasis on individual doctors accepting the need to formally record their clinical decisions, alongside the reasoning behind them, in patient case notes. They found that there had been *'a clear reduction in autonomy in the sense of GP's ability to determine their own clinical practices and to evaluate their own performance without normally having to account to others'* (Harrison and Dowswell 2002: 221).

Harrison and Dowswell (2002) argue that their findings demonstrate the contingent nature of individual 'rank and file' doctor's day to day clinical autonomy, and in doing so provide further evidence for the restratification thesis. Similarly, the increased emphasis placed by portfolio based performance appraisal upon doctor's formally recording their decisions about student performance, and the reasons for them, does seem to indicate that they are becoming more 'bureaucratically accountable' to medical elites. The accounts provided by consultants and general practitioners concerning the introduction of portfolio based performance appraisal for trainees certainly revealed that appraisal is placing them under a greater degree of collegiate surveillance and control as educational supervisors. Not least of all because they were responsible for coordinating and undertaking the assessment of trainees during clinical training placements, planning and recording assessment events within a trainees portfolio, as well as 'signing them off' as 'fit to practice'. Nevertheless, as the chapter will discuss, further investigation revealed that doctor's 'bureaucratic accountability' to medical elites within the clinical education context currently possesses a 'ritual quality' (Pym 1973). Portfolio appraisal was viewed as something of a 'paper chasing' and 'form filling' exercise by the doctors interviewed, such as Dr Green (General Practitioner):

'In medicine in general they are more pieces of paper flying around these days. So you would expect that medical education would be the same. But I think there is a general kind of automation to filling in forms, on behalf of both trainees and supervisors. You see, you are going in, doing this and doing that, filling out this and filling out that; and not because you want to but because you have to. So I am not sure how much is actually being done properly as our medical education masters require'.

This tendency to view portfolio based performance appraisal as a paper-chasing exercise was due to a mixture of 'structural' and 'ideological' factors. These will be defined and discussed in detail later in the chapter. First, the 'ritual nature' of doctor's 'bureaucratic accountability' must be discussed in greater detail. A good place to begin is Annual Appraisal.

Annual Appraisal and the Shipman Affect

'You do realise, don't you, that this is all because of Shipman?'
Dr Violet (Physician)

When I discussed the introduction and affects of portfolio based performance appraisal interviewees, I found that they recognised the system of medical training had undergone extensive change in the last decade. Furthermore, it had moved towards emphasising a structured competency focused, outcomes based, approach to training and career progression by means of formal appraisal (Bruce 2007). The introduction of Annual Appraisal for general practitioners and consultants and recent modernisation of junior doctor and later specialist training are bound up with this process (BMA 2005, Slater 2007). As chapter three discussed, the drive to introduce formal appraisals for doctors as part of their employment contract formed a key part of the government programme to introduce clinical governance across the NHS (Slater 2000 2002 2003). As the following extract from a key Department of Health document relating to the implementation of appraisal for doctors notes:

'Appraisal should include data on clinical performance, training and education, audit, concerns raised and serious clinical complaints, application of relevant clinical guidelines, relationships with patients and colleagues, teaching and research activities, and personal and organisational effectiveness'.
(Department of Health 2001: 34)

In chapter three, appraisal was seen as a political response to the growing number of high profile medical malpractice scandals, such as Shipman, Bristol and Alder Hay. These had led to calls for an end to medical self-regulation, or at least, the introduction of greater non-medical input into the regulation and monitoring of doctor's fitness to practice (Stacey 2000, Slater 2003, Davies 2004). Interviewees such as Dr Yellow (Surgeon) recognised that appraisal had not been initiated by elites within the medical profession:

'I don't think you can honestly say that we as a profession wanted appraisal. It is a government thing, because of the events at Bristol, and because of Shipman of course...I think Tony Blair and his mates wanted to bring us doctors inline and make us more accountable, at least on paper, and the (royal) colleges and the BMA and GMC knew that the tide was against them, so they had no choice but to get on board'.

Dr Yellow's comments reinforce that appraisal met with a mixed press within medicine when it was first proposed, not least of all because it could lead to a doctor being referred to their employer and the GMC for underperformance (Graham 2002). It is therefore perhaps not surprise to learn that although open to NHS managerial input, because of intensive lobbying from the Royal Colleges, the GMC and the BMA, Annual Appraisal was introduced firmly under collegiate control (Irvine 2003). It was successfully argued by the professional elites that this was the only valid and acceptable method by which Annual Appraisal could be undertaken (Slater 2002).

Appraisal is completed by a consultants' Clinical Director in the hospital context, or a Primary Care Trust registered GP trainer in the general practice setting. Both have undergone training in their role by the Royal Colleges (Black 2002). Appraisal essentially involves a review of a doctor's achievements to identify their developmental needs (Rughani 2000). Appraisers may occasionally report to their NHS employer and the GMC that a particular doctor's professional performance is unacceptably poor. However, for most doctors, appraisal is said to be a positive process, focused upon maintaining and recognising good standards of clinical care (Department of Health 1999). In principle, it can lead to promotion, managerial and administrative duties being contractually recognised, an increase in secretarial or clinical support, or even a Royal College merit award (Black 2002).

Appraisal requires that doctors maintain a portfolio of evidence relating to their practice achievements, just as medical students and junior doctors must maintain a personal portfolio. The Annual Appraisal portfolio is themed into sections relating to the GMCs *Good Medical Practice* (1995): Good Medical Care, Maintaining Good Medical Practice, Working Relationships with Colleagues, Relations with Patients, Teaching and Training, Probity, Health, Management Activity and Research. The appraisal interview revolves around discussing the evidence doctors provide in each section to prove they are maintaining basic professional standards. For example, the results of clinical audit and information relating to clinical caseload should be recorded under Good Medical Care. Evidence of continuing medical education in the form of conference attendance and training programs completed should be included under Maintaining Good Medical Practice. The results of peer reviews of a doctor's clinical practice should be included under Working Relationships with Colleagues. Examples of good practice relating to gaining informed consent and general interaction with patients should be included in Relations with Patients. A summary of formal teaching activity and any feedback on its quality should be included under Teaching and Training. Relevant critical incidents and issues should be included in the Probity and Health sections. Administrative and managerial commitments should be placed under Management Activity. Information relating to research activity, such as ethical approval applications and research publications should be held under the section entitled Research (Black 2002). Finally, each portfolio includes a professional development plan that summarises actions agreed because of the appraisal interview (Rughani 2000). For example, it may be decided that targeted training in a specific surgical technique is necessary. This plan will subsequently include an account by the doctor of how they went about meeting agreed goals (and the reasons why they did not achieve them if they did not) (Gentleman 2001). This shows that Annual Appraisal is a further example of how rank and file doctors are becoming more 'bureaucratically accountable' for their activities to medical elites, in terms of having to formally document what they do, and provide reasons for doing it, for subsequent review by their peers (Harrison and Dowswell 2002).

Given the politicised background to the introduction of Annual Appraisal, it was anticipated that interviewees would possess a range of positive and negative views. The forty-six doctors interviewed were split into two opposing camps, with eighteen viewing appraisal positively:

'There is a lot of paperwork involved in appraisal, which can be quite a pain, and I know a few colleagues who are really negative about it. But I have to say that I found it a very useful exercise. At least for establishing in my own mind where I am career wise and what I want to be doing in a years time'.
Dr Purple (Surgeon)

As Dr Purple's comments illustrate, interviewees who viewed appraisal positively tended to emphasise how it helped them *'keep track of how I am getting on'* (Dr Brown General Practitioner). This contrasted to the twenty-eight interviewees who viewed appraisal negatively, and tended to regard it as a *'waste of energy and time, nothing more than a paper exercise'* (Dr Blue Surgeon). The following comments from Dr Violet's (Physician) are typical:

'Appraisal is a waste of time. I get nothing from it at all. It's just another thing I have to do because 'the powers that be' require it be done for their own purposes. I mean, do you think if I did have a problem it would help solve it? No, it's just a superficial exercise that achieves nothing concrete, and it takes up time that could be better spent doing other things'.

While some interviewees held that they found appraisal a personally meaningful exercise, many found it an onerous task. All reported that Annual Appraisal involved a lot of 'paper chasing' and 'form filling' (just as they did when discussing portfolio appraisal for trainees). They said that maintaining their portfolio took a considerable amount of time and effort. A key difference between the two 'camps' was that those who viewed appraisal negatively tended to stress how it interfered with their clinical workloads. More often than not, they would be highly dismissive of appraisal and argued that it was formalising something that medical practitioners did anyway as a matter of professionalism:

'These days it is all about accountability, and that is fine, but I do think it needs to be remembered by the government and management that they are dealing with professional people, not with the cleaning or canteen staff, and to my mind being a professional means that you have high standards and make sure you achieve them, and keeping up to date forms a necessary part of that professionalism .Without having to complete some form or other so that management can double check to make sure you are doing what you are supposed to be doing.'
Dr Scarlet (Physician)

In contrast, those who viewed appraisal positively acknowledged that appraisal took time and effort. Furthermore, they often also held that it was indeed something that a doctor's professionalism had always required them to do anyway. Nevertheless, they said they had found it a personally rewarding exercise:

'It takes up a lot of time...(but) you get out a lot out of preparing your portfolio. It certainly makes you sit down and think about what you need to do to improve as a doctor'.
Dr Red (Surgeon)

Appraisal and the Elitist Nature of the Medical Club

Comments such as Dr Scarlet's on the previous page demonstrate how there is a propensity within the medical club for club members to possess exclusory, paternalistic and elitist attitudes towards the issue of ensuring doctors continued competence to practice (Allsop 2002). It also shows how there is a propensity for doctors to hide such attitudes behind the 'service ideal' of their professionalism (i.e. that it is in the best interests of patients that they be left alone to manage their own affairs) (Gladstone 2000). Critical social commentators have argued that such attitudes have been a pervasive feature of the occupational culture of the medical profession since the 1858 Medical Act established the

GMC and institutionalised the principle of professional self-regulation under the banner of serving 'the public interest' (i.e. Stacey 1992, Allsop and Saks 2002, Davies 2004, Slater 2007). Whether they viewed appraisal positively or negatively, interviewees comments showed that they possessed exclusory 'closed shop' attitudes concerning Annual Appraisal. The following extract from Dr Black's (Physician) interview is typical in this regard:

'What worries me is the question of if a ball has started rolling that will eventually roll in the direction of including non-medical staff and even patients in the appraisal interview...I would argue that your appraisal should be managed by your colleagues. As they are the only ones who can really judge if you are performing satisfactorily. There is no way I would be happy doing it if somebody other than medical members of staff were actively involved'.

Interviewees' accounts may pay 'lip service' to the contemporary requirement that medical governance be open and accountable to the public. However, there accounts were nevertheless replete with paternalistic, elitist and exclusory attitudes concerning performance appraisal and professional accountability:

'Talk of transparency and accountability is all well and good. You certainly find a lot of it in today's NHS with its obsession with meeting targets and reducing waiting lists. But at the end of the day you don't ask the airplane passengers to judge the quality of a pilots landing past a very basic level. It is the same with doctors and clinical work. And I think that fact needs to be acknowledged, and we need to be left alone to get on with the job ourselves'.
Dr Silver (General Practitioner)

Along with this antagonism towards attempts by the state to 'open up' medical governance, of which Annual Appraisal is one example, was the belief that as its stands appraisal *'is a paper exercise and doesn't really change a thing'* (Dr Green General Practitioner). Indeed, interviewee's who were positive about appraisal said they were positive despite a frequent lack of 'follow up' on the outcomes of appraisal. Dr Purple (Surgeon) and Dr Lime (Physician) highlight this point:

'It does give you an opportunity to step back and look at the work you do and what problems you face doing your job on a day to day basis. Like in terms of its management; in terms of organising things like clinical and secretarial support in order to operate effectively. But the problem is that when things are highlighted, and it is agreed that changes need to be made. For instance, it was agreed in my last appraisal that we needed another medical secretary in the department. But here we are still waiting for that to happen eight months later'.
Dr Purple

'I can see that you could argue that appraisal is a positive thing as it can encourage a consultant to take study leave for developmental and career reasons. The fact remains that such things need financial resources behind them and staff to cover absences. And that can be a major problem.'
Dr Lime

Dr Lime's comments illustrate how interviewees believed that the appraisal process lacked 'follow through' and that this was due to financial and human resource factors. Furthermore, it was this criticism of appraisal that interviewees frequently used to justify a cynical attitude toward the argument, put forward by the state and NHS management, that Annual Appraisal improves the performance and working conditions of doctors and the quality of NHS service provision (i.e. Department of Health 2001). They felt that appraisal had been unnecessarily forced upon the profession for political reasons, and without adequate consideration of its resource implications. For them it was essentially a 'knee jerk' response to recent high profile medical malpractice cases, such as the Harold Shipman case. As Dr Indigo (Physician) argues:

'Appraisal does not make a blind bit of difference to your average doctor who performing well. And you need to remember that 95% of doctors are doing a very good job. Of the remaining 5%, well, I think they would have been picked up anyway by their colleagues. And I also think that you can say without a doubt that Shipman would not have been picked up by Appraisal. He was a one off, a killer, and he knew how to cover his tracks. You know don't you that he always got good feedback on his performance from patients? He was well liked by them you see, which is ironic really (laughs). So the question is why was appraisal introduced? So the politicians could appear to be doing something; that is why! You can talk about Shipman and Bristol and the need for good clinical governance, everyone does these days, but at the end of the day it's about appearing to doing something for political reasons'.

Like Dr Indigo above, it was generally held by interviewees that poor performance would be detected by clinical colleagues *'at the day to day level on the ward, not in an appraisal meeting'* and furthermore would be dealt with *"outside of the appraisal system"* (Dr Purple Surgeon). Interviewee's accounts highlighted that the traditional 'informal processes' of the medical club, such as 'having a quiet word', were being collegially relied upon to deal with underperformance (Stacey 1992). They were also preferred to more formal approaches such as appraisal. The following comments from Dr Silver (General Practitioner) reinforce this point:

'I would say that it is pretty much self-evident if you aren't doing your job properly. And that my colleagues here will quickly say something to me if I don't do my job right. Because that is what has happened in the past in medicine and it is how we still do things now. Somebody has a quiet word with you and you sort yourself out. And if the problem continues, well, then things may get more formal. But most of the time there is no need'.

When this issue of the preference for 'informal processes' by doctors was explored in more detail, it was apparent that in spite of being dismissive of appraisal interviewees recognised that a key outcome of the appraisal process was a formal, individualised, 'career record'. In short, if a complaint is made, it becomes a matter of 'appraisal record'. This has negative connotations in terms of career progression. A fact that seemed to reinforce to interviewees' the need to advocate the use of 'informal processes', which are a known feature of the medical club, such as 'having a quite word' (Stacey 1992 2000, Allsop 2006). As Dr Burgundy (Surgeon) argues:

'I think you do have to say you have concerns with a colleague's ability to do the job if you have them. I just don't think you should 'jump the gun' and do it in such a way that it leaves a 'black mark' against their name for the rest of their career. Which is essentially what appraisal can do if, say, you were reported to your clinical director but nothing came of it; well even then it would have to go in your portfolio, and so would be part of your appraisal discussion. So it would be recorded and 'out there' for people to see. And I think that is unfair. We all have out bad days, even the best of us, and mistakes and accidents do happen because we deal in risk everyday. You don't have to be a bad doctor for something adverse to happen and patients to complain'.

Whatever the truth of Dr Burgundy's assertions regarding the 'risk laden' nature of medical work, his argument that a doctor's failings should not be 'out there' as a matter of public record, belie the inherently 'protectionist' nature of the medical club (Gladstone 2000). As chapter two discussed, Dame Janet Smith undertook a thorough evaluation of Annual Appraisal as part of her review of how Shipman was able to murder his patients over a prolonged period of time (Smith 2005). She felt that the appraisal process as it stands would not have identified Shipman, and furthermore does *'not offer the public protection from under performing doctors'* (Smith 2005: 1048). This is because it is undertaken under 'closed shop' collegiate conditions. She is concerned that a culture of 'mutual protectionism' lingers on within the medical club. Despite protestations by medical elites that things have changed (i.e. Irvine 2003, Catto 2007).

Certainly, the doctors interviewed possessed elitist and exclusory attitudes about doctor appraisal. They shared a propensity to argue that the monitoring of a doctor's performance was something that should remain within the medical fraternity. Interviewees argued that *'your appraisal very much depends upon your relationship with your clinical director, if that's generally good on a day to day level then your actual appraisal meeting usually lasts for as long as it needs to complete and sign all the forms'* (Dr Brown General Practitioner). What is more, they also reported that their appraisers approached the appraisal process as a 'paper exercise'. They were not concerned with identifying areas of poor performance, but with *'ensuring I had done all the necessary paperwork so we could get it over with as quickly as possible'* (Dr Pink Physician)

Statements such as Dr Brown's and Dr Pink's above, about how their peers approached the appraisal process, support Dame Smith's arguments that the medical club remains inherently 'protectionist' and appraisal fails to protect the general public from underperforming doctors. Furthermore, they reinforce the need for a system of 'checks and balances' to collegiate control over medical training and regulation (Slater 2000 2003).

It does seem logical to argue that if poor performance is identified and dealt with; it will be recognised and addressed at an informal level outside of the formal Annual Appraisal process. If a doctor fails to perform in an operating theatre or an outpatient's clinic, then one can hardly imagine such matters would be 'put on hold' by clinical colleagues until they can be addressed at a later point in an appraisal interview. As Dr Orange (Physician) notes:

'If there is a problem it's going to be handled immediately and quite informally at first too. Nine times out of ten that will solve it I think'.

Yet it is difficult to imagine that the parents of the children involved in Bristol and Alder Hay, or the family of the victims of Dr Shipman, would agree with interviewees that 'having a quite word' 'off record' is a satisfactory response when underperformance is identified. They would more than likely argue that such methods have persistently proved to be ineffective in ensuring the public is protected from 'failing doctors' (Gladstone 2000, Llyod-Bostock and Hutter 2008). Furthermore, their arguments may appear logical to members of the medical club, but to an outsider it is somewhat surprising to that interviewees argued on one hand that appraisal would not pick up 'another Shipman', while on the other hand maintaining that a 'closed shop' collegiate approach is the most appropriate regulatory model. For it is generally recognised that the 'closed shop' of the medical club enabled Shipman to commit the crimes he did, and similarly allowed the heart surgeons at Bristol to underperform for as long as they did (Davies 2004, Smith 2005). Certainly, as chapter two discussed, the medical club has historically possessed a culture that frowns upon members 'whistle blowing' (Stacey 1992 2000). This makes it difficult for a member to confront a colleague who is performing poorly (Smith 1995, Irvine 2003 2006). It also goes some way to explaining why 'informal processes' were preferred by interviewees, and 'formal processes' such as appraisal treated with some caution.

It needs to be noted at this point that doctor's accounts of Annual Appraisal are just that, accounts. It was not possible to confirm if what interviewees said happened did in fact happen. Additionally, no interviewees admitted to underperforming or knowing of particular instances where underperformance had been addressed within the appraisal process (although they were well aware of instances were underperformance had been dealt with informally). This means that it was not possible to identify rigorously if Annual Appraisal does:

- "Lack depth', in the context of if it does indeed operate under the cloak of 'mutual protectionism' traditionally found in the medical club when problems are identified and have to be addressed by a doctors peers (Waring 2005).
- 'Lack teeth', in the context of actually being able to identify underperforming doctors in the first place (Smith 2005).
- 'Lack follow up', in the context of the general financial and human resource backing necessarily to ensure appraisal outcomes have a positive impact upon service delivery and doctor performance (Slater 2007).

Investigating such matters would require direct observation of actual appraisal 'events', alongside a thorough longitudinal investigation of the concrete effects of the outcomes of appraisal on doctors performance and working conditions. Although the fact is that 46 doctors from different hospitals and general practice surgeries possessed the same experiences and perceptions concerning Annual Appraisal. Which does lend substantial weight to the validity and reliability of this studies finding that, as it currently stands, appraisal does not operate as a thorough evaluation of a doctor's 'fitness to practice' (Smith 2005).

The Appraisal Ritual Outside of the Medical Club

Relevant literature in the public sector, higher education and industry contexts frequently report similar findings to that found by this research (Bruijn 2001, Armstrong 2005). Academic research on the implementation of performance appraisal has long highlighted that *'for the majority of employees... (the appraisal) interview either did not take place or was of little consequence'* (Pym 1973: 232). For instance, Hill's (1992) study of academic appraisal found that just 15.3% of respondents agreed that post-appraisal follow-up action had been undertaken. The value of appraisal for individuals and organisations has been questioned due to the fact that there is meagre evidence to support the assertion that staff appraisal improves individual and organisational effectiveness (Meyer 1991, Bruijn 2001). Additionally, it is often argued that for managerial staff performance appraisal is an onerous and time consuming process, which does not deliver what it promises, in terms of productivity, efficiency or accountability (Armstrong 2005). This is frequently due to its human resource and financial implications (Fletcher 1997). Often it is up to individuals to extract what personal benefit they can from the appraisal process. This usually results in their reporting, similar to my interviewees, that it is the fact that they personally took time to prepare for their appraisal, rather than the appraisal interview itself, which helped identify how they are doing in their job, as well as decide what the 'next steps' in their career should be (Bruijn 2001). Consequently, it has been argued, *'if appraisals fail to meet their manifest purpose, they succeed rather as rituals of employment'* (Pym 1973: 233). In the sense that they may appear to be occur 'on paper', but in reality a mixture of human resource and financial pressures mean they frequently fail to achieve their manifest purpose of improving individual and organisational effectiveness (Fletcher 1997, Armstrong 2005). The contribution of an organisations 'working culture' to this state of affairs also must be recognised. The accounts collected by this research suggest that Annual Appraisal for doctors has been implemented because of a shift in the governing conditions under which 'medical collegitism' is practiced (Catto 2006 2007). Yet they also reinforce that it possesses a real propensity to become a 'ritual of employment' (Pym 1973). This may be in part due to justifiable doubts concerning its ability to identify underperformance and support change. Clearly human and financial resource factors do impact upon the implementation of Annual Appraisal. However, as the previous section discussed, the 'exclusory' and 'elitist' nature of organisational culture of the medical club also seemed to stop the appraisal process initially identifying, formally recording and subsequently addressing, underperforming doctors (Smith 2005).

'Paperwork Compliance': A Definition

It may appear that doctors are becoming more 'bureaucratically accountable' for what they do to their peers, for they must now formally record their decisions and the reasons for them (Harrison and Dowswell 2002). Nevertheless, the data collected shows that this accountability possesses 'a ritual quality'. In the sense it exists 'for the sake of appearances' (Pym 1973, Slater 2002). This can be seen in the adoption of a stance by interviewees toward the completion of portfolio based performance appraisal, defined as 'paperwork compliance'.

The concept of 'paperwork compliance' was generated from interviewees' accounts of how portfolio based performance appraisal was undertaken, especially how they approach trainee supervision and assessment during clinical placements. Interviewee's accounts of their own appraisal experiences highlighted the ritual nature of the conduct of portfolio based performance appraisal within the medical club. Consequently, they did play a significant part in the development of this construct. Certainly, doctor's accounts of how their appraisers approached Annual Appraisal in a 'paper filling' 'tick box' manner means that 'paperwork compliance' may be present in the Annual Appraisal context too. However, verification of this fact would require that the doctors involved as appraisers in Annual Appraisal were interviewed to identify if they adopt this stance when conducting appraisals. This task was outside of the aims of this research, which investigated 'rank and file' practitioner's experiences of portfolio based performance appraisal.

'Paperwork compliance' exists when the paperwork completion requirements of appraisal are fulfilled, with relevant sections of a portfolio completed and an appraisee 'signed off' by their appraiser as either having meet minimum performance criteria or not. However, though the paperwork has been completed, the technical aspects of the appraisal procedures have not been adhered to by the appraiser, that is past a highly superficial 'tick box', 'paper filling', level. The following comments from Dr Lime (Physician) encapsulate 'paperwork compliance' succinctly:

'Its like this, you fill in the forms in a workmanlike 'doting the I's and crossing the T's', fashion. But its all for the look of the thing. It doesn't mean that you actually have done what you are meant to have done, or for that matter believe in what you have written past a very superficial level. You see, you tend to 'bend' the paperwork because you have checked out that everything is OK your own way. So you are just complying with the bureaucratic need to get the paperwork done, and that's all really'.

Stated in formal terms, 'paperwork compliance' gives the impression that an appraisee has been appraised using collegially agreed minimum performance standards. These have been predefined with regards to occupational specific knowledge, skills and attitudinal 'competency domains'. Yet, in reality these have played a superficial role in helping an appraiser form an opinion in regards to: a) Which tasks an appraisee should undertake and be assessed in to be defined as 'competent' at a level appropriate to their career level (i.e. compare a final year medical student and a senior house officer). b) The level of proficiency possessed by an appraisee about these tasks. As this section of the chapter will now discuss, this is because medicine possesses a high level of 'indetermination' within the indetermination/technicality ratio, which forms the basis of its expertise (Jamous and Peloille 1970).

Sociologists have argued that as a profession, medicine possesses a particularly high ratio of indetermination/technicality (Turner 1995). As chapter four discussed, all occupations are marked by a mixture of 'explicit' and 'implicit' expertise (Jamous and Peloille 1970). This refers to publicly available 'techniques and procedures' and private and personal 'rules of thumb'. The explicit 'technical mode of knowledge' can be expressed as a precise list of unambiguous specifications. This is unlike the implicit 'indeterminate mode of knowledge', which remains imprecise, ineffable and only graspable through the acquisition of personal insight. It is always therefore bound up with the personal career biography of a practitioner. The 'technicality' and 'indeterminate' elements of occupational expertise share in common that a trainee acquires them by observing and following 'the example' of a more experienced practitioner. But in the final analysis, the 'indeterminate' elements can only be 'picked up' by a trainee through the acquisition of direct personal experience (Bosk 1979). In Jamous and Peloille's (1970) terminology, indeterminate knowledge is located in personal attributes (or 'virtualities' as they call them) of its producer herself. The producer is the 'owner' of their means of production and reproduction, rather than simply a user of them This is why sociological accounts of medical education highlight how practitioners reinforce trainees need to maximize 'exposure' and gain as much clinical experience as possible during clinical placements (Sinclair 1997). Furthermore, these accounts highlight that an experienced doctor's 'clinical acumen' is used to 'trump' formal academic knowledge and 'best evidenced' clinical guidelines (Bosk 1979, Harrison 2004). In effect, this 'trumping' happens within the portfolio appraisal process, causing 'paperwork compliance'. This 'trumping' was also present in Armstrong's (2002) study of GPs, which was discussed in chapter three. Armstrong found that the GPs he interviewed asserted the need to exercise personal judgment during doctor-patient encounters due to the 'indeterminate' aspects of their expertise, and furthermore, they did so in the face of the 'technicality' being promoted by medical elites operating in 'the guideline industry' and producing clinical protocols and evidenced based guidelines.

In summary, 'paperwork compliance' occurs the doctor as appraiser 'trumps' with their personal 'clinical acumen' the formal 'technicality' bound up with portfolio based performance appraisal. As the chapter will demonstrate, she succeeds in doing so because of structural factors within the clinical training context and a cultural tendency within the medical club to reinforce, first, the need for a clinician to rely upon her 'gut feeling' when making a professional judgment, and second, the need for one club member to respect another's clinical expertise and right to independent practice, as long as this remains within acceptable 'club limits' (Freidson 1970, Stacey 2000). As Watkins (1987: 21) rightly notes *'the medical profession is organised along the principle that once you have ensured that people conform loyally to the right ideas you can allow them a considerable degree of independence of action'.*

The concept of 'paperwork compliance' was prevalent within interviewee's accounts of portfolio based performance appraisal for medical students and junior doctors. The next section of the chapter will discuss this issue.

The Appraisal Ritual within the Medical Club: 'Bureaucratic Accountability' and 'Paperwork Compliance'

Thus far chapter has discussed how the implementation of portfolio based performance appraisal ensures that rank and file doctors are 'bureaucratically accountable' for their educational activities to their peers. Appraisal requires doctors document their decisions and the reasons for them in a manner that is open to collegiate surveillance and correction (Harrison and Dowswell 2002). Interviewees admitted that portfolio appraisal leaves a 'paper trail'. In doing so, it places them under greater surveillance and control from medical elites, such as medical schools, postgraduate deaneries and Royal Colleges. As Dr Yellow (Surgeon) points out:

'With portfolios being used more and more like they are you could argue that there is a 'paper trail' now leading up from medical school and junior doctor levels to the senior registrar and consultant level. And I really don't think we are far off having some kind of administrative system that joins all these portfolios together so if I have signed off my house officer as competent, but a later on he has problems and messes up, then the colleges or GMC could come knocking on my door with questions'.

From interviewees accounts it became clear that this 'paper trail' produced a situation whereby knowledge that appraisal records can be inspected was enough proof for doctors to act as if they would be inspected. This encouraged doctors to autonomously and independently self-discipline themselves and change their behaviour (Foucault 1977, Rose and Miller 1992). In terms of how interviewees supervise and assess trainees, as well as how they monitor their own continued 'fitness to practice' in preparation for Annual Appraisal. As the respective extracts from Dr Gold (Physician) and Dr Green (General Practitioner) illustrate:

'Having to use a portfolio to help me plan and record student assessment has changed in some ways how I go about supervising them...because the portfolio approach requires I fill in forms saying I have tested them on such things I am much more focused now on making sure their clinical and communication skills are thoroughly tested, even if I do do it my own way'.
Dr Gold

'I would say that (annual) appraisal can make you a little more focused upon making sure that you are using clinical protocols and guidelines at a day to day level. Because, well, it's like having done one appraisal you realise what you can do to make the next one less of a hassle. At least at a basic administrative level of form completion. And that is bound to have some knock on affects on clinical practice'.
Dr Green

Dr Gold and Dr Green both note that the implementation of portfolio based performance appraisal has caused them to alter some aspects of their behaviour. However, interviewee's accounts also showed that these changes were largely highly superficial and had little true effect on how they went about their educational activities. For example, portfolio appraisal draws upon a rationalistic-bureaucratic discourse of outcomes based performance assessment utilising explicit standards to establish norms to govern what is reasonable, desirable and efficient (Challis 1998, Searle 2000). Supervisors are expected to use these standards when judging a trainees' clinical performance, as well as their own practice achievements in Annual Appraisal (Snadden and Thomas 1999, Southgate 2001). Yet interviewees' accounts revealed that they were not prepared to accept these norms and standards without question. Furthermore, they were not prepared to accept them without interpretation of their meaning and appropriate application, given that they see themselves as experts in their medical specialty. As Dr White (General Practitioner) notes:

'The competency domains that are listed in the student portfolio try to be prescriptive. By saying that students need to be able to do a, b, c and d clinically by the end of a placement. As well as that I need to make sure that they can do a, b, c and d to such and such

standard. But try as they (the medical school) might they can't turn core practice skills like taking a good history into a simple yes/no 'tick box' exercise...it is still down to you to judge how well they have done...and nine times out of ten you really are just fitting what you have done yourself to test them into the appropriate box on the portfolio forms'.

As Dr Turquoise (Surgeon) comments below show, interviewees were not prepared to allow themselves to be judged without judging the utility of the process their judgers were using to judge them:

'I certainly made sure I got across how utterly worthless I thought the whole appraisal process was. Come to think of it, that is probably why the meeting only lasted around fifteen minutes and mainly involved "John' (his clinical director) apologising for the excessive amount of paperwork involved (laughs)'.

Dr White's comments on the previous page touch upon the important role played by the personal 'indeterminate-tacit' dimension in justifying, on behalf of interviewees, a stance of 'paperwork compliance' towards the formalised procedures and standards bound up with the introduction of portfolio based performance appraisal. Doctor's accounts may have emphasised how clinical placements for trainees are more structured, given recent reforms in undergraduate medical education and junior doctor training (BMA 2005). They may also have shown how medical elites are increasingly providing prescriptive 'outcome based' standards by which to judge clinical performance (Searle 2000, Wilkinson 2002). In doing so, they highlighted how the implementation of portfolio based performance appraisal can be said to be linked with this growing process of formalisation and standardisation across clinical education and provide support for the restratification thesis (Challis 1999, Southgate 2001). However, interviewee's accounts also reinforced how within medicine a significant degree of emphasis is placed upon gaining direct personal experience of clinical phenomena, in order to develop that 'ineffable' occupational quality, 'clinical acumen'. What is more, interviewees accounts also showed how this emphasis upon gaining clinical experience leads 'rank and file' doctors to resist the codified 'rules and procedures' associated with the new rationalistic-bureaucratic governing regime being imposed upon them by medical elites (Armstrong 2002). The chapter will now turn to discussing how interviewees reported they formed an opinion of trainees 'fit to practice' in order to illustrate this important point.

Based upon interviewee's accounts, three broad camps emerged in terms of how far their actions conformed to the requirement that they meet with trainees at certain points during clinical placements, as well as use the competency domains and performance criteria contained within a trainee's portfolio documentation to initially agree, and then subsequently record the achievement of, learning goals. First, and most dominant, were the 'non-compliers' (nineteen out of forty-six interviewees). These individuals may support the need for changes in medical training, and be passionate about their medical specialty and the supervision of trainees, but they ignored completely a trainees' portfolio when assessing them. They preferred instead to do things their own way and 'sign off' a trainees' portfolio documentation at the end of the placement i.e. *'I don't tend to look at their portfolios really. There really is no need for me to do that past scanning it to make sure all the boxes have been ticked and the right pieces of paper completed and signed at the end of the placement...When they (a trainee) turns up on day one I tell them what I expect of them and will be looking out for, and*

I tend to just fill in the portfolio paperwork around those expectations of them...the portfolios are not for me but for the medical school or the deanery; so they can say they have met whatever political requirements they must these days' (Dr Violet, Physician).

'Non-compliers' did not use a portfolio to help them manage and undertake students assessment. Typically, trainee's portfolios were viewed as 'paper tasks' that *we have been asked to complete by the medical school and deanery so they can say they have up to date records when the GMC comes to visit'* (Dr Red, Surgeon). This was a viewpoint shared by the second group, the 'minimalists'. Like 'non-compliers', 'minimalists' (seventeen out of forty six interviewees) viewed portfolios as tools introduced by the medical school and postgraduate deanery to meet the changing training and regulatory requirements of the broader socio-political context surrounding medical governance. Unlike 'non-compliers', they reported that they held some, albeit highly informal and often irregular, one to one meetings with students to check on their progress. They had some 'minimal' contact with a trainees' portfolio during a clinical placement. Unlike their 'non-complier' counterparts who only saw a trainees portfolio at the end of a placement. 'Minimalists' reported that having minimal contact with trainee's portfolios helped them check on an ongoing basis that the paperwork was up to date. This they felt made its completion an easier task i.e. *'I do try to arrange things so that we meet and record what is happening in the portfolio as I think it is important to keep a record of their progress as they go along...I find that approach is liked by students as it makes them feel that you are keeping an helpful eye on them. And it certainly makes checking and completing portfolio documentation less of an onerous task than it is when you try to do everything all at once at the end'* (Dr Yellow, Surgeon).

'Minimalists' tend to 'use the portfolio to make sure they [students and junior doctors] have completed the necessary sections as they go along, so we don't end up doing it all at the end, as that can be very time consuming' (Dr Brown, General Practitioner). Like the 'minimalists', 'enthusiasts' (ten out of forty six interviewees), held meetings with trainees during a clinical placement. However, with 'enthusiasts' these were more formally planned to take place at the beginning, the middle and the end of a trainees' clinical placement. They were enthusiastic about the use of a portfolio to record student progress, arguing, 'the portfolio approach is useful as it helps you keep track of a junior or student' (Dr Orange, Physician). They felt that this reinforced to trainees that they must keep a record of their activities. Unlike the 'non-compliers' and 'minimalists', 'enthusiasts' used portfolio documentation to guide the practice areas in which they would assess students, albeit in a basic, high superficial, manner. However, although they used portfolio documents to inform and guide them, like 'non-compliers' and 'minimalists', 'enthusiasts' reserved the right to assess students as and how they thought fit. They used their own personal standards of judgment i.e. 'I do try and make sure to meet regularly with students and that I do assess them in the key areas in the portfolio documentation Like communication skills with patients, or their ability to use clinical protocols when formulating a diagnosis...But at the end of the day what I am most concerned with is satisfying in my own mind that they are basically competent to do the job as I see it, not with filling in the portfolio paperwork. Don't get me wrong. I like the portfolio approach. It's just that, well, I think if you talk to my colleagues they will tell you much the same thing. That it does tend to be too prescriptive and tell you want to do assessment wise with a student or a junior (doctor)...It's like they (the medical school and deanery) are trying to remove the need for you to exercise your personal judgment by giving you a form to fill in, in a set way, using prescriptive criteria. And I think you can't expect us as experienced clinicians to agree with that approach' (Dr White, General Practitioner).

In spite of the presence of relatively minor differences between the three groups, all forty-six interviewees self-reported that they adopted a stance of 'paperwork compliance' towards portfolio appraisal. Furthermore, they held that the medical school and postgraduate deanery were aware that supervisors were *'handling student assessment in our own way as we have always done'* (Dr Blue, Surgeon). Supervisors believed that medical school and postgraduate deanery staff left them alone as they trusted their judgments. While there was also the fact that supervisors are not directly employed by, or accountable to, medical schools and postgraduate deaneries (a point the chapter will return to shortly). As Dr Purple (Surgeon) points out:

'It's my job to look after students when they are here and report back about how they have got on. That is all. Don't get me wrong. I like teaching them. But I don't really care if the medical school or the deanery are happy or not with the way I have filled out one of their forms'.

Interviewees accounts of how they supervised and assessed students, and the role the portfolio plays within this, are just that: accounts. It was not possible to substantiate whether or not they behaved in the way they said they did when supervising students or junior doctors. Nevertheless, the doctors interviewed provided corroborating accounts independently from each other (Bryman 2004). This inevitably lends some weight to the validity and reliability of the key finding of this research: a trainee's portfolio played a superficial role in helping supervisors, first, decide what work tasks an appraisee should undertake and be assessed in, and second, form an opinion about the level of technical proficiency possessed by an appraisee about these tasks. Dr Silver (General Practitioner) makes this point succinctly:

'I know that in many ways medical education is a different beast these days; is more structured, more 'best evidenced' and more standard driven. I certainly think that is what the likes of the GMC and the medical school want you to believe that. And on the surface it does look different. But beneath it is exactly as it was when I was a junior...If you want to get on and pass a placement you do as your consultant says. And you do what they tell you to do in the way they want you to do it, or else you end up in trouble. And I don't see anything wrong with that. After all, they are here to learn'.

The need for trainees to conform to their consultant's expectations of them, alongside the need for trainees to maximize the 'clinical experience' obtained during a placement, was used repeatedly by interviewees to justify the view that portfolio appraisal for trainees was essentially a 'form filling' exercise. Given the nature of clinical training and work, it was seen as 'natural' by interviewees for portfolio paperwork to be ignored or paid superficial regard. This attitude is perhaps to be expected, after all clinical placements are the sites where 'clinical acumen' is developed and tested (Atkinson 1995). Indeed, although supervisors may ask medical and nursing staff their thoughts on a student, they preferred to *see for myself what they can do in clinic, on the ward and in theatre, before I make a decision on how good they are'* (Dr Red, Surgeon). In short, interviewees 'trumped', with their personal 'clinical acumen', the formal 'technicality' bound up with portfolio based performance appraisal documentation. This included the requirement to consult other individuals concerning a trainee. This approach was further justified in the mind of interviewees by the fact that it is they, not their clinical colleagues, who must finally 'sign off' a trainee as 'fit to practice'. While the heavy emphasis placed upon gaining clinical experience also seemed to lead trainees to be complicit in the adoption of a stance of 'paperwork compliance', on behalf of interviewees, toward portfolio based performance appraisal. With interviewees, like Dr Black (Physician) below, frequently reported that trainees also viewed portfolios as 'paper chasing exercises':

'All the students I meet complain about the amount of form filling involved in maintaining a portfolio, so I don't think it really matters to them how it is done as they want to get on and learn, not sit around and fill in and discuss portfolio forms'.

In spite of the recent rhetoric of medical elites (i.e. GMC 2003, BMA 2005) today's trainees are no more 'stakeholders' and 'equal partners' in their education than their predecessors. According to interviewees, trainees must keep their mouths shut and do as they are told if they want to 'get on' during placements and gain a good reference in order to climb up the career ladder. The following comments from Dr Bronze (Physician) reinforce this view:

'I know with things like the portfolio you are meant to ask them (junior doctors) what they want to do and achieve. And you do pay lip service to that. As you are trying to get to know then so you can mentor them along a bit, and knowing their career aspirations and the like helps you do that. But, come on, who is the consultant here? I don't think you really should expect that they will have a say over what they should do. They are here to learn from me and that means they do as I say...(and) that's how they get a good reference at the end from me'.

Similar to Annual Appraisal, a general preference amongst interviewees was to deal with underperformance through 'informal mechanisms'. While as the following comments from Dr Green (General Practitioner) reinforce, interviewees also preferred not to report a student or junior if they could help it:

'I do tend to let them off with minor things like poor attendance or if they talk down to the support staff, which can happen... I'll have a word with them about things like that even though it may say that everything is OK in the portfolio...(because) I'm not going to mention things to the medical school or deanery unless I really need to...I just think they deserve the benefit of the doubt We all do I think (laughs) But particularly them as they are still learning the ropes...(So) when there is a problem I just have words with them, and I think that is most appropriate in most cases'.

Furthermore, when they did report a student or junior they preferred to bypass the formal referral documentation held within a trainee's portfolio, as noted by Dr Orange (Physician):

'There was one lad who was a real problem. His practice skills were diabolical He really needed intensive support. To tell you the truth I don't know how he managed to pass medical school. Anyway, the upshot was that I did refer him. But I didn't use the portfolio documentation. Nothing was written down on paper. I just phoned the deanery and we arranged some extra skills training for him. I thought that the best way of doing it really, without making a fuss or bringing too much attention to it.'

The comments from Dr Orange and Dr Green reinforce how doctors may view portfolio based performance appraisal as a 'paper chasing' exercise, but are wary of processes which formally record poor performance. This is in no small part due to the high level of 'indetermination' and 'uncertainty' involved in medical work (Atkinson 1995). For as chapter two and three discussed, this reinforces that they should not be party to giving a fellow member of the medical club a 'black mark' on their career record, no matter how junior they are, unless it be absolutely necessary (Stacey 1992).

Two points need to be made about these findings. First concerns the issue of supervisors reporting that they were reluctant to refer underperforming trainees for formal remedial action by medical elites. This does not mean that the 'informal processes' they used to remedy this situation were inadequate or failed to improve a trainee's performance. Furthermore, it must be admitted that it is impossible to know exactly what happened when underperformance was identified. Consequently, the data obtained should not be taken to indicate that underperforming, and so potentially dangerous, medical students and junior doctors are passing assessments of their 'fitness to practice'. Interviewee's accounts do not provide information on the prevalence of underperformance amongst trainees. This was not the purpose of this research. Yet their accounts do reinforce the notion that there is reluctance to formally report such incidents due to the existence of cultural barriers within the medical club to 'incident reporting' (Waring 2005). Quite possibly as a result of general acceptance between club members that there is a potential for clinical error to occur no matter how competent an individual doctor is, so it is necessary to 'close ranks' and deal with such matters 'of the record' as far as possible (Stacey 2000).

Second, findings should not be interpreted to imply that trainee's clinical placements, or their general level of supervision and clinical teaching, were not of the highest quality. The quality of clinical education received should not be judged by the fact that supervisor's accountability for their actions and judgments to medical elites possesses a 'ritual quality', or that they adopt a stance of 'paperwork compliance' towards trainee performance appraisal. It was clear from interviewees that they demanded the highest standards from students and tested them in a rigorous manner. However, they did so in their own personal idiosyncratic way, instead of adopting the more rigid approach required by portfolio appraisal.

Yet doctor's accounts do reinforce the fact that there is good reason to doubt the legitimacy of portfolio based performance appraisal as an accurate administrative record and governance tool which promotes medicines 'new professionalism', through supporting individual and organisational accountability in the training and regulatory arena. Certainly, medicines 'new markers of trust' appear less than trustworthy (Kuhlmann 2006b). In conclusion, the central finding of this empirical research was that portfolio based performance appraisal might make 'rank and file' doctors 'bureaucratically accountable' to medical elites, for they must now record their decisions and the reasons behind them, but nevertheless, this accountability possesses a 'ritual quality', as illustrated by interviewee's adoption of 'paperwork compliance' towards portfolio appraisal for trainees. Two contextual factors sustain 'paperwork compliance' amongst interviewees: 'structural' and 'ideological'.

Supporting 'Paperwork Compliance': The Structural Factor

The factor themed as 'structural' is defined as such because it comes about due to the structural relationship which currently exists between the hospitals and general practice surgeries that act as clinical education sites, and the medical schools and postgraduate deaneries who are responsible for medical training. It is estimated they are some 16,000 NHS clinical staff involved in some way with the teaching of medical students and junior doctors (Bligh 2001). The vast majority of these are not directly employed by medical schools or postgraduate deaneries. These include doctors similar to those interviewed for this research who act as clinical placement supervisors. The arrangements for allocating clinical placement supervisors have traditionally been 'ad hoc' and decided 'in-house' within a clinical specialty. The notion was 'somebody has to do it'. Furthermore, this supervision was arranged outside of the direct control of medical schools or postgraduate deaneries (Stewart 2002). As chapters two, three and four discussed, there exists a cultural tendency for different elements within the medical club to respect each other's right to self-determination and autonomy. In the context of clinical education, this reinforced the right for specialties to organise their own clinical teaching arrangements (Sinclair 1997).

Clinical teaching attracts SIFT money (Service Increment For Teaching) (Irby 1994). A doctor's hospital department or GP practice, receives SIFT money for the clinical supervision and teaching they provide. This means that unlike their peers working in the medical school classroom, or medical school management, individual practitioners are not personally contractually accountable to the medical school or postgraduate deanery (Lowry 1993, Bligh 2001). Rather, they remain NHS employees. The lack of formal contractual accountability of clinical placement supervisors to medical elites raises four key issues. First, although they are not directly employed by the medical school or postgraduate deanery, senior doctors have a professional obligation to teach and 'pass on the science and the art' to the next generation of clinicians (Bligh 1998, Irvine 2003). However, there is little formal recognition in doctor's NHS contracts for the educational work they do. Contractually, there is little time allocated for educational activities, and no personal reward, either monetary or in terms of status and recognition, for what is done (Sinclair 1997). Furthermore, doctor's NHS contracts actually place teaching duties in formal competition with other non-clinical responsibilities; including audit, research and continuing professional development (Stewart 2002). It was not uncommon for interviewees to complain about the amount of paperwork involved in portfolio appraisal due to service pressures and other interests and responsibilities that placed demands upon their time. Second, and related to this, educational activities have traditionally been seen within medicine as coming a poor third behind clinical work and research. It has been argued that there is a competing triad of education, research and service within medicine, with medical education coming last (Elston, 1991, Bligh 2001). It needs to be remembered that trainees' clinical placements are first working environments, and a doctor's priority remains the care of his patients (Lowry 1993, Seabrook 2004). Additionally, traditionally clinical research has taken precedence over educational activities because it offers opportunities for prestige and career enhancement (Leinster 2003). This leads into the third issue. The relegation of education behind service and research commitments has meant that doctors receive little formal preparation and training in their supervisory role, or in general teaching and assessment techniques (Bligh 2001, Irvine 2003). Only six interviewees said they had completed one or more training courses run by the Royal Colleges on teaching and learning in medicine. None had participated on a formal training programme in performance appraisal and the role of appraiser. None possessed a recognised educational qualification. Furthermore, they had not received formal training from medical elites in the portfolio systems they were meant to be using to assess trainees. This point is illustrated by the following interview extract from Dr Brown (General Practitioner):

'No there was no training programme or general introduction to the portfolio. Obviously I did receive information about what changes were going to be introduced... (and) I think that is all I needed really'.

Doctors were expected to supervise and assess trainees using a portfolio system without receiving any formal training. However, they were not concerned that they had not received such training. This general lack of formal training in educational theory and practice reflects a cultural tendency within the medical club to equate clinical expertise with the ability to teach (Lowry 1993). Recent reforms in medical training have seen the introduction of new educational methods, such as problem based learning and portfolio learning, which bring with them certain procedural and technical requirements. It is arguable that these methods require a doctor receive formal training in their implementation (Leinster 2003). This leads into the fourth issue. It is arguable that the successful implementation of new educational methods such as portfolio appraisal within medicine require clinical teachers possess a closer, more supportive and 'managed' relationship with training providers, such as medical schools, than they currently do (Bligh 2001). Yet, because of their current lack of contractual obligation to the medical school and postgraduate deaneries, interviewees' felt remote from the medical school and the postgraduate deanery. They did not feel they possessed a close and supportive relationship with either of them. Here Dr White (General Practitioner) reflected the general experience of interviewees when he said: *'I don't really have much contact with the medical school. When I do it mostly involves speaking to the administrative support staff...who I must say are good at their job and very efficient'.* Indeed, Dr White's comments go some way to explain why interviewees did not feel that their supervision of trainees was recognised and valued by the medical school or the postgraduate deanery. As Dr Lilac (General Practitioner) notes: *'No what we do as supervisors isn't really valued I think...Despite your contribution you don't as a clinical teacher get to have much of a say over what happens there. But I suppose they don't have much say over what happens here either (laughs)'.*

In summary, the structural relationship between clinical education sites and educational elites such as medical schools highlights four key issues. These are:

1. Lack of accountability for clinical supervisors to medical school and postgraduate deanery management, as well as a lack of adequate recognition and reward for educational duties via NHS employment contract
2. Lack of priority for educational duties compared to service delivery needs and clinical research activities

3. Lack of formal training for clinical supervisors in educational theory and practice, including specific educational methods such as portfolio appraisal
4. Lack of consultation and inclusion, by medical schools and postgraduate deaneries, of clinical supervisor's views concerning the organisation and delivery of undergraduate and postgraduate medical education

Taken together these four issues form the contextual backdrop against which interviewees adopted 'paperwork compliance' towards portfolio based performance appraisal. They reinforced the 'ritual quality' of rank and file doctor's 'bureaucratic accountability' to medical elites. Due to recent challenges to the principle of medical self-regulation, medical elites involved in regulation of medical education utilise transparent quality assurance mechanisms, such as 'best evidenced' performance standards, to enhance institutional and individual accountability. Nevertheless, the four issues highlighted by the structural factor show that recent educational reforms for trainees, specifically *Tomorrows Doctors* (GMC 1993 2002 2003) and *Modernising Medical Careers* (BMA 2005), appear to have failed to address key human resource issues. Even though these have a powerful negating influence upon attempts to enhance an individual doctor's accountability for their educational activities past a superficial level.

Supporting 'Paperwork Compliance': The Ideological Factor

Although of clear importance, it may well be that the 'ideological' factor is most important in comparison to the structural one. For the 'structural factor' reinforces the 'ritual quality' of doctors 'bureaucratic accountability' to medical elites. In doing so, it contributes to the adoption of 'paperwork compliance' by 'rank and file' doctors. Nevertheless, the concept of 'paperwork compliance' is grounded firmly in the epistemological makeup of medical expertise and therefore remains at the ideological root of the occupational culture of the medical profession (Stacey 1992 2000). The empirical findings discussed here illustrate how attempts to enhance accountability within the medical club utilising a rationalistic-bureaucratic discourse of outcome based standard setting and performance appraisal will encounter inevitably a certain amount of resistance 'on the shop floor' (that is at the level of the individual practitioner) due in no small measure to that 'ineffable' and 'charismatic' quality known as 'clinical acumen' (Bosk 1979). The formal 'technicality' of the rules and procedures linked with medicine's new governing tools such as portfolio based performance appraisal are designed to ensure quality control and accountability. These are being 'trumped' by the 'indeterminacy' that lies at the basis of modern medical expertise. This state of affairs reflects what Armstrong (2002) found in his study. He noted that doctors are now required to record their clinical decisions and the reasons for them in order to ensure compliance with the 'technicality' of evidenced based guidelines (Grey and Harrison 2004). However, he also noted that they 'trump' the clinical protocols of the medical elite operating within in the 'guideline industry'. Furthermore, they do this by reaffirming at the level of everyday clinical practice the inherent 'indeterminacy' that lies at the basis of much of medical work.

It has been noted by sociologists that a cloud of uncertainty surrounds much of medical work to the extent that 'training for uncertainty' became long ago a defining characteristic of the occupational culture and internal social organisation of the medical profession (Fox 1975, Atkinson 1981, Stacey 1992, Gladstone 2000). Freidson (1970, 1994, 2001) argues that because of this a thoroughgoing 'epistemological individualism' lies at the basis of the 'clinical mentality'. This is due to the need for doctors to exercise personal judgment and discretion because of the inherently specialist nature of their work. The faith of the 'clinical mentality' in firsthand perception and personal experience is so entrenched within the medical club that, as Armstrong (1980: 167) notes, *'whether this skill is described as 'clinical sense', 'clinical ability' or the 'art of diagnosis' the (individual) doctor is ranked according to his facility with the technique'.* Furthermore, as chapter three showed, the work of historically minded sociologists such as Berlant (1975) and Larson (1977) reinforces the foundational role played by the 'indeterminate' realm of 'clinical acumen', in justifying the institutionalisation of the principle of professional self-regulation in the form of the GMC.

Yet two interrelated issues have been recognised amongst sociologists since the 1970s about the 'indeterminate' foundations of modern medical expertise. First, as medical practice and technology develops today's 'indeterminacy' becomes tomorrows 'technicality'. The general public becomes increasingly aware of the possibilities and limitations of modern medical practice as this process unfolds. Therefore, they demand ever more say over their treatment and care (Haug 1973). While also increasingly requiring doctor's account for their actions and how they organise members training, practice and discipline to ensure quality control. Second, the indeterminate foundations of modern medical expertise have reinforce a propensity within the medical club to justify exclusory, paternalistic and elitist attitudes concerning who controls the governance of medical training, practice and discipline. The doctors interviewed for this research certainly possessed paternalistic and elitist attitudes concerning the issue of doctor appraisal and the reporting of underperformance. Such attitudes are typically hidden by doctors behind the 'service ideal' of their professionalism (i.e. that it is in the best interests of patients that they be left alone to manage their own affairs). However, as chapter three discussed, medicine's self-image of being special and 'set apart' from the rest of society is no longer held to be as justifiable as it once was (Irvine 2006). Modern medicine may still be treated with awe and respect, and its members possess considerable status and influence within society, but the medical club has to come to terms with the fact that it no longer commands as much unquestioning respect as it used to (Lupton 1997, Elston 2004, Allsop 2006). Certainly, in the last three decades critical social commentators have argued that many occupations possess 'formal' and 'tacit' dimensions to their expertise; but they do not demand the same degree of exclusive collegiate control over members training, practice and discipline that the medical profession typically has done (Polanyi 1967, Jamous and Peloille 1970, Allsop and Mulcahy 1996). Why should doctors be able to claim they are so special that they should be completely exempt from non-medical surveillance and accountability, particularly within a modern democratic society? Certain elements of the profession have recognised this fact, as chapter three detailed. Indeed, recent attempts to establish a 'new medical professionalism' recognise the need to for the medical club to be open and accountable if the principle of professional self-regulation is to continue (i.e. Irvine 1997 2001 2003 2006, Catto 2006 2007).

Conclusion: An Invaluable Baseline

As this last point illustrates, the empirical work of this research takes place against a socio-political backdrop which since the re-emergence of liberalism in the last three decades has seen an intensification in the external and internal governance of expertise across the public and private spheres, the health and social service sector, as well as the higher education system (Stacey 1992, Taylor 1997, Hanlon 1998, Biggs 1999, Allsop and Saks 2002). Power (1997) and Rose (1999) note that a key facet of advanced liberal society is its central concern with disciplining the population without recourse to direct or oppressive intervention. Yet it also sees the encroachment of demands for standardisation and transparent accountability associated with Audit into all aspects of social life (Burchell, Gordon and Miller 1991). Rose (1999) argues that Audit is a key large-scale activity for governing the activities of experts 'at a distance' in order to minimise the costs and risks associated with the application of specialist expertise. Is it a surprise, therefore, that the rationalistic-bureaucratic discourse of outcomes based standard setting and performance appraisal is also found within occupations other than medicine, such as accountancy, law and education for example (Slater 2000, Allsop 2002)? Indeed, elite collegiate training and regulatory bodies in occupational groups concerned with teaching, social work and nursing (to name but a few) are increasingly subjecting the practices of their members to surveillance and standardisation. The changes underway in medicine can be found in other occupations and other contexts, and research into the changing nature of the governance of medical expertise should keep this comparative issue in mind.

The findings of this research may not indicate an intractable situation whereby the tacit foundation stones of professional expertise will always be used to 'trump' measures that seem to act to survey and curtail professional autonomy. Its interviewees belong to a different generation than ones who will experience the full affect of recent changes in medical training and regulation. Will it be different for the next generation of doctors: those whose training, practice and disciplinary arrangements will increasingly operate under a different set of cultural expectations concerning the appropriate limits of professional autonomy, as one generation of doctors gives away to the next? Indeed, it is arguable that the research bears witness to the fact that we are standing at the beginning of a long-term process of change and reform within medical training, practice and regulation. What is more, it is also arguable that the full affects of this process will gradually unfold over the coming decades as the political renewal of liberalism continues to bring with it a fundamental shift in the grounds upon which 'good governance' is practiced. Interviewee's accounts did reveal that a process of restructuring is underway in medicine and that they do feel that over time this will increasingly formalise and standardise clinical education. What is more, they felt this process is placing them under more and more surveillance. It is making them ever more accountable to medical elites for their decisions and the reasons behind them. Aren't we then talking about a process of organisational and cultural change that actually is just beginning? Certainly, chapter three reinforced that it takes time to achieve substantive change within the medical club (Irvine 2003 2006, Bruce 2007).

It needs to be remembered that this research was conducted on the cusp of recent changes in undergraduate and postgraduate medical education (GMC 1992 2002 2003). It is just five years since the first 'new curriculum' medical students began to graduate nationally. It is only three years since the new junior doctor-training program began (BMA 2005). Additionally, Annual Appraisal for senior doctors has also only been in operation for a relatively short period of time (Black 2002). Given these three facts, it is arguable that this research reports what is happening at the beginning of a process of far reaching changes in medical training and regulation, whose full affects will not be known for another generation of doctors. Could it be that these findings have provided an invaluable 'baseline' from which the affect of subsequent changes in the governance of medical expertise can be compared longitudinally? This conclusion seems appropriate given that at the time of writing we are still waiting for revalidation to be implemented nationally in 2010, and furthermore, it will be at least a decade more before the full effects of revalidation's implementation are known. However, at this time we can be confident of two things. First, revalidation will bring about far reaching changes in medical training and regulation. Second, the state will continue to move away from emphasising 'professional autonomy' and towards emphasising 'professional accountability' within the health and social care arena. Additionally, it will continue to rely upon a rationalistic-bureaucratic discourse of standard setting and performance appraisal to achieve this goal. Given these circumstance it is best for the moment to conclude that these findings reinforce that a process of change has only just begun within the medical club. Consequently, it is perhaps most appropriate to allow Dr Blue (Surgeon) to have the final say on what he thinks the future may bring:

'I don't know what will exactly happen in medical education over the next few years...I do think we will look back and say that this was when the big changes were starting to occur. But having said that, going on what is happening at the moment I expect whatever does happen will in some way involve me having to fill out more paperwork. It generally does'.

Chapter 7

THE GOVERNANCE OF DOCTORS
UNDER NEO-LIBERAL MENTALITIES OF RULE

The research detailed in chapter six was undertaken after a review of the sociological literature revealed that, first, little research had been undertaken by social scientists on recent challenges to medical autonomy from the perspective of doctors themselves, and second, what had been undertaken had been concerned with analysing doctors perceptions of challenges to their clinical freedom 'at the bedside', rather than with what is happening within the training and regulatory sphere. It therefore represents the first attempt to analyse doctors educational autonomy in the context of contemporary sociological debate concerning 'the decline and fall' of medical autonomy and the future of the principle of professional self-regulation.

The research findings provide direct empirical evidence to support the central argument of the 'restratification thesis'. Namely that medical elites are seeking to maintain collective rights and freedoms in the form of collegiate control over training, practice and discipline. Furthermore, to achieve this goal they are introducing administrative and managerial strategies, which not only place the 'rank and file' under greater collegiate surveillance, but also subject them to a rationalistic-bureaucratic discourse of outcomes based standing setting and performance appraisal. The empirical findings certainly do indicate that 'rank and file' practitioners are becoming more 'bureaucratically accountable' to 'medical elites', in the sense that they are required to record their decisions and the reasons for them (Harrison and Dowswell, 2002). As in the clinical arena, doctor's activities within the educational domain are becoming subject to greater peer surveillance and control. Yet the empirical evidence also shows that this 'bureaucratic accountability' possesses a 'ritual quality', and furthermore, this state of affairs is due to a mixture of structural and ideological factors, with doctors adopting a stance of 'paperwork compliance' towards portfolio based performance appraisal as a consequence. This finding has significant consequences. Particularly given that portfolio based performance appraisal fills an important function as a 'signifier of quality control' under the more open and accountable governing regimes advocated by medical elites.

Clearly further research is needed to verify and expand upon the 'core theme' of chapter six - 'paperwork compliance' - in other contexts. In particular, given that this is the first empirical study to examine specifically the introduction of portfolio based performance appraisal within the medical club, it is necessary to undertake comparative research in other medical schools to identify if regional variation exists. Factors such as variations in curricula design, as well as trainer and trainee characteristics, need to be taken into account when undertaking comparative research between 'Blue School' and other medical schools and postgraduate training providers. While, as chapter six discussed, further research needs to be undertaken that is specifically concerned with identifying if appraisers involved in Annual Appraisal adopt a stance of 'paperwork compliance'. Identifying this is important because they are part of the medical elite and will play a significant role in Revalidation. Furthermore, it is important to specifically focus upon exploring the issue of 'paperwork compliance' from the perspective of trainees themselves, including how it interacts with key factors that could be involved in shaping their experience of medical education and performance appraisal, such as their gender, ethnicity, age or personal career aspirations. But perhaps most importantly, the findings reinforce the need to look at reforms in medical education from a long-term perspective. It is necessary to conduct longitudinally based research to develop further the concept of 'paperwork compliance'. Finally, given its conceptual grounding within the restratification thesis and the neo-Weberian and Governmentality theoretical perspectives, the concept of 'paperwork compliance' could also be applied other similar occupational contexts, such as in nursing, law, accountancy or dentistry for example.

The Restratification Thesis

In spite of possessing clear theoretical and empirical relevance to the contemporary regulatory policy context, the restratification thesis has not received a great deal of attention from sociologists since its initial formation by Freidson in the 1980s (Harrison 2004). Rather, they have focused upon exploring contemporary challenges to professional autonomy through the respective lenses of the deprofessionalization and proletarianization theses (Elston 2004). As chapter five outlined, the deprofessionalization thesis tends to focus on topics that indicate that there has been a decline in public trust of medicine and the threat this poses to the principle of professional self-regulation. The growth of media coverage of gross medical malpractice cases like Harold Shipman is a good example (see chapter three). It focuses upon the fact that attitudes to traditional forms of authority are changing and highlights that the public increasingly expects their governing institutions to operate in a transparent and accountable manner (Moran 1999). In contrast, the proletarianization thesis highlights the existence of the potential for expert work in general, and medical work in particular, to become subject to rationalisation and routinization (see chapter four). Today's 'indeterminacy' becoming tomorrows 'technicality'. It focuses upon how this causes medical work to become subject to managerial bureaucratic control in the name of controlling costs and promoting consumer choice.

It is undoubtedly the case that the proletarianization and deprofessionalization theses possess a great deal of descriptive value. They illustrate that two broad general trends – the rise of heath care managerialism and the growth of consumer power - are actively challenging internationally traditional professional freedoms. Including the historical right of occupations classified as professions in the Anglo-American context to manage their own affairs and so possess monopolistic occupational control over members training, practice and discipline (Gladstone 2000). Nevertheless, the deprofessionalization and proletarianization theses do not fully encapsulate the nature of the contemporary situation faced by professions such as medicine, law, nursing, dentistry, teaching and social work (Allsop and Saks 2002). It is not a simple case where professional autonomy is in long-term decline due to the rise of health care managerialism and a more critically aware and demanding general public. Rather, two key points need to be noted.

First, the applicability of the deprofessionalization and proletarianization theses inside and outside of their point of origin, the United State of America, is open to serious question (Elston 2004). Certainly, critical commentators within the UK context, such as Elston (1991), have argued convincingly that neither the proletarianization thesis nor the deprofessionalization thesis fully reflect the nature of the contemporary professional training and practice context. Additionally, even the most ardent advocate of the proletarianization or deprofessionalization theses must acknowledge that there is a distinct lack of empirical evidence to support their claims (Harrison and Ahmed 2000). While, as chapter five discussed, when such evidence is found, it further reinforces their limitations as explanatory frameworks due to their inability to fully encapsulate the impact current challenges to traditional professional privileges are having on 'rank and file' professional practitioners autonomy 'at the front line' (Lupton 1997, Grey and Harrison 2004).

Second, the proletarianization and deprofessionalization theses focus solely upon external factors held to be acting upon the professions, such as the growth of a more informed and demanding general public. They do not consider the internal changes professions such as medicine are currently undergoing, as professional elites response to challenges to professional privileges by subjecting 'rank and file' practitioners to greater peer surveillance and control. The dominance of the deprofessionalization and proletarianization theses within the sociological literature, regarding current trends in the governance of professional expertise, belies the fact that sociologists are guilty of paying little attention to internal reforms within the professions, when analysing current changes in how professional expertise is regulated.

It is certainly arguable that sociologists have paid little attention to how professions such as medicine are reforming their training and regulatory arrangements as they respond to calls to become more open and accountable for how they manage their affairs (Davies 2004). By focusing mainly upon external threats to professional autonomy, through their advocacy of the deprofessionalization and proletarianization theses, sociologists have only considered half of the picture in relation to the changing position of professions within contemporary society. The restratification thesis redresses this imbalance by firmly refocusing sociological analysis so it also considers internal reforms occurring within professions such as medicine. There can be no doubt that in advocating a 'new medical professionalism', medical elites are seeking to maintain collective rights and freedoms, in the form of collegiate control over training, practice and discipline (Catto 2006 2007).

Debate exists between neo-Weberian commentators (i.e. Freidson 1985 1994 2000, Elston 1991 2004) and neo-Marxist commentators (i.e. McKinley and Stoeckle 1988, Coburn 1997, Barnett 1998) over whether the process of restratification signifies a further decline in professional autonomy (the neo-Marxist viewpoint) or the retention of profession prerogatives (the neo-Weberian viewpoint). Yet the fact of the matter is that unlike their neo-Weberian counterparts, neo-Marxists fail to recognise that professional prerogatives do not rest solely upon the control of occupational work tasks. Control over educational credentials plays an important role in ensuring the legitimacy of occupational control over regulatory and disciplinary arrangements surrounding group members activities. Certainly, neo-Marxist commentators are guilty of neglecting the fact that the restratification thesis argues occupational control over members training arrangements is vital to maintaining professional privileges (Freidson 1994).

By directing the attentions of sociologists to the important role played by control over training arrangements in maintaining professional borders and privileges, the restratification thesis opens up an important area for empirical inquiry, which the research detailed here has only begun to address. There certainly is a need to conduct empirical research into how doctor's educational activities are changing over time as they become more 'bureaucratically accountable' to medical elites for what they do. There is a clear need for sociologists to analyse changes in the nature and extent of the educational autonomy possessed by 'rank and file' medical practitioners, in order to more fully understand the consequences of the restratification process currently occurring within the medical profession.

The empirical findings presented in chapter six do reinforce that sociologists need to undertake urgently a dedicated research programme into reforms occurring within medical education at undergraduate, postgraduate and continuing levels. Here it needs to be acknowledged that the empirical work discussed here relies solely upon doctors own accounts of their educational activities. It was not able to provide an independent report of what actually happened between appraisers and appraisees during appraisal meetings. Nor does it explore in depth with doctors themselves the reasons why they approached portfolio based performance appraisal as they did. Further research is therefore required to verify and expand upon the research findings presented in chapter six. Preferably using a mixture of methods, including direct observation of portfolio based performance appraisal events. Additionally, comparative research with other professions needs to be undertaken. Medicine is not alone in becoming subject to a process of restratification as a result of the state acting to open up the previously 'closed shop' field of professional regulation (Slater 2007). Comparative research, concerned with the strategies by which different professional elites are reacting to contemporary challenges to the principle of professional self-regulation, would enable sociologists to obtain a clearer picture of what the future may bring, in regards to how the experts who provide us with much valued public services are regulated to ensure the welfare of the general public.

The Neo-Weberian and Governmentality Viewpoints

Finally, it needs to be noted that an additional advantage of the restratification thesis is that it reinforces the value of synthesising the neo-Weberian and Governmentality perspectives when analysing the governance of professional expertise. As chapter three discussed, the new-Weberian viewpoint has dominated the sociological study of professional regulation in the UK for the last four decades. In addition to the important insights the neo-Weberian standpoint offers into the fundamentally exclusory nature of 'club governance', it encapsulates the socio-legal and political realities of the regulatory context with regards to the professions in general and medicine in particular. Yet the fact is the dominance of the neo-Weberian perspective has led social scientists to somewhat neglect the symbiotic nature of the development of professional expertise and the modern liberal democratic state. Although the neo-Marxist perspective may avoid this error, as discussed in chapter five, it does so by advocating a largely negative and overly simplistic view of the relationship between the state, the professions and the general population. In contrast, the Governmentality perspective focuses upon the productive affects of the close relationship that exists between the professions and the state. It does this by highlighting how professionals enable the state to govern legitimately the population in such a way that an individual's capacity for self-determination is enhanced, while simultaneously being brought into line with overarching governing objectives.

The Governmentality perspective highlights the key role professions, such as medicine, have played in the governance of the population. In doing so, it adopts a similar critical view of the emergence of professionalism as a form of regulatory control as the neo-Marxist and neo-Weberian perspectives. Importantly, it reinforces the need for current debate surrounding recent challenges to the principle of professional self-regulation, to also consider the changing nature of the relationship between subject-citizens and the state, as a result of the political and economic re-emergence of liberalism since the mid to late-1970s. For the Governmentality perspective notes the ascendancy of the concept of the 'enterprise self' into all spheres of contemporary life. In doing so it highlights how challenges to the principle of professional self regulation and concurrent calls to reform elite regulatory bodies such as the GMC can be seen to be directed towards the object of Governmentality - the population in general and the individual subject-citizen in particular – as much as they are the medical profession. For medicine (and indeed the health and social care professions as a whole) form but one part of a complex array of governing calculations, strategies and tactics which seek to promote the security, wealth, health and happiness of the population. It is important for social scientists interested the study of the professions and professional regulation to recognise this fact. For changes in the conditions under which 'good governance' can be practiced within previously closed off public institutions such as the GMC highlight how society as a whole is currently undergoing a period of far reaching transformation. This in turn reinforces the fact that study of the professions and the principle of professional self-regulation must always remain grounded within broader sociological theorising concerning the nature of modern world in which we live.

LIBRARY, UNIVERSITY OF CHESTER

APPENDIX

Biographical details of the participants interviewed for the study (all names are pseudonyms):

Dr White, General Practitioner, age 38, Female, White
Dr Lilac, General Practitioner, age 44, Male, Chinese
Dr Green, General Practitioner, age 47, Male, White
Dr Brown, General Practitioner, age 43, Male, White
Dr Silver, General Practitioner, age 55, Male, White
Dr Purple, General Practitioner, age 57, Male, Black: Caribbean
Dr Saffron, General Practitioner, age 41, Female, White
Dr Terra-Cotta, General Practitioner, age 54, Male, Asian: Pakistani
Dr Wisteria, General Practitioner, age 49, Male, White
Dr Magenta, Accident and Emergency, age 44, Male, White
Dr Ruby, Accident and Emergency, age 37, Male, White
Dr Rose, Accident and Emergency, age 41, Male, White
Dr Sapphire, Accident and Emergency, age 39, Male, White
Dr Tawny, Accident and Emergency, age 42, Male, White
Dr Taupe, Accident and Emergency, age 44, Male, Chinese
Dr Ginger, Accident and Emergency, age 38, Female, White
Dr Orange, General Medicine, age 61, Male, White
Dr Indigo, General Medicine, age 39, Male, White
Dr Black, General Medicine, age 41 , Male, White
Dr Bright, Clinical Chemistry, age 45, Male, White
Dr Gold, Medical Microbiology, age 38, Male, White
Dr Scarlet, Obstetrics and Gynaecology, age 49, Male, Asian: Pakistani
Dr Sparkle, Obstetrics and Gynaecology, page 53, Male, White
Dr Pink, Dermatology, age 55, Male, White
Dr Lime, Gastroenterology, age 46, Male, White
Dr Ultramarine, Gastroenterology, age 45, Male, White
Dr Tangerine, Biochemistry, age 37, Female, White
Dr Violet, Geriatric Medicine, age 55, Male, White
Dr Tan, Geriatric Medicine, age 57, Male, White
Dr Bronze, Endrocology, age 45, Male, White
Dr Blaze, Endrocology, age 59, Male, White
Dr Dark, Surgeon (ENT), age 54, Male, White

Dr Wheat, Surgeon (ENT), age 47, Male, Asian: Indian
Dr Sandy, Surgeon (ENT), age 54, Male, White
Dr Tan, Surgeon (Cardio), age 43, Male, White
Dr Purple, Surgeon (Cardio), age 47, Male, White
Dr Turquoise, Surgeon (Cardio), age 41, Male, White
Dr Ingot, Surgeon (General), age 52 , Female, White
Dr Lime, Surgeon (General), age 61 , Male, White
Dr Light, Surgeon (General), age 42, Male, Chinese
Dr Blue, Surgeon (General), age 48, Male, White
Dr Red, Surgeon (General), age 51, Male, White
Dr Burgundy, Surgeon (General), age 45, Male, White
Dr Teal, Surgeon (General), age 47, Male, White
Dr Grey, Surgeon (General), age 43, Male, White
Dr Yellow, Surgeon (General), age, 46, Female, Asian: Pakistani

ACKNOWLEDGEMENT

I would like to take this opportunity to thank all the doctors who agreed to participate in this research for giving up their time to speak to me, as well as staff and old friends at 'Blue School' for their continued support and friendship.

BIBLIOGRAPHY

[1]   Academy of Royal Medical Colleges (2006) Response to 'Good Doctors, Safer Patients' Published by The Academy of Royal Medical Colleges

[2]   Agar, M (1980) The Professional Stranger London: Academic Press

[3]   Ahmed, W I U and Harrison, S (2000) Medical Autonomy and the UK State: 1975 to 2025 *Sociology,* Volume 34, Number 1, 129-46

[4]   Albrecht, G.L, Fitzpatrick, R and Scrimshaw, S.C (2000) The Handbook of Social Science and Medicine Sage Publications

[5]   Alford, R R (1975) Health Care Politics: Ideological and Interest Group Barriers to Reform University of Chicago Press

[6]   Allen, I (1995) Doctors and The Careers: A New Generation London: Policy Studies Institute

[7]   Allsop, J and Mulcahy, L. (1996) Regulating Medical Work: Formal and Informal Controls Open University Press

[8]   Allsop, J and Saks, M. (2002, editors) Regulating the Health Professions Sage Publications

[9]   Allsop, J. (2002) Regulation and the Medical Profession *in Allsop, J and Saks, M (2002, editors)* Regulating the Health Professions Sage Publications

[10] Allsop, J. (2006) Regaining Trust in Medicine: Professional and State Strategies *Current Sociology*, Volume 54, Number 4, 621-36

[11] Alment, A. (1976) Competence to Practice: Report of the Enquiry set up for the Medical Profession in the United Kingdom. Published by the Alment Committee

[12] Anthias, F and Yuval-Davis, N (1993) Contextualising Feminism: Gender, Ethnic and Class Divisions *Feminist Review,* Volume 15, 62-75

[13] Armey, R and Bergen B (1984) Medicine and the Management of Living Taming the Last Great Beast University of Chicago Press

[14] Armstrong, D (1980) Health Care and the Structure of Medical Education *in Noack, H (1980, editor)* Medical Education and Primary Health Care Croom Helm London

[15] Armstrong, D (1983) Political Anatomy of the Body Medical Knowledge in Britain in the Twentieth Century Cambridge University Press

[16] Armstrong, D. (1995) Outline of Sociology as Applied to Medicine Arnold

[17] Armstrong, D (2002) Clinical Autonomy, Individual and Collective: The Problem of Changing Doctors Behaviour Social Science and Medicine, Volume 55, 1771-1777

[18] Armstrong, M (2005) Managing Performance London Institute of Personal development

[19]   Atkinson, P. (1981) The Clinical Experience: The Construction and Reconstruction of Medical Reality Farnborough: Gower

[20]   Atkinson, P (1995) Medical Talk and Medical Work Sage Publications

[21]   Atkinson, P Coffey, A L Delamont, S Loftland, J and Loftland L (2001) Handbook of Ethnography Sage Publications

[22]   Barber, B (1963) Some Problems in the Sociology of the Professions *Daedalas*, Volume 92, 669-689

[23]   Barker-Penfield J (1979) Sexual Surgery in the Late Nineteenth Century *in Dreifus,*

[24]   *C (1979, editor)* Seizing Our Bodies New York Vintage

[25]   Barnett, M (1991) The Politics of Truth Cambridge Polity

[26]   Barrett, J R, Barrett, P and Kearns, R A (1998) Declining Professional Dominance? Trends in the Proletarianization of Primary Care in New Zealand *Social Science and Medicine,* Volume 46, Number 2, 193-207

[27]   Barrett, M and Philips, A. (1992) Destabilising Theory Cambridge Polity Press

[28]   Barrows, H.S and Pickell, G.C. (1991) Developing Clinical Problem-Solving Skills Norton and Company

[29]   Barry, A, Osborne, T and Rose, N (1996) Foucault and Political Reason University College London Press

[30]   Bateman, T. (2000) A visit from the Quality Assurance Agency: A Reflection From One Medical School *Medical Education,* Volume 34, Number 12, 1026-28.

[31]   Baggot, R. (2002) Regulatory Politics, Health Professionals, and the Public Interest in

[32]   *Allsop, J and Saks, M (2002, editors)* Regulating the Health Professions Sage Publications

[33]   Bauman, Z (1996) From Pilgrim to Tourist: A Short History of Identity *in Hall, S and du Guy, P (1996, editors)* Questions of Cultural Identity Sage Publications

[34]   Becker, H.S, Geer, B, Hughes, E.C and Strauss, A.L. (1961) Boys in White: Student Culture in Medical School Chicago and London: University of Chicago Press

[35]   Berg, M (1997) Problems and Promises of the Protocol *Social Science and Medicine*, Volume 44, Number 8, 1081-88

[36]   Berlin, I. (1969) Two Concepts of Liberty *in I. Berlin (2002),* Four Essays on Liberty London: Oxford University Press

[37]   Bell, C (1978) Studying the Locally Powerful: Personal Reflections on a Research Career *in Bell, C and Encel, S* (1978, editors) Inside the Whale Sydney: Pergamon

[38]   Ben-David (1977) Centres of Learning: Britain France and the United States New Yor McGraw Hill

[39]   Bendelow, G and Carpenter, M, Vautier, C and Williams, S. (2001, editors) Gender, Health ad Healing Routledge

[40]   Berg, M. (1997) Problems and Promises of the Protocol *Social Science and Medicine*, Volume 44, Number 8, 1081-88

[41]   Berlant, J.L. (1975) Profession and Monopoly: A Study of Medicine in the United States and Great Britain University of California Press

[42]   Biggs, J (1999) Teaching for Quality Learning at University Open University Press

[43]   Black, D (2002) Consultant Appraisal *GMC News Supplement on Appraisal and Revalidation 1- 4.* The GMC: London

[44]   Blaikie, N (1993) Approaches to Social Inquiry Cambridge Polity Press

[45] Blake, C. (1990) The Charge of the Parasols: Women's Entry to the Medical Profession The Women's Press; London

[46] Bligh, J (1995) Identifying the Core Curriculum *Medical Teacher,* Volume 17, 383-90

[47] Bligh, J (1998) Trends in Medical Education *European Journal of Dental Education,* Volume 2, 2-7

[48] Bligh, J (2001) Learning From Uncertainty: A Change of Culture Medical *Education,* Volume 35, Number 1, 2

[49] BMA (2005) The Foundation Programme: A Rough Guide Stationary Office London

[50] BMJ News (1995) Performance Bill will give GMC new powers *BMJ,* Volume 310, 759-60

[51] BMJ Editorial (1999) Time for Evidence Based Medical Education *BMJ,* Volume 318, 1223-24

[52] BMJ Career Focus (2003) Formal and Informal Suspensions and the NCAA *BMJ,* Volume 327, 163

[53] Bosk, C.L. (1979) Forgive and Remember: Managing Medical Failure Chicago and London: University of Chicago Press

[54] Bonner, T.N. (1995) Becoming a Physician: Medical Education in Britain, France, Germany and the United States, 1750-1945 Oxford University Press

[55] Bradley, J and Bligh, J (1999) One Year's Experience with a Clinical Skills Resource Centre *Medical Education,* Volume 17, 383-90

[56] Bristol Royal Infirmary Inquiry (2001) Learning From Bristol: The Report of the Public Inquiry Into Children's Heart Surgery at the Bristol Royal Infirmary, 1984-1995 Stationary Office London

[57] Bridgens J (2003) Medical Education in the Real World *Medical Education,* Volume 37, 470

[58] Bruce, D.A. (2007) Regulation of Doctors *BMJ,* Volume 334, 436-37

[59] Bryman, A. (2004, 2nd Edition) Social Research Methods Oxford University Press

[60] Bullimore, D (1998) Study Skills and Tomorrows Doctors London:WB Saunders

[61] Bulmer, M (1984) The Chicago School of Sociology Chicago University Press

[62] Burchell, G, Gordon, C and Miller, P (1991, editors) The Foucault Effect: Studies in Governmentality Harvester Wheatsheaf

[63] Burchell, G (1993) Liberal Government and Techniques of the Self *Economy and Society,* Volume 22, Number 3, 267-282

[64] Burchell, G (1996) Liberal Government and Techniques of the Self in *Barry, A, Osborne, T and Rose, N (1996)* Foucault and Political Reason University College London Press

[65] Burrage, M (1988) Revolution and the Collective Action of the French, American and English Legal Professions *Law and Social Enquiry: The Journal of the American Bar Foundation,* Volume 13, Number 2, 225-277

[66] Burrage, M and Torstendahl, R (1990, editors) Professions in Theory and Practice Sage Publications

[67] Butler, J (1993) Bodies That Matter: On The Discursive Limits of Sex Routledge

[68] Bruijn, H (2001) Managing Performance in the Public Sector Routledge

[69] Byrum, W.F. (1985) Physicians, Hospitals and Career Structures in Eighteenth Century London in *Bynum W.F and Porter, R (1985, editors)* William Hunter and the Eighteenth Century Medical World Cambridge University Press

[70] Bynum W.F and Porter, R. (1985, editors) "William Hunter and the Eighteenth Century Medical World" Cambridge University Press

[71] Calman, K. (1993) Hospital Doctors: Training for the Future DOH London

[72] Calman, K. (1994) Continuing Medical Education DOH London

[73] Calman, K and Williams, S (1995) Challenges to Professional Autonomy in the United Kingdom: The Perceptions of General Practitioners *International Journal of Health Services,* Volume 35, 219-241

[74] Carr-Saunders, A.M. and Wilson, P.A. (1933) The Professions The Clarendon Press

[75] Carter, K.C. (1991) The development of Pasteur's concept of disease: causation and the mergence of specific causes in nineteenth century medicine *Bulletin of the History of Medicine,* Volume 2, 528-548

[76] Cassell (1988) The relationship of the observer to the observed when 'studying up' *in Burgess, R.G (1988, editor)* Studies in Qualitative Methodology London JAJ Press

[77] Catto, G. (2006) GMC News, 3

[78] Catto, G (2007) Will We Be Getting Good Doctors and Safer Patients? *BMJ,* Volume 334, 450

[79] Carvel, J. (2002) Concern as Women Outnumber Men in Medical Schools *The Guardian,* 4.7.2002, 11

[80] Chadwick, J and Mann, W N. (1950) The Medical Works of Hippocrates Oxford Blackwell

[81] Challis, M (1999) AMEE Medical Education Guide Number 11 (Revised): Portfolio Based Learning and Assessment in Medical Education *Medical Teacher,* Volume 21, Number 4, 370-86

[82] Chamberlain, T.C (1965) The Method of Multiple Working Hypothesis *Science* Volume 148, 745-749

[83] Charmaz, K (1983) The Grounded Theory Method: An Explication and Interpretation *in Emerson, R.M (1983, Editor)* Contemporary Field Research Boston Little Brown

[84] Charmaz, K (2000) Grounded Theory: Objectivist and Constructivist Methods *in Denzin, N.K and Lincoln, Y.S (2000, Editors Second Edition).* Handbook of Qualitative Research Sage Publications

[85] Charmaz, K (2004) Grounded Theory *in Lewis-Beck, M.S, Bryman, A, and Liao, T.F (2004, Editors)* The Sage Encyclopaedia of Social Science Research Methods Sage Publications

[86] Charmaz, K (2006) Constructing Grounded Theory: A Practical Guide Through Qualitative Analysis Sage Publications

[87] Clay, B. (1999) Medical Workforce and the Gender Shift *Hospital Medicine,* Volume 60, Number 12, 901-3

[88] Coburn, D Rappolt, S and Bourgeault, I (1997) Decline vs Retention of Medical Power Through Restratification: An Examination of the Ontario Case *Sociology of Health and Illness,* Volume 19, Number 1, 1-22

[89] Coburn, D and Willis, E (2000) The Medical Profession: Knowledge, Power and Autonomy in *Albrecht, G.L, Fitzpatrick, R and Scrimshaw, S.C (2000)* The Handbook of Social Science and Medicine Sage Publications

[90] Copeman, W.S.C. (1960) Doctors And Disease in Tudor Times London: Dawson and Sons

[91] Connell, R.W. (1995) Masculinities Allen and Unwin

[92] Conrad, L, Nee, M, Nutton, V, Porter, R and Wear, A (1995) The Western Medical Tradition: 800 BC to AD 1800 Cambridge University Press

[93] Conrad, P (1992) Medicalization and Social Control *Annual Review of Sociology,* Volume 18, 209-32

[94] Cox, D. (1991) Health Service Management – A Sociological View: Griffiths and the Non-Negotiated Order of the Hospital *in Gabe, J, Calman, M and Bury, M (Editors)* The Sociology of the Health Service Routledge

[95] Cutler, A and Waine B (1994) Managing the Welfare State Oxford:Berg

[96] Davies, C. (1987) Viewpoint: Things to come – the NHS in the Next Decade *Sociology of Health and Illness,* Volume 9, 302-17

[97] Davies C and Beach A (2000) Interpreting Professional Self-Regulation: A History of the United Kingdom Central Council for Nursing midwifery and Health Visiting London Routledge

[98] Davies, C (2001) Lay involvement in professional self-regulation: a study of public appointment-holders in the health field The Open University Press

[99] Davies, C (2002) Registering a Difference: Changes in the Regulation of Nursing in *Allsop, J and Saks, M. (2002, editors)* Regulating the Health Professions Sage Publications

[100] Davies, C. (2004) Regulating the Health Care Workforce: Next Steps for Research *Journal of Health Services Research and Policy,* Volume 9, Supplement 1, January

[101] Davis, M.H, Friedman B.D, Harden, R.M, Howie, P, Ker, C, McGhee, MJ, Pipard, MJ and Snadden, D. (2001) "Portfolio Assessment in medical students' final examinations" *Medical Teacher,* Vol 23, No 4, 231-250

[102] Day, P and Klein, R. (1992) Constitutional and Distributional Conflict in British Medical Politics: The Case of General Practice 1911 – 1991 *Political Studies,* Volume 40, 462-78

[103] Dean, M (1999) Governmentality: Power and Rule in Modern Society Sage Publications

[104] Delamothe, T. (1998) Who Killed Cock Robin? *BMJ,* Volume 316, 1757

[105] Deleuze, G (1988) Foucault University of Minnesota Press

[106] Department of Health (1989a) Working for Patients DOH London

[107] Department of Health (1989b) Medical Audit; NHS Review. Working Paper 6 . DOH London

[108] Department of Health (1991) The Patient's Charter DOH London

[109] Department of Health (1991) Junior Doctors: The New Deal DOH London

[110] Department of Health (1998) A First Class Service: Quality in the New NHS DOH London

[111] Department of Health (1999) Supporting Doctors, Protecting Patients DOH London

[112] Department of Health (2000) The NHS Plan DOH London

[113] Department of Health (2000) Patient and Public Involvement in the NHS DOH London

[114] Department of Health (2001) NHS Appraisal: Appraisal for Consultants Working in The NHS DOH:London

[115] Department of Heath (2001) Assuring the Quality of Medical Practice: Implementing Supporting Doctors, Protecting Patients DOH London

[116] Department of Heath (2001) Modernising Regulation in the Health Professions DOH London

[117] Department of Health (2001) Hospital, Public Health Medicine and Community Health Services Medical and Dental Staff in England 1990 – 2000. DOH London

[118] Dilthey, W (1911) Descriptive Psychology and Historical Understanding The Hague, The Netherlands: Martinus Nijhoff

[119] Dingwall, R and Lewis, P (1983, editors) The Sociology of the Professions: Lawyers, Doctors and Others McMillan

[120] Dingwall, R, Fenn, P and Quan, L (1991) Medical Negligence: a Review of the Literature Oxford Centre for Legal Studies Wolfson College

[121] Dolmans and Schmidt (1996) The Advantages of Problem Based Learning Curricula *Postgraduate Medicine,* Volume 72, 535-38

[122] Donaldson, L. (2006) Good Doctors Safer Patients: Proposals to Strengthen The System to Assure and Improve the Performance of Doctors and to Protect the Safety of Patients DOH London

[123] Doolin, B. (2002) Enterprise Discourse, Professional Identity and the Organization Control of Hospital Clinicians *Organization Studies* (23) 3: 369-390

[124] Doyal, L and Pennell I (1979) The Political Economy of Health London: Pluto Press

[125] Drolet, M (2004, editor) The Postmodernism Reader Routledge

[126] du Guy, P (1996a) Consumption and Identity at Work Sage Publications

[127] du Guy, P (1996b) Organising Identity making people up at work. Paper presented at the Southampton *Space and Identity* Seminar Series May 1996

[128] du Guy, P (1996c) Organising Identity: Entrepreneurial Governance and Public Management , *in Hall, S and du Guy, P (1996, editors)* Questions of Cultural Identity Sage Publications

[129] Dumm, T.L (1996) Michel Foucault and the Politics of Freedom Sage Publications

[130] Durkheim, E (1957) Professional Ethics and Civic Morals Routledge and Kegan Paul

[131] Editorial (1858) *The Lancet,* Volume 2, 148

[132] Elliott (2001) Concepts of the Self Cambridge Polity Press

[133] Elston, M.A. (1991) The Politics of Professional Power: Medicine in a Changing Medical Service *in Gabe, J, Calman, M and Bury, M (1991, editors)* The Sociology of the Health Service Routledge

[134] Elston, M A (1997) The Sociology of Medical Science and Technology Oxford Blackwell

[135] Elston, M.A. (2004) Medical Autonomy and Medical Dominance, in, *Gabe, J, Bury, M and Elston, M.A. (2004)* Key Concepts in Medical Sociology Sage Publications

[136] Ellwood, P.M. (1988) Outcomes Management: A Technology of Patient Experience *New England Journal of Medicine,* Volume 318, 1549-56

[137] Engels, F (1974) The Condition of the Working Class in England Progress Publishers

[138] Enthoven, A.C. (1985) Reflections on the Management of the National Health Service Nuffield Provincial Hospitals Trust

[139] Ehrenreich, B and English, D. (1973) Witches, Midwives and Nurses: A History of Women Healers Writers and Readers Publishing Cooperative: London

[140] Ettorre, E (2004) Dealing with a Difficult Interview: Professionalism and Research Ethics *in Hallowell, N, Lawton, J and Gregory, S (2004)* Reflections on Research: The Realities of Doing Research in the Social Sciences Open University Press

[141] Etzioni, A (1969) The Semi-Professions and their Organisation New Your Free Press

[142] Fitzpatrick, R, Hinton, J, Newman, S and Scambler, G (1984) The Experience of Illness London Tavistock

[143] Exworthy, M (1998) Clinical Audit in the NHS Internal Market: From Peer Review to External Monitoring *Public Policy and Administration,* Volume 13, Number 2, 40-53

[144] Fetterman, D.M (1998) Ethnography: A Step By Step Guide Sage Publications

[145] Finucane, P.M (1998) Problem Based Learning: Its Rationale and Efficacy *Medical Journal Australia,* Volume 168, 445-8

[146] Fletcher C and Williams R (1985) Performance Appraisal and Career Development London: Hutchinson

[147] Fletcher C (1997) Appraisal: Routes to Improved Performance Short Run Press

[148] Flew, A. (1984, Editor) A Dictionary of Philosophy New York: St Martin's

[149] Flynn, R. (1992) Structures of Control in Heath Management Routledge

[150] Flynn, R (2002) Clinical Governance and Governmentality *Health Risk and Society* Volume 4, Number 2, 134-167

[151] Freddi, G and Bjorkman, J.W. (1989, editors) Controlling Medical Professionals: The Comparative Politics of Health Governance Sage Publications

[152] Freidson, E. (1970) The Profession of Medicine New York: Dodds Mead

[153] Freidson, E (1970) Professional Dominance: The Social Structure of Medical Care

[154] New York: Atherton Press

[155] Freidson, E (1985) The Reorganisation of the Medical Profession *Medical Care Review* Volume 42, Number 1, 1-20

[156] Freidson, E. (1994) Professionalism Reborn: Theory, Prophecy and Policy Cambridge Polity Press

[157] Freidson, E. (2001) Professionalism: The Third Logic Cambridge Polity Press

[158] Friedman, M (1962) Capitalism and Freedom University of Chicago Press

[159] Foucault, M (1965) Madness and Civilisation: The History of Insanity in the Age of Reason New York: Random House

[160] Foucault, M (1970) The Order of Things London: Tavistock

[161] Foucault, M (1972) The Archaeology of Knowledge London Tavistock

[162] Foucault, M (1977) Discipline and Punish: The Birth of the Prison London Allen Lane

[163] Foucault, M (1979) The History Sexuality Volume 1London Allen Lane

[164] Foucault, M (1980) Two Lectures in *Gordon, C (1980, editor)* Power/Knowledge Selected Interviews and Other Writings 1972: 1977 Brighton: Harvester Press

[165] Foucault, M (1982) The Subject and Power *Critical Inquiry,* Volume 7, 777-95

[166] Foucault, M (1985a) The History Sexuality Volume 2 The Use of Pleasure London Allen Lane

[167] Foucault, M (1985b) Sexuality and Solitude in *Blonsky, M (1985 editor)* On Signs:A Semiotics Reader Blackwell

[168] Foucault, M (1986) The History Sexuality Volume 3 The Care of the Self   London Allen Lane

[169] Foucault, M. (1989) The Birth of the Clinic: An Archaeology of Medical Perception Routledge Classics

[170] Foucualt, M (1991a) The Ethic of Care for the Self as a Practice of Freedom: An Interview *in Bernauer, J and Rasmussen, D (1991, editors)* The Final Foucault Cambridge MIT Press

[171] Foucault, M (1991b) Governmentality *in Burchell, G, Gordon, C and Miller, P (1991, editors)* The Foucault Effect: Studies in Governmentality Harvester Wheatsheaf

[172] Fournier, V and Grey C (1999) Too Much, Too Little and Too Often: A Critique of du Guy's Analysis of Enterprise *Organisation,* Volume 61, 107-28

[173] Fox, R (1975) Training For Uncertainty *in Cox, C Mead A (1975, Editors)* A Sociology of Medical Practice London: Collier: Macmillan

[174] Fox-Keller, E (1985) Reflections on Gender and Science Yale University Press

[175] Fukuyama, F (1992) The End of History and the Last Man Penguin

[176] Gabe, J and Calman, M (1989) The Limits of Medicine Womens Perception of Medical Technology *Social Science and Medicine,* Volume 28, 223-31

[177] Gabe, J, Calman, M and Bury, M. (1991, editors) The Sociology of the Health Service Routledge

[178] Gabe, J, Kelleher, D and Williams, G. (1994) Challenging Medicine Routledge

[179] Gabe, J and Bury, M. (1996) Halcion Nights: A Sociological Account *Sociology,* Volume 30, 447-469

[180] Gabe, J, Bury, M and Elston, M.A (2004) Key Concepts in Medical Sociology Sage Publications

[181] Giddens, A. (1986) Sociology A Brief But Critical Introduction Macmillan

[182] Giddens, A. (1990) The Consequences of Modernity Cambridge Polity

[183] Gilbert (2001) Reflective Practice and Clinical Supervision: Meticulous Rituals of the Confessional *Journal of Advanced Nursing*, Volume 36,199-205

[184] Geertz, C (1983) Local Knowledge: Further Essays in Interpretative Anthropology Basic Books

[185] Gerth, H H and Wright Mills, C (1946) Introduction *in Weber, M* (1946) Essays in Sociology Oxford University Press

[186] General Medical Council (1993, 2002 and 2003) Tomorrows Doctors GMC London

[187] General Medical Council (1995b, 2005) Good Medical Practice GMC London

[188] General Medical Council (1995a) Duties of a Doctor GMC London

[189] General Medical Council (1999) Report of the Revalidation Steering Group GMC London

[190] General Medical Council (2000) Revalidating Doctors Ensuring Standards Ensuring the Future GMC London

[191] General Medical Council (2008) Bulletin Issue 42 February 2008 GMC London

[192] Gentleman, D. (2001) The Changing Face of Medical Regulation in the UK *Clinical Risk,* Volume 7, 169-75

[193] Gladstone, D. (2000, editor) Regulating Doctors Institute for the Study of Civil Society

[194] Glaser, B.G and Strauss, A.L (1967) The Discovery of Grounded Theory: Strategies for Qualitative Research Chicago:Aldine

[195] Gordon, C (1989) The Soul of the Citizen: Max Weber and Foucault on Rationality and Government *in Whimster, S and Lask, S (1989, editors)* Max Weber: Rationality and Modernity Allen and Unwin

[196] Gordon, C (1991) Governmental Rationality: An Introduction *in Burchell, G, Gordon, C and Miller, P (1991, editors)* The Foucault Effect: Studies in Governmentality Harvester Wheatsheaf

[197] Gordon, C (1996) Foucault in Britain *in Barry, A, Osborne, T and Rose, N (1996)* Foucault and Political Reason University College London Press

[198] Gould, D. (1985) The Black and White Medicine Show London: Hamish Hamilton

[199] Graham, D (2002) View From The Top *Hospital Doctor,* Volume 30 (May), 22

[200] Graham, D and Clark, P (1986) The New Enlightenment The Rebirth of Liberalism Macmillan

[201] Gray, A and Harrison, S. (2004, editors) Governing Medicine: Theory and Practice Open University Press

[202] Grey, C (1994) Career as a Project of the Self and Labour Process Discipline *Sociology,* Volume 28, Number 2, 479-98

[203] Green, D (1987) A Missed Opportunity? *In Green, D, Neuberger, J, Young, M and Burstal, M (1987, editors)* The NHS Reforms: Whatever Happened to Consumer Choice? London Institute of Economic Affairs

[204] Hackett, M C (1999) Implementing Clinical Governance in Trusts *International Journal of Health Care Quality Assurance,* Volume 12, 210-13

[205] Hacking, L (1986) Making Up People *in Heller, T , Sosna, M and Wellbery, D (1986, editors)* Reconstructing Individualism: Autonomy, Individuality and the Self in Western Thought Stanford University Press

[206] Hall, S (1996) Introduction: Who Needs Identity? *in Hall, S and du Guy, P (1996, editors)* Questions of Cultural Identity Sage Publications

[207] Hall, S and du Guy, P (1996, editors) Questions of Cultural Identity Sage Publications

[208] Ham, C. (1988) Health Care Variations: Assessing the Evidence Kings Fund Institute

[209] Hammersley, M and Atkinson, P (1995, second edition) Ethnography: Principles in Practice London: Routledge

[210] Hanlon, G (1994) The Commercialisation of Accountancy London Macmillan

[211] Hanlon, G (1998) Professionalism as Enterprise *Sociology,* Volume 32, Number 1, 43-63

[212] Harrison, S and Schultz, R.L. (1989) Clinical Autonomy in the UK and the USA: Contrasts and Convergence in *Freddi, G and Bjorkman, J.W (1989, editors)* Controlling Medical Professionals: The Comparative Politics of Health Governance Sage Publications

[213] Harrison, S and Ahmad, W.I.U. (2000) Medical Autonomy and the UK State: 1975 to 2025 *Sociology,* Volume 34, Number 1, 129-46

[214] Harrison S and Dowswell G (2002) Autonomy and Bureaucratic Accountability in Primary Care: What English General Practitioners Say *Sociology of Health and Illness* Volume 24, Number 2, 217-241

[215] Harrison, S. (2004) Governing Medicine: Science and Practice *in Gray, A and Harrison, S (2004, editors)* Governing Medicine: Theory and Practice Open University Press

[216] Haug, M. R (1973) Deprofessionalization: An Alternative Hypothesis for the Future *in Halmos, P (1973, editor)* Professionalization and Social Change *Sociological Review* Monograph No 20 University of Keele

[217] Hayek, F (1973) Law, Legislation and Liberty Routledge and Kegan Paul

[218] Hawkins, J M (1979, editor) The Oxford Paperback Dictionary Third Edition Oxford University Press

[219] Hill P J (1992) Is Your Academic Appraisal Scheme Working Effectively? Paper Presented at the BEMAS Conference University of Nottingham 6th to 8th April

[220] Holliday (1987) Beyond Monopoly London University of Chicago

[221] Holloway, T. (1966) The Apothecaries Act, 1815: A Reinterpretation (part 1) *Medical History* 10th July 1966, 107-29

[222] Holmes, H (1980) Birth Control and Controlling Birth Clifton, NJ: Humana Press

[223] Hood, C. (1991) A Public Management for all Seasons? *Public Administration* Volume 69 (Spring), 3-19

[224] Hood, C. (1995a) Contemporary Public Management: A New Global Paradigm? *Public Policy and Administration,* Volume 10, Number 2, 104-117

[225] Hood, C. (1995b) The New Public Management in the 1980s; Variations on a Theme *Accounting Organizations and Society,* Volume 20, Number 2/3, 93-109

[226] Hopkins, A. (1990) Measuring Quality of Medical Care Published by The Royal College of Physicians, London.

[227] Hornsby-Smith, M (1993) Gaining access in *Gilbert, N* (1993, editor) Researching Social Life Sage Publications

[228] Hoy, D C (1986) Foucault: A Critical Reader Oxford Basil Blackwell

[229] Hughes, D, McGuire, A and McKenzie, L (1988) Medical Decision Making – A Bibliography Oxford Centre for Socio-Legal Studies

[230] Hughes, E (1963) Professions Daedalus, Volume 92, 655-668

[231] Irby, D M (1994) What Clinical Teachers in Medicine Need to Know *Academic Medicine,* Volume 69, 334-342

[232] Irvine, D. (1997) The Performance of Doctors 1:Professionalism and Self-Regulation in a Changing World *BMJ,* Volume 314, 1540-50

[233] Irvine, D (2001) Doctors In the UK: Their New Professionalism and Its Regulatory Framework *The Lancet*, Volume 358, Issue 9295, 1807-10

[234] Irvine, D. (2003) The Doctors Tale: Professionalism and the Public Trust Radcliffe Medical Press

[235] Irvine, D. (2006) Success Depends Upon Winning Hearts and Minds *BMJ,* Volume 333, 965-6

[236] Jackson, J.E (1990) I Am A Fieldnote in *Sanjek, R* (1990, editor) Fieldnotes: The Making of Anthropology Cornell University Press

[237] Jamous, H and Peliolle, B. (1970) Changes in the French University-Hospital System in *Jackson, J.A. (1970)* Professions and Professionalization Cambridge University Press

[238] Johnson, T.J. (1972) Professions and Power MacMillian Press Ltd

[239] Johnson, T J (1977) Professions in the Cass Structure *in Scase, R (editor)* Class Cleavage and Control Allen and Unwin

[240] Johnson, T.J (1994) Expertise and The State in *Gane, M and Johnson, T.J* Foucault's New Domains Routledge

[241] Johnson, T.J (1995) Governmentality and the Institutionalization of Expertise *Johnson, T, Larkin, G and Saks, M (1995, editors)* Health Professions and The State in Europe Routledge

[242] Johnson, T, Larkin, G and Saks, M (1995, editors) Health Professions and The State in Europe Routledge

[243] Jewson, N.D. (1974) Medical Knowledge and the Patronage System in Eighteenth Century England *Sociology,* Volume 8, 369-85

[244] Jewson, N.D. (1976) The Disappearance of the Sick-Man from the Medical Cosmology *Sociology,* Volume 10, 225-44

[245] Kitchener, M (2000) The Bureaucratization of Professional Roles: The Case of Clinical Directors in UK Hospitals, *Organization*, Volume 7, Number 1, 129-54

[246] King, H (2001) Greek and Roman Medicine. London: Bristol Classical Press

[247] King, R and Wincup, E (2000, editors) Researching Research on Crime and Justice Oxford University Press

[248] Kelly, M and Field, D (1994) Comments on the Rejection of the Biomedical Model in Sociological Discourse *Medical Sociology News,* Volume 19, Number 2, 34-7

[249] Kennedy, I. (1983) The Unmasking of Medicine: A Searching Look at Health Care Today London: Granada Publishing

[250] Klein, R.E. (1983 first edition and 1989, second edition) The Politics of The National Health Service London: Longman

[251] Klein, R.E. (1998) Why Britain is Reorganising its National Health Service – Again *Health Affairs,* Volume 17, Number 4, 17-19

[252] Kmietowicz, J (2006) BMA Rejects Chief Medical Officers Proposals on Medical Regulation *BMJ,* Volume 333, 967

[253] Kogan, M and Redfern, S. (1995) Making Use of Clinical Audit: A Guide to Practice in the Health Profession Open University Press

[254] Krause, E.A (1996) Death of the Guilds: Professions States and the Advance of Capitalism Yale University Press

[255] Kuhlmann, E (2006a) Modernizing Health Care: Reinventing Professions, the State and the Public Policy Press: Bristol

[256] Kuhlmann, E (2006b) Traces of Doubt and Sources of Trust: Health Professions in an Uncertain Society *Current Sociology,* Volume 54, 607-19

[257] Kuhlmann, E and Allsop, J. (2008) Professional self-regulation in a changing architecture of governance: Comparing health policy in the UK and German *Policy and Politics* (36) 2: 173-89

[258] Kullmann, E and Saks, M. (2008) Rethinking Professional Governance: International Directions in Healthcare, Bristol:Policy Press

[259] Larkin, G (1983) Occupational Monopoly and Modern Medicine London Tavistock

[260] Larkin, G. (1995) State Control and the Health Professions in the United Kingdom *in Johnson, T, Larkin, G and Saks, M (1995, editors)* Health Professions and The State in Europe Routledge

[261] Larson, M.S. (1977) The Rise of Professionalism: A Sociological Analysis University of California Press

[262] Lash S and Urry, J (1994) Economies of Signs and Space Sage Publications

[263] Lane, J. (1985) The Role of Apprenticeship in Eighteenth Century Medial Education in England. in *Bynum W.F and Porter, R (1985, editors)* William Hunter and the Eighteenth Century Medical World Cambridge University Press

[264] Laqueur, T. (1987) Organism, Generation and the Politics of Reproductive Biology in *Gallagher, C and Laqueur (1987, editors)* The Making of the Modern Body: Sexuality and Society in the Nineteenth Century University of California Press

[265] Leinster, S (2003) Medical Education in the Real World *Medical Education,* Volume 37, 397-398

[266] Likert R (1961) New Patterns in Management New York: McGraw-Hill

[267] Lindeman, M. (1999) Medicine and Society in Early Modern Europe Cambridge

[268] Light, D.W (1998) Managed Care in A New Key: Britain's Strategies for the 1990s *International Journal of Health Sciences,* Volume 28, Number 3, 427-44

[269] Lloyd-Bostock, S and Hutter, B (2008) Reforming Regulation of the Medical Profession: The Risks of Risk Based Approaches *Health, Risk and Society,* Volume 10, Number 1, 69-83

[270] Lock, M and Gordon, D. (1988) Biomedicine Examined London : Kulwer Academic Publishers

[271] Long P (1986) Performance Appraisal Revisited Institute of Personnel Management: London

[272] Louden, I. (1995) Medical Education and Medical Reform in *Nutton, V and Porter, R (1995, editors)* The History of Medical Education in Britain Amsterdam and Atlanta

[273] Lowry, S. (1993) Medical Education: teaching the teachers *British Medical Journal,* Number 306, 127–30

[274] Lupton, D. (1994) Medicine as Culture: Illness, Disease and the Body in Western Societies Sage Publications

[275] Lupton, D (1995) The Imperative of Health: Public Health and the Regulated Body Sage Publications

[276] Lupton, D (1997) Doctors on the Medical Profession *Sociology of Health and Illness,* Volume 9, Number 4, 480-97

[277] Lynn, K (1963) Introduction to the Professions *Daedalus,* Volume 92, 653

[278] Lyotard, J F (1984) The Postmodern Condition A Report on Knowledge University of Manchester Press

[279] Macpherson (1962) The Political Theory of Possessive Individualism Oxford Clarendon Press

[280] Marshall, J (1996) Personal Autonomy and Liberal Education *in Peters, M, Hope, W, Marshall, J and Webster, S (1996, editors)* Critical Theory, Post-Structuralism and the Social Context Palmerston North Dunmore Press

[281] Marquand, D. (1988) The Unprincipled Society: New Demands and Old Politics London: Jonathon Cape

[282] Marx, K and Engels, F (1958) Selected Works Volume 1 Penguin

[283] Maudsley, G (1999) Do We All Mean The Same Thing By 'Problem Based Learning'? *Academic Medicine,* Volume 74, 178-85

[284] Maulitz, R.C (1987) Morbid Appearances: The Anatomy of Pathology in the Early Nineteenth Century Cambridge University Press

[285] McDonald, K.M. (1995) The Sociology of the Professions Sage

[286] McGregor, D (1957) An Uneasy Look at Performance Appraisal *Harvard Business Review,* Volume 35, 89-94

[287] McKee, M and Black, N (1993) Junior Doctors Work at Night *Journal of Public Health Medicine,* Volume 15, Number 1, 16-24

[288] McKinlay J B (1977) The Business of Good Doctoring or Doctoring as Good Business: Reflections on Freidson's views on the Medical Game *International Journal of Health Services,* Volume 7, 459-83

[289] McKinlay, J B and Arches, J (1985) Towards the Proletarianization of Physicians *International Journal of Health Services,* Volume 15, 161-95

[290] McKinlay, J B and Stoeckle, J D (1988) Corporatization and the Social Transformation of Doctoring *Health Services,* Volume 18, 191-205

[291] McManus, I.C. (1997) From Selection to Qualification: How and Why Medical Students Change, in *Allen, I (Editor)* Choosing Tomorrows' Doctors Policies Studies Institute

[292] McManus, I.C. and Sproston, K.A. (2000) Women in Hospital. Medicine in the United Kingdom: Glass Ceiling, Preference, Prejudice or Cohort Effect? *Journal for Epidemiology and Community Health,* Volume 54, Number 1, 10-16

[293] Mead, G.H. (1934) Mind, Self and Society Chicago University Press

[294] Merrison Report (1975) Report of the Committee of Inquiry into the Regulation of the Medical Profession HMSO London

[295] Meyer, H.H (1991) A Solution to the Performance Appraisal Feedback Enigma *Academy of Management Executive,* Volume 5, 68-76

[296] Miles, M.B and Huberman, A.M (1994, second edition) Qualitative Data Analysis: An Expanded Sourcebook Sage Publications

[297] Miller, P and Rose N (1990) Governing Economic Life *Economy and Society* Volume 19, 1-31

[298] Mishler, E, Amara-Singham, L and Hauser, S (1981) Social Contexts of Health and, Illness and Health Care Cambridge University Press

[299] Mishler, E (1989) Critical Perspectives on the Biomedical Model in *Brown, P (1989 editor)* Perspectives in Medical Sociology Belmont: Wadsworth

[300] Ministry of Health and Department of Health for Scotland (1944) A National Health Service. CMND 6502 London: HMSO

[301] Moran, M and Wood, B. (1993) States, Regulation and the Medical Profession Open University Press

[302] Moran, M. (1999) Governing the Health Care State; A Comparative Study of the United Kingdom, the United States and Germany Manchester University Press

[303] Moran, M. (2004) Governing Doctors in the British Regulatory State , in *Gray, A and Harrison, S (2004, editors)* Governing Medicine: Theory and Practice Open University Press

[304] Morrision, K. (1996) Developing Reflective Practice in Higher Degree Students through a Learning Journal *Studies In Higher Education* Volume 21, Number 3, 317-32

[305] Morse, J.M (2004) Purposive Sampling *in Lewis-Beck, M.S, Bryman, A, and Liao, T.F (2004, Editors)* The Sage Encyclopaedia of Social Science Research Methods Sage Publications

[306] Moldow, G. (1987) Women Doctors in Gilded-Age Washington University of Illinois Press, Urbana and Chicago

[307] Muirhead-Little, E. (1932) The History of the British Medical Association: 1832 to 1932. BMA Publishing.

[308] Murphy, R (1988) Social Closure Oxford Clarendon Press

[309] Navarro V (1976) Medicine Under Capitalism New York Prodist

[310] Navarro V (1980) Work Ideology and Medicine *International Journal of Health Services,* Volume 10, 523-50

[311] Navarro V (1986) Crisis, Medicine and Health: A Social Critique New York Tavistock

[312] Navarro V (1988) Professional Dominance or Proletarianization? Neither *Millbank Quarterly,* Volume 66 Supplement 2, 57-75

[313] NCCA (28th October, 2003) NCAA Finds Suspension of Doctors Not Always Necessary (www.ncaa.nhs.uk/news/index)

[314] Nettleton (1995) The Sociology of Health and Illness Cambridge Polity Press

[315] Newton, T (1998) Theorising Subjectivity in Organisation: The Failure of Foucauldian Studies? *Organisation Studies,* Volume 19, Number 3, 415-47

[316] Newton T and Findlay P (1996) Playing God? The Performance of Appraisal *Human Resource Management Journal,* Volume 6, Number 3, 42-58

[317] Newman, C. (1957) The Evolution of Medical Education in the 19th Century Oxford University Press

[318] NHS Executive (1994) Risk Management in the NHS Leeds NHSE

[319] Norman, G.R (1988) Problem-Solving Skills, Solving Problems and Problem Based learning *Medical Education*, Volume 22, 279-86

[320] Nutton, V and Porter, R (1995, editors) The History of Medical Education in Britain Amsterdam and Atlanta

[321] Oakley, A (1984) The Captured Womb Blackwell Oxford

[322] Oakley, A. (1993) Essays in Women, Medicine and Health Edinburgh University Press

[323] Osborne, T (1993) On Liberalism, Neo-Liberalism and the Liberal Profession of Medicine *Economy and Society,* Volume 22, Number 3, 345-56

[324] Olesen, V. (2001) Resisting 'fatal unclutteredness' Conceptualising the sociology of health and illness into the millennium *in Bendelow, G and Carpenter, M, Vautier, C and Williams, S (2001, editors)* Gender, Health ad Healing Routledge.

[325] O'Malley, C.D. (1970) The History of Medical Education Berkley and Los Angeles

[326] Oppenheimer, M (1973) The Proletarianization of the Professional in *Halmos, P (1973, editor)* Professionalization and Social Change *Sociological Review* Monograph No 20 University of Keele

[327] Pattern, P (1987) Michel Foucault in *Austin-Bross (1987, editor)* Creating Culture Allen and Unwin

[328] Parry, N and Parry, J. (1976) The Rise of The Medical Profession: A Study of Collective Social Mobility Croom Helm Ltd

[329] Park, K. (1985) Doctors and Medicine in Early Renaissance Florence Princeton: NJ

[330] Parsons, T (1949) Essays in Sociological Theory Glencoe Free Press

[331] Parsell, G.J and Bligh, J (1995) The Changing Context of Undergraduate Medical Education *Postgraduate Medical Journal,* Volume 71, 397-403

[332] Perkin, H (1989) The Rise of Professional Society: England Since 1980 Routledge

[333] Peters, M (2001) Poststructuralist, Marxism and NeoLiberalism: Between Theory and Practice Rowman and Littlefield

[334] Peterson, A (1997) Risk, Governance and the New Public Health *in Peterson, A and Bunton, R (1997, editors)* Foucault Health and Medicine Routledge

[335] Peterson, A and Bunton, R (1997, editors) Foucault Health and Medicine Routledge

[336] Pfeffer, N (1985) The Hidden Pathology of the Male Reproductive System *in Homans, H (1985, editor)* The Sexual Politics of Reproduction Aldershot Gower

[337] Pidgeon, N (1996) Grounded Theory: Theoretical Background in *Richardson, J.T.E (1996, editor)* Handbook of Qualitative Research Methods for Psychology and Social Sciences Leicester: the British Psychological Society

[338] Plummer. K (2001) Documents of Life 2 Sage Publications

[339] Pollitt, C. (1990) Managerialism and the Public Services Oxford: Blackwell

[340] Pollitt, C. (1993) Audit and Accountability: The Missing Dimension? *Journal of the Royal Society of Medicine,* Volume 86 (April), 209-11

[341] Polanyi, M (1967) The Tacit Dimension Routledge

[342] Porter, J (1996) Representing Reality: Discourse, Rhetoric and Social Construction Sage Publications

[343] Porter, R. (1995, editor) Medicine in the Enlightenment Amsterdam and Atlanta

[344] Porter, R. (1997) The Greatest Benefit to Mankind: A Medical History of Humanity from Antiquity to the Present London McMillan

[345] Porter, R. (2002) Blood and Guts: A Short History of Medicine Allen Larve the Penguin Press , London

[346] Poynter, F.N.L. (1966, editor) The Evolution of Medical Education in Britain London McMillan

[347] Power, M (1997) The Audit Society Oxford University Press

[348] Prior, P (1999) Gender and Mental Health Macmillan London

[349] Pym, D (1973) The Politics and Ritual of Appraisal *Occupational Psychology,* Volume 47, 231-35

[350] Ranson, S. (1994) Towards the Learning Society Cassell

[351] Redman, W (1995 second edition) Portfolios For Development: A Guide for Trainers and Managers Kogan Page

[352] Reed, M (2000) The Limits of Discourse Analysis in Organisational Analysis *Organization,* Volume 7, Number 3, 524-30

[353] Reiser, S.J. (1978) Medicine and the Reign of Technology Cambridge University Press

[354] Rhodes, R (1994) The Hollowing Out of the State: The Changing Nature of Public Services in Britain *Political Quarterly,* Volume 65, 138-51

[355] Riddell, P. (1989) The Thatcher Decade Oxford:Blackwell

[356] Riska E and Wegar K (1993). Gender, Work and Medicine Women and the Medical Division of Labour London Sage

[357] Riska, E (2001) Medical Careers and Feminist Agendas: American, Scandinavian and Russian Women Physicians London Sage

[358] Ritzer, G and Walczzak , D (1988) Rationalization and the Deprofessionalization of Physicians *Social Forces,* Volume 67, 1-22

[359] Robinson, J. (1988) A Patients Voice at the GMC: A Lay Member's View of the General Medical Council Health Rights: London

[360] Rock, P (2001) Ethnography and Symbolic Interactionism *in Atkinson, P Coffey, A L Delamont, S Loftland, J and Loftland L (2001)* Handbook of Ethnography Sage Publications

[361] Rose, N (1985) The Psychological Complex Routledge and Kegan Paul

[362] Rose, N (1990) Governing the Soul The Shaping of the Private Self Routledge

[363] Rose, N (1992) Governing the Enterprise Self *in Heelas, P and Morris, P (1992, editors)* The Values of the Enterprise Culture Routledge

[364] Rose, N and Miller, p (1992) Political Power Beyond the State: Problematics of Government *British Journal of Sociology,* Volume 43, Number 2, 173-205

[365] Rose, N (1993) Government, Authority and Expertise in Advanced Liberalism *Economy and Society,* Volume 22, Number 3, 283-299

[366] Rose, N (1996a) Governing Advanced Liberal Democracies *in Barry, A, Osborne, T and Rose, N (1996)* Foucault and Political Reason University College London Press

[367] Rose, N (1996b) Identity, Genealogy, History *in Hall, S and du Guy, P (1996, editors)* Questions of Cultural Identity Sage Publications

[368] Rose, N (1999) Powers of Freedom: Reframing Political Thought Cambridge University Press

[369] Royal College of Obstetricians and Gynaecologists (2006) Response to 'Good Doctors, Safer Patients Published by The Royal College of Obstetricians and Gynaecologists

[370] Royal College of General Practitioners (2006) Response to 'Good Doctors, Safer Patients' Published by Royal College of General Practitioners

[371] Rughani, A (2000) The GPs Guide to Personal Development Plans Radcliffe Medical Press Oxford

[372] Russett, C.E. (1989) Sexual Science: The Victorian Construction of Womanhood Harvard University Press

[373] Saks, M (1995) Professions and the Public Interest: Medical Power, Altruism and Alternative Medicine Routledge

[374] Schrift, A. D (1995) Reconfiguring The Subject as a Process of Self *New Formations,* Volume 25, 28-39

[375] Schubert, M.K. (1998) The Relationship Between Verbal Abuse of Medical Students and their Confidence in their Clinical Abilities *Academic Medicine*, Volume 73, Number 8, 907-9

[376] Shutz, A (1962a) The Stranger: An Essay in Social Psychology in *Shutz, A, (1962)* Collected Papers 2: Studies in Social Theory The Hague, The Netherlands: Martinus Nijhoff

[377] Shutz, A (1962b) Collected Papers 1: The Problem of Social Reality The Hague, The Netherlands: Martinus Nijhoff

[378] Seabrook, M. (2004) Intimidation in Medical Education: Students and Teachers Perspectives *Studies in Higher Education*, Volume 29, Number 1, 59-74

[379] Searle, C (1999) The Quality Of Qualitative Research Sage Publications

[380] Searle, J (2000) Defining Competency: The Role of Standard Setting *Medical Education,* Volume 34, 363-366

[381] Sharma, U (1992) Complementary Medicine Today: Practitioners and Patients Routledge

[382] Shaw, B. (1957) The Doctors Dilemma Penguin Books

[383] Sheaff, R, Marshall, M, Rogers, A, Roland, M, Sinbald, B and Pickard, S (2004) Governmentality by Network in English Primary Care *Social Policy and Administration,* Volume 38, 89-103

[384] Silver, H.K and Glicken, A.D. (1990) Medical Student Abuse: Incidence, Severity and Significance *Journal of the American Medical Association*, Volume 263, 527-32

[385] Silverman, D. (2005, 2nd Edition) Doing Qualitative Research: A Practical Handbook Sage Publications

[386] Sinclair, S. (1997) Making Doctors: An Institutional Apprenticeship Berg

[387] Siraisis, N. (1990) Medieval and Early Renaissance Medicine: An Introduction to Knowledge and Practice Chicago

[388] Slater, B. (1998) The Politics of Change in the Health Service MacMillan Press Ltd

[389] Slater, B. (2000) Medical Regulation and Public Trust: An International Review Kings Fund Publishing

[390] Slater, B. (2001) Who Rules? The New Politics of Medical Regulation *Social Science and Medicine,* Volume 52, 871-83

[391] Slater, B. (2002) Medical Regulation: New Politics Old Power Structures *Politics* Volume 22, Number 2, 59-67

[392] Slater, B. (2003) Patients and Doctors: Reformulating the UK Health Policy Community *Social Science and Medicine,* Volume 57, 927-36

[393] Slater, B (2007) Governing UK Medical Performance: A Struggle For Policy Dominance *Health Policy,* Volume 82, Number 3, 263-75

[394] Smith, C and Wincup, E *(2000)* Breaking In: Researching Criminal Justice Institutions *in King, R and Wincup, E* (2000, editors) Researching Research on Crime and Justice Oxford University Press

[395] Smith, J. (2005) Shipman: Final Report DOH London

[396] Smith, R. (1992) The GMC on Performance: Professional Self-Regulation is on the line *BMJ,* Volume 304, 1257

[397] Smith, R. (1993) The End of the GMC? The Government not the GMC is Looking at Underperforming Doctors *BMJ,* Volume 307, 957

[398] Smith, R. (1995) The future of the GMC: An interview with Donald Irvine *BMJ,* Volume 310, 1515-18

[399] Smith, R. (1998) All changed, changed utterly *BMJ,* Volume 316, 1917-18

[400] Smith, R.G. (1994) Medical Discipline: The Professional Conduct of the GMC 1958 – 1990 Oxford University Press

[401] Snadden, D and Thomas, M. (1998) The use of portfolio learning in medical education *Medical Teacher*, Volume 20, Number 3, 244-65

[402] Southgate, L. (2001) The General Medical Councils Performance Procedures Study of the Implementation and Impact *Medical Education,* Volume 35, Supplement 1, 23-45

[403] Spencer, A and Podmore D (1986) In A Mans World London Tavistock

[404] Spencer, J (2000) Ethnography after Postmodernism *in Atkinson, P Coffey, A L Delamont, S Loftland, J and Loftland L (2001)* Handbook of Ethnography Sage Publications

[405] Stacey, M (1988) The Sociology of Health and Illness London Uwin Hymen

[406] Stacey, M. (1992) Regulating British Medicine John Wiley and Sons

[407] Stacey, M. (2000) The General Medical Council and Professional Self-Regulation in *Gladstone, D. (2000, editor)* Regulating Doctors Institute for the Study of Civil Society

[408] Starr, P. (1982) The Social Transformation of American Medicine New York: Basic Books

[409] Strauss, A.L. (1987 Qualitative Data Analysis for the Social Scientist Cambridge University Press

[410] Strauss, A.L and Corbin, J.M. (1990) Basics of Qualitative Research: Grounded Theory Procedures and Techniques Sage Publications

[411] Strauss, A.L and Corbin, J.M. (1998) Basics of Qualitative Research: Procedures for Developing Grounded Theory Sage Publications

[412] Stewart, P M (2002) Academic Medicine: A Faltering Regime *BMJ,* Volume 324, 347-48

[413] Stones, R (1996) Sociological Reasoning: Towards a Postmodern Society London: Mcmillan

[414] Taylor, I (1997) Developing Learning In Professional Education Open University Press

[415] Tawney, R.H (1921) The Acquisitive Society New York Harcourt Brace

[416] Tenkin, O. (1973) Galenism: Rise and Decline of a Medical Philosophy Ithaca, NY

[417] Thatcher, M (1987) Interview *Women's Own,* October 1987, 8-10

[418] Turner, B.S. (1992) Regulating Bodies: Essays in Medical Sociology Routledge

[419] Turner, B.S. (1995, second edition) Medical Power and Social Knowledge Sage Publications

[420] Van Maanen, J (1979) The fact of fiction in organisational ethnography *Administrative Science Quarterly,* Volume 24, 539-611

[421] Van Maanen, J and Kolb, D (1985) The Professional Apprentice: Observations on Fieldwork Roles in two Organizational Settings *Research in the Sociology or Organizations* Volume 4, 1-33

[422] Vernon, D.T.A and Blake, R.L. (1993) Does Problem Based learning Work? A Meta-Analysis of Evaluative Research *Academic Medicine,* Volume 68, 550-63

[423] Vogel, D. (1986) National Styles of Regulation: Environmental Policy in Great Britain and the United States. London: Cornell University Press

[424] Waitzkin H (1989) A Critical Theory of Medical Discourse *Journal of Health and Social Behaviour,* Volume 30, 220-39

[425] Ward, S. (1994) Education for Life *British Medical Association, News Review* (September), 18-19

[426] Waring, J.J. (2005) Beyond Blame: Cultural Barriers to Medical Incident Reporting *Social Science and Medicine,* Volume 60, 1927-35

[427] Waring, J J (2007) Adaptive Regulation or Governmentality: Patient Safety and the Changing Regulation of Medicine *Sociology of Health and Illness,* Volume 29, Number 2, 163-179

[428] Wakins (1987) Medicine and Labour: the Politics of a Profession Lawrence and Wishart: London

[429] Weber, M (1946, edited by Gerth, H.H and Wright Mills, C) Essays in Sociology Oxford University Press

[430] Weber, M (1947) The Theory of Social and Economic Organisation New York: Free Press

[431] Weber, M (1949) The Methodology of the Social Sciences Glencoe:Free Press

[432] Weber, M. (1978) Economy and Society London: The University of California Press

[433] Weiss M and Fitzpatrick R (1997) Challenges to Medicine: The Case of Prescribing *Sociology of Health and Illness,* Volume 19, Number 3, 297-327

[434] Wennberg, J. (1988) Practice variations and the need for outcomes research *in Ham, C (1988, Editor)* Health Care Variations: Assessing the Evidence Kings Fund Institute

[435] White, K (2001) The Early Sociology of Health London Routledge

[436] White Paper (2007) Trust, Assurance and Safety: The Regulation of Health Professionals in the 21st Century London: Stationary Office

[437] Wilensky, J L and Wilensky H.L (1951) Personnel Counselling: The Hawthorne Case *American Journal of Sociology,* Volume 17, 265-80

[438] Williams, S J and Calman M (1996) Modern Medicine University College London Press

[439] Willis, P (2000) The Ethnographic Imagination Cambridge Polity

[440] Wilson, E (1990) Hallucinations: Life in the Post-Modern City Hutchinson: Radius, London.

[441] Wilkinson, TJ, Challis, M, Hobma, SO, Newble, DI, Parbossingh, JT, Sibbald, RG and Wakefield, R (2002) The use of portfolios for assessment of the competence and performance of doctors in practice *Medical Education*, Volume 36, Number 1, 23-46

[442] Witz, A. (1992) Professions and Patriarchy Routledge: London and New York7

[443] Wright, P and Treacher, A (1981, editors) The Problem of Medical Knowledge Examining the Social Construction of Medicine Edinburgh University Press.

INDEX

D

E

H

I

O

N

P

T